RESTITUTION

Restitution

A family's fight for their heritage
lost in the Holocaust

KATHY KACER

Second Story Press

Library and Archives Canada Cataloguing in Publication

Kacer, Kathy, 1954-
Restitution : a family's fight for their heritage lost in the Holocaust /
by Kathy Kacer.

ISBN 978-1-897187-75-3

1. Holocaust, Jewish (1939-1945)—Reparations—Fiction. 2. Reeser
family—Fiction. 3. Art thefts—Europe—History—20th century—Fiction. 4.
Jewish property—Europe—History—20th century—Fiction. 5. World War,
1939-1945—Confiscations and contributions—Fiction. I. Title.

PS8571.A33R48 2010   C813'.54   C2010-900608-9

Edited by Colin Thomas
Copyedited by Alison M. Kooistra
Designed by Melissa Kaita
Cover photo and frames © iStockphoto

Printed and bound in Canada

*Second Story Press gratefully acknowledges the support of the Ontario Arts Council
and the Canada Council for the Arts for our publishing program. We acknowledge the
financial support of the Government of Canada through the Book Publishing
Industry Development Program.*

ONTARIO ARTS COUNCIL
CONSEIL DES ARTS DE L'ONTARIO

Canada Council   Conseil des Arts
for the Arts   du Canada

Published by
SECOND STORY PRESS
20 Maud Street, Suite 401
Toronto, ON M5V 2M5
www.secondstorypress.ca

AUTHOR'S NOTE

The names of three of the people in this story, Theofil Král, Adolfo Flores, and George Harwood, have been changed to protect their identities. Král's and Flores's identities have been further obscured by changing events in their lives.

To Karl Reeser, with my deepest appreciation,
and for Ian, with love

PROLOGUE

Toronto, March 14, 1990

THEO PICKED UP THE ENVELOPE and quickly counted the money inside. One thousand, two thousand, three thousand, and one, two, three, four, five hundred dollars – and double that when this mission was completed and the paintings had been delivered. He placed the envelope of cash inside the drawer of his bedside table, pulled a suitcase from the top shelf of the closet, opened it on the bed, and began to pack.

"Will you be gone a long time?" A young woman entered the bedroom, carrying a glass of wine. Theo reached for the glass and placed it on the bedside table before drawing her into his arms. She nestled there for a moment.

"Not too long," he murmured before pulling away. The young woman rested languidly on the bed while Theo resumed his packing, chiding himself for allowing the momentary distraction. He paused and closed his eyes, mentally ticking off the list of tasks facing him, and ordering them in sequence.

The trip to Prague would last exactly one week, barely enough time to do everything that was needed in order to retrieve these paintings. First and foremost, he needed to arrange a meeting with the diplomat at the Canadian embassy. Securing the custom-made equipment to transport the artwork was next, but that would not be a problem; his sources were always on standby for such jobs. Then there was the issue of getting the paintings out of the country and across the border. That could prove difficult. Many people would be watching his movements and too many would be all too willing to report a smuggler to the authorities. If anyone caught wind of an illegal scheme, the consequences would be swift and severe.

The young woman roused herself from the bed and moved to his dresser. She rummaged through a pile of clothing and retrieved a thick woolen sweater. "It'll be cold and damp in Prague," she said. "I checked in the newspaper. You'd better take this, just to be on the safe side." Theo didn't respond. He took the sweater and threw it onto a stack of clothing next to his case.

This was not the first time he had undertaken to retrieve fine art from Prague. His dealings were legal most of the time; he bought and sold paintings with the consent and authorization of the state-controlled National Gallery. But every now and then, a special job would come up, one that required circumventing official regulations. This was one such assignment. And it called for an expertise that few other than Theo possessed. He referred to it as *recovering* art, and this was an art form in and of itself as far as he was concerned. Some might call it stealing, and it was certainly no secret that Theo profited from these excursions. But he was not a dishonest person, and, in this case, his mission would be to reunite a family with what was rightfully theirs.

The man who had contacted him had presented a convincing case that had moved Theo. This man and his family had been denied their property for fifty years, ever since they had been forced from their homeland at the start of the Second World War. *Now that's stealing*, thought Theo, smiling wryly. That was the real crime. Not what he was about to do. He was doing a good deed, helping someone recover his lost property. Besides, there was something wonderfully dangerous about this mission, and Theo was attracted to risk like a moth to light. *After all, what is life without adventure?* he often asked.

The young woman came up behind him, wrapping her arms around his chest. "I don't like the idea of you going to Czechoslovakia," she whispered. "I don't think it's safe."

"Don't worry about me," he said easily. "I'll be fine."

There were many who thought Theo was careless or indifferent to the details and dangers of his work, and he sought to cultivate that impression. In a business such as his, it was easier to pass under the radar of suspicion if one appeared detached. But when it came to his business affairs, he was meticulous and thorough.

"I've heard you say that before," she replied, trying to make her voice sound light.

"And I've been right each time, haven't I?" He checked himself. It wasn't good to joke about this or to get too cocky. He knew all too well that in Communist Czechoslovakia state spies were everywhere and few people could be trusted. Recently, the politics of all the Soviet Bloc countries had been changing, governments crumbling before the eyes of the world. There was talk of democracy and a lifting of restrictions. But Theo knew that talk was just that. In practice, people could still be searched, property confiscated. He could certainly be arrested and imprisoned if his activities were discovered. But he knew how to deal with the Communists. After all, he had been a loyal member of the party himself at one time.

Theo turned back to his packing. It was too late to worry about any of this. He had thirty-five hundred dollars burning a hole in his bedside table, and thirty-five hundred more to come when he was home with the merchandise. He had to remain focused on the task at hand. He had his connections in Prague – trusted accomplices in the foreign diplomatic mission. They would help as they had done in the past. Theo was confident of that. Besides, if the situation became too tricky, he would back off immediately. He was no fool when it came to his own safety.

"Will I hear from you when you get back?" This woman was as persistent as she was beautiful.

Theo didn't respond. He threw the last articles of clothing into his suitcase and zipped it up. Then he turned back to the woman.

"I'll miss you," she said. "You never answered my question about how long you'd be away."

This time, he smiled and replied, "With luck, I'll be back in a week."

PART I

WAR IN
THE WORLD

CHAPTER ONE

Rakovník, Czechoslovakia, August 1937

IT WAS EARLY MORNING in the Reiser household. The sun crept up over the wide window ledge and floated into the second floor bedroom, casting a warm glow over sixteen-year-old Karl's face as he slept. Noises of an awakening city followed. Shopkeepers released their awnings and pulled their stalls into place on the street below. Cars honked their horns in the busy square, their engines sputtering and popping as they drove by. Voices blended into a fusion of salutations and acknowledgments. The town of Rakovník in western Czechoslovakia was coming alive. Karl resisted the urge to join in and nestled into his blankets. He had been dreaming, and for a moment he pushed his mind to go back to that place just before awakening, where fantasy and reality merged. He had imagined himself bicycling through the countryside, deep into the woods, and then past fields of sunflowers en route to the river. School had broken up for the summer vacation and Karl had dreamed of lazy adventures and swims in fresh water so cold it took his breath away.

The sounds from the street below his window were daily background music to Karl's mornings, lulling him in and out of wakefulness. But on this morning something was different, interfering with the peacefulness of the approaching day. This wasn't a sound, but a feeling, and it was strangely wet and sloppy! The dream forgotten, Karl rolled over in bed to see the panting face of Lord, his Great Dane, licking his hand and urging him to get up. Lord's ears perked up at the sign of movement from his young owner.

Karl reached over to pat his dog, wondering briefly how Lord had managed to get into his room, past the watchful eyes of his mother. She would not be pleased to discover the dog here. Karl groaned and rolled back over, burying himself under the covers and trying to find that quiet place where sleep might once again claim him. But Lord would have none of it. He nuzzled the bed sheets, and gave a low raspy growl.

"Shhhh," Karl commanded, rolling over once more. "Don't you realize you'll be banished from the house forever?" He reached over to scratch affectionately behind Lord's ear. Everyone, his parents included, had thought it was brazen of him to name his dog "Lord." But Karl had insisted on the name for this majestic creature. Lord sighed and rested his head on Karl's bed. "Those pleading eyes won't help you," Karl whispered. "And mother will think I'm the one who let you in here." *How did Lord get past everyone in the first place?* he wondered again.

Too late to go back to sleep, Karl realized. By now, his father would be up and in his office. Mother would be busy with the household and the family servants. Perhaps she was already supervising the preparation of that evening's dinner. With luck, there would be a roast chicken with *houskové knedlíky* – bread dumplings – and *palačinky* – crepes filled with jam – for dessert. Any minute now, Leila, his nanny, would knock softly at Karl's bedroom door, telling him it was time to get up and come downstairs for breakfast. Perhaps Leila would protect him from his mother's displeasure at discovering Lord in his bedroom. Leila Adrian had been with the family for years, and she had a soft spot for young Karl, whom she had practically raised from birth. Leila was from Sudetenland, the northern part of Czechoslovakia, a region that was home to an ethnic German population that had clashed with the Czechs over the years. But that was politics, and

Leila didn't care about that. She was ferociously loyal to this family, and her love had grown over her years of devoted service. She had never married and had no children. And while she would occasionally visit her sister in their hometown of Ústí nad Labem, the Reiser family was her true family. Karl knew Leila would try to defend him, but, more than likely, he and the dog were going to be in trouble this morning.

Another sound drifted up from the downstairs salon. Karl listened for a moment, hearing his parents' voices rise and fall. He sensed some kind of alarm in their tone, and wondered briefly what his father was doing here when normally he would be in his office by this time. As a commodities broker, Father bought future grain crops from large farms in the area and sold these contracts to domestic and foreign markets. His company, A. Reiser, had been started by Karl's grandfather Abraham. But Karl's father had taken ownership at a young age, achieving great success and making his family one of the wealthiest in Rakovník. His offices were on the ground floor of the house, though he was often away on business.

"Come, Lord," Karl finally said. "Let's see what's going on. Maybe I can sneak you past Mother without her noticing." Lord snorted an acknowledgment and Karl rolled out of bed. He paused briefly to look at his reflection in the mirror above his bookshelf. His long, thin face and lanky physique reflected back. Like his father, Karl had a strong, angular nose. His sparkling eyes were a gift from his mother. He dressed quickly, ran a brush through his thick hair – the red hair and freckles also came from his father's side of the family – and sprinted down the long staircase to the main floor. Lord followed, sending the Oriental carpets flying as he rounded the corner at the bottom of the stairs. But Karl needn't have worried about his dog. When he entered the living room, his parents were deep in discussion, oblivious to all other activity.

"But, Victor, who could have done such a thing?" his mother asked. She paced anxiously back and forth.

Karl's father shook his head. "Calm down, Marie. I'm sure it's nothing. Children. Pranksters. That's all. You mustn't be so upset. There's nothing personal in this."

"Nothing personal! How can you say it's nothing? We've never been targeted like this. It's shocking, disgusting! We are fully assimilated in this town."

This was an understatement. There were only thirty Jewish families who lived in this town of about thirty thousand people. And though the Jewish families all knew one another, Karl and his family only saw them a couple of times a year when they met at the big synagogue on Vysoká Street for the High Holidays. These events, and the occasional Yiddish word that Victor would drop into a conversation, were the only indications of the family's Jewish background. First and foremost, the Reisers thought of themselves as Czechs – loyal citizens of their country.

Karl had rarely seen his mother this agitated. An attractive and cultured woman, she was typically reserved and in control. But not this morning. She wrung her hands and tugged nervously at the collar of her lace blouse. Father eased his ample bulk out of an armchair and took his wife by the hand.

"And that's why you mustn't worry," he said. "This is a minor incident. But I've called the police to report it, just to be on the safe side. Please, calm down."

The telephone rang shrilly and Father moved to answer it. He responded in clipped sentences to the caller; perhaps a police official, Karl guessed. Mother continued to pace, ignoring Karl, who had taken a seat in the corner of the living room next to his sister, Hana. Leila stood in another corner of the room, casting nervous glances at her two young charges. Their nanny was grandmotherly in appearance, a small, gray-haired, kind woman. She too looked more troubled than Karl could ever remember.

Karl leaned over to his sister and whispered, "What's going on?"

Hana was usually talkative, but not so this morning. She sat perched on the edge of her chair, holding her dog, Dolinka, in her lap and stroking its head. Hana shrugged. "Go outside and see for yourself," she replied. Hana was four years younger than Karl. They were as close as a brother and sister could be, though Karl sensed at times that Hana thought of him as the favorite – the older of the two and the only boy in the family.

Karl walked out the door and onto the streets of Rakovník. The family's three-storey house was in the main part of town, facing Husovo Náměstí, the central square. Their property consisted of three buildings side by side. The first contained the grain warehouse for his father's business, and the second housed several servants and employees. The last house on the corner was the family home. Theirs was one of several impressive buildings in this section of the city.

By now, the main square was full of people and cars, everyone rushing about their business. Karl walked a few paces from his home and then turned around. He sucked in his breath at the sight that greeted him. In bold, white letters, the word *Žid* – Czech for Jew – had been painted across the brick wall of the house. The thick letters stood out on the street, emblazoned across the face of their home, their intent unmistakably menacing. Karl was not one for emotional outbursts. But this time was different. This time, he was overwhelmed with contempt for whoever had committed this crime. He stood rooted to the spot, his face flushed, his chest pounding.

There was no such thing as hiding your Jewish identity in a town as small as Rakovník. You were saddled with it within a country where anti-Semitism had deep roots. In 1541, during the Habsburg dynasty, there had been a complete expulsion of the Jewish population. Over the centuries, the Jewish ghetto in Prague had been burned to the ground on several occasions, forcing Jews to rebuild their community each time. Even though his family thought of themselves as fully integrated into the Rakovník community, Karl was often bullied by his schoolmates. Not only were the Reisers Jewish, they were wealthy to boot, making Karl an easy target. As a child he frequently had been followed to school and taunted by the other children. "Hey *Žid*, did you fall asleep under a strainer?" they teased, suggesting that the sun had passed through a sieve to create the pattern of red freckles that lay across his nose and cheeks. He hated the reference, and felt self-conscious about his appearance. Nothing seemed worse than being a red-haired, freckle-faced *Jewish* boy living in a small town in Eastern Europe in the 1930s.

The worst assault had happened a year earlier when Karl was walking home from school. He could hear them approaching from behind – several boys, thugs who attended his school. But this time, the taunts were louder and more menacing than before.

"Žid, do Palestiny!" – *Jew, go to Palestine!* – one boy shouted, as Karl glanced over his shoulder and quickened his pace, anxious to get to the safety of his house. Though he was tall and muscular, Karl was not athletic, and certainly not a fighter. He would be no match for these tougher boys. The footsteps behind him came closer and then a thick, meaty hand reached out and grabbed Karl by the shoulder, spinning him around. It was over in seconds. Karl lay on the ground doubled over as the boys laughed easily and moved on. He limped home and spent the evening nursing the painful bruises on his stomach and the welts across his arms. He hid the marks from his parents, who would have been outraged by the attack. Eventually, Karl put it behind him.

There had been other beatings, but each time he would shake them off and let the incidents pass. And, relatively speaking, he knew that these confrontations were minor, not at all like the real dangers that existed these days in other countries where Jews were being systematically targeted. Adolf Hitler's name had been spoken with disdain in Karl's home for years. "A madman," his father often said. "He'll never last." And yet the preceding years had seen the steady rise of anti-Semitic laws in Germany. With the Nuremberg Laws of 1935, Jews had lost their status as legal citizens there. They could no longer hold public office, and were barred from various professions and occupations.

But it seemed inconceivable that the harsh measures being implemented in Germany would ever come to Karl's homeland. Tomáš Masaryk, their country's beloved previous president, would never have allowed the Jews of Czechoslovakia to be targeted in that way. He respected the worth and dignity of all people, regardless of religion. And his successor, Edvard Beneš, appeared to rule with the same spirit of liberalism. Despite the hostility toward Jews that had marked the history of the Czech lands, both of these leaders expounded a democratic political philosophy that kept anti-Semitism in check. Karl could handle those occasional beatings by local thugs. However, this was an attack on his home, on his family; this was much more serious. As he stood staring at the graffiti on the wall, Karl's mind was so preoccupied that he didn't notice his father, who had come out of the house to join him on the sidewalk.

"In this country, I'm afraid they think they can smell a Jew. Anti-Semitism is bred here, and singling us out is sport," his father said, breaking Karl's concentration. It was unlike his father to speak so plainly about the centuries of political and social discrimination toward Jewish people. Usually he shrugged the history off. "History and reality are two different entities," Victor had been fond of saying. Today, the two seemed to merge in his frank acknowledgment, taking Karl aback. "The police will do nothing about this," his father added, gesturing toward the paint that had dripped down onto the sidewalk, leaving a line of small white puddles like stars dotting a dark sky. "They say it's probably just some kids playing."

"And you?" Karl asked. "What do you think?"

Once again, his father retreated to a place where he seemed willing to dismiss the vandalism. "I'm sure it's nothing," he said with a shrug. "Kalina, come here and help clean this off," Father called to his chauffeur, who stood awkwardly to one side. By now there was a crowd of onlookers gathering in front of the house. "We're not here to create a spectacle for everyone." Kalina nodded and ran to get supplies from the garage. When he returned, Karl stepped forward to assist him.

"What do *you* think of this?" Karl asked as he and the chauffeur began to scrub at the paint that covered the wall.

"It's a sign," Kalina replied, glancing nervously at the sky and then shaking his head. Only in his early thirties, Kalina seemed much older, due in part to his many superstitions. He would spit three times if he passed a nun on the road, or if a black cat crossed in front of the car while he was driving. Karl was amused by the assortment of rituals and routines that controlled Kalina's life. Still, Kalina was a loyal employee, and had secretly taught Karl to drive, well before the legal age. Once a year, the chauffeur would perform a general maintenance of the family automobile. He would disassemble the engine, clean the parts, and then reassemble it.

Karl was fascinated with the mechanical working of the car and eagerly followed Kalina around like a puppy, lapping up as much information as he possibly could.

"The Germans are going to take over the country. Mark my words," Kalina continued brusquely as he rolled up his sleeves and began to scrub the wall with sweeping brush strokes. The muscles stood out on his burly arms and sweat glistened on his forehead. But Kalina was an inconsistent forecaster, one month raging about a possible German invasion and the next month equally adamant about a Russian takeover.

With the help of strong ammonia and several steel brushes, the paint was removed in no time. But even after all traces of the graffiti were gone, Karl still felt uneasy. He was putting the pails and brushes away just as Kalina brought the car around for his father.

Father eased himself into the back seat of the black Peugeot and rolled down the window. "Karl," he called to his son. "I have to see a client today. Go and look after your mother. She's more worried about this than she ought to be." With that, he gestured to the chauffeur and the car moved forward, leaving Karl alone on the street.

He glanced again at the house. *Should Mother be so worried?* he wondered. *Shouldn't father be more worried?*

"Such a terrible thing," Leila cried as Karl reentered the house. She spoke in German, the language in which she had been raised and the one she had taught to Karl and Hana. Leila clasped and unclasped her hands, shaking her head, and gathering her apron into a knot. "Who would do such a thing to this family?"

Leila wasn't helping the situation, Karl thought. She was merely adding fuel to the frenzy of worry that gripped the household. He needed to escape the overheated city and his agitated family. He walked out the door, grabbed his bicycle from the garage, and rode quickly out of town and toward the pond. A long ride and swim would make him feel better.

Karl wound his way through the streets, passing the town hall, the brewery, the library, and the theater. His journey took him past the old synagogue with its twin Roman towers and matching minarets. A large stone Star of David adorned the archway over the double doors at its entrance, surrounded by stucco ornaments and gilded windows. The building dated back to 1763, and its interior always felt dark and slightly mysterious to Karl. The presiding rabbi did not live in town. He came in from Saatz* to celebrate the High Holidays and to give Jewish instruction to young boys. Karl often skipped the monthly classes. He had had a bar mitzvah of sorts, just a small service in the rabbi's study, attended by his parents. It was a rite of passage that meant little to Karl or his family.

Close to the synagogue was the Jewish cemetery where marble and granite stones were engraved with Stars of David, crowns, and hand symbols. Here the memories were powerful. As a small boy, Karl had walked here with his father almost every Sunday to visit the graves of his grandparents. Before entering, Victor would remove a handkerchief from his pocket, tie a knot in each of the four corners, and place this makeshift skull cap on Karl's head. Karl would place pebbles on the gravestones of his grandparents, following the biblical practice of marking graves with a pile of stones. He never fully understood what this ritual meant, though he knew it was a sign of love and respect.

In the distance, Karl could hardly miss the splendor of the lofty High Gate, which dominated the landscape. Everyone in town took pride in this majestic landmark. Built in 1517, the High Gate was really a tower constructed of rough stone and mortar in an almost perfect square. Jutting out from each of the building's three levels, stone gutters shaped like pigs, frogs, and knights channeled water from the roof. Rakovník's coat of arms had been carved prominently above the archway at the entrance.

Karl left the town behind him and rode south along the river Berounka, passing deep woods interspersed with large, sun-soaked meadows. Fifty kilometers to the east lay the capital city of Prague. Karl's father did business there on an almost weekly basis, chauffeured by Kalina across

---

* Now known as Žatec in the Czech Republic.

the intersections of roads and railways, undulating hills and flat fields. Occasionally, Karl had joined his father on these trips. Though he reveled in the bustle of the big city, today he was grateful for the tranquility of the countryside.

The pond was quiet, just the way he had hoped it would be on this warm summer day. Karl enjoyed his time alone. He had few friends and tended to keep to himself. Perhaps it was the casual anti-Semitism that prevailed. Even the teachers couldn't hide their contempt for the few Jewish students at the school. When teaching a lesson one day, Mr. Ulrich, the geography teacher, had posed a question and commented, "Even the Jews should be smart enough to know this."

There was one Christian boy with whom Karl was friendly, Miloš Nigrin, the son of the local druggist. Miloš never joined in when others taunted Karl. He was a frequent guest at the Reiser dinner table and the two boys often cycled together. Karl's other friend was George Popper, the only other Jewish boy at the school and a year ahead of Karl.

But today, Karl was relieved and grateful that none of his fellow students were at the pond. He didn't want conversation; he certainly didn't want anyone to interrogate him about the graffiti – and by now word might have spread. He even wondered if some might doubt the incident had ever happened, or worse, might use it as an excuse for further assaults upon his family. Either way, all Karl wanted was peace and seclusion. In those moments of solitude, he could slip out of himself and reflect more clearly on events.

The pond was his favorite retreat. The water here was deep and clean, and the surrounding fields provided an inviting area to picnic and relax with friends and family. Flanking the field were tall pine trees that grew in a tight formation. Sparrows and robins nestled atop the swaying branches and sang their endless symphony. Each year, a competition was held here. Those who swam three times around the pond and jumped off the tall wooden diving tower at one end were awarded with flowers.

Karl was a strong and natural swimmer. He dropped his bicycle in the tall grass, stripped down to his bathing trunks, and dove in. The water was cool and refreshing. Each stroke around the perimeter of the swimming pond seemed to calm him. His arms cut silently and efficiently through the water, propelling him forward and clearing his mind.

By the time he returned home, the heat of the day had begun to recede; he was feeling refreshed and had placed the vandalism in the back of his mind. *It was just another stupid kid in town doing something cowardly,* Karl thought. *And we're the easy target.* But when Father walked in at the end of the day, the conversation about the graffiti resumed and within minutes the good feeling from the swim was gone.

"We're deluding ourselves if we think this is nothing," his mother ranted, picking up where she had left off that morning. "Look at what's happening in Germany."

"Honestly, Marie. You're blowing this out of proportion," Victor replied, removing a silk handkerchief from his pocket and wiping his brow and balding head. Sweat poured from his red face. "Czechoslovakia is not Germany and it never will be! We're a democracy. Czechs would never tolerate having the Nazis and their rules here." Like so many others, Karl's father held fast to the belief that if Germany threatened to invade, Britain and France would come to Czechoslovakia's aid.

"But, Victor, how do you know that?" Mother was pacing, moving across the floor of the salon like a tiger striding back and forth in its cage. Strands of hair from her perfectly coifed bun had loosened and floated across her flushed cheeks and forehead. Her brow was furrowed and her mouth was drawn in a tight, determined line. "Germany used to be a democracy, and now the Germans are rallying behind Hitler," she declared. "There is no protection for Jews under the law in Germany, none whatsoever."

Victor was equally adamant. "We are more Czech than Jewish," he insisted.

Karl watched this exchange from his chair in the corner of the room. As his eyes moved back and forth from his mother to his father, he imagined he could see their arguments flying across the room like a ping pong ball from one of the tournaments he had played in at school. As always, he was pensive during these discussions, weighing what his parents had to say, and wondering who was more right. He had listened to his parents argue about the political situation in their country many times. Mother was typically negative and apprehensive during these exchanges, while Father was quick to placate her and neutralize her anxiety.

"It's as if it's open season on Jews in Germany," mumbled Marie, oblivious to her husband's comments. "It seems that with his promise of prosperity for all German citizens, people are quick to overlook Hitler's darker side."

"In this country it's different. There are still many who will stand up for their Jewish friends and neighbors," Victor insisted.

"You're blind, Victor," Marie finally said, shaking her head. "Czechoslovakia will not escape Hitler's wrath. We should think about leaving," she announced suddenly.

Karl's eyes shot up. This was a first. Mother was actually suggesting that the family run from their country.

"Ridiculous!" snapped his father. "There is no reason to leave. Besides, Jews are coming here to Czechoslovakia for their safety."

"It's true!" Karl interjected from his spot on the sidelines. "I read in the newspaper that there are Jews from Austria, Hungary, and Germany who have been flooding across our borders to escape persecution in their own homelands." If Czechoslovakia was considered a safe haven by those from other countries, then surely it was safe for Karl and his family.

His mother shook her head. "Then they are naive if they think this country will protect them. I say we pack up the family and get out while we still can."

"We are secure here in this community," Victor insisted, "in a country that will defend itself, and defend us if necessary."

It seemed as if the conversation would end there, but Marie perched herself on the edge of one of the settees. She glanced over at Karl and then turned to face her husband. "I have to tell you something, Victor," she began. "I've been sending some of our money to a bank in Paris."

Victor's jaw dropped and for once he seemed at a loss for words.

"I've been doing it for several months now," she continued.

"But how?" sputtered Victor.

Marie sat up straighter and thrust her chin forward defiantly. "I've been buying up foreign currency and transferring it to the Crédit Lyonnais."

Victor was furious. "But Marie, this is an illegal activity!" Foreign currency exchanges were not permitted unless they were declared to the government.

"I don't care," replied Marie. "I'm creating a nest egg, a safety net for our family in the event that we need to get out of Czechoslovakia. And judging from recent events, this may happen sooner than you think." She leaned forward now, pleading with her husband. "Don't you see, Victor? We'll have money waiting for us outside these borders."

Karl gazed at his mother. It was so unlike her to take a stand like this against Father – to do something without his consent.

"Don't you realize that you are putting us in grave danger?" Victor asked. By now his father's face had turned such a deep shade of crimson that Karl feared he might pass out if further provoked.

Marie was undeterred. "I'm glad I've done it," she replied. "And I plan to send some of our belongings as well – clothing and household goods. I'll send them to Mr. Kolish, that associate of yours in Holland. He can keep some things for us in case we need them. I won't stand back and watch this country and our lives fall apart," she added firmly. "If no one else is going to plan for this family, then I will."

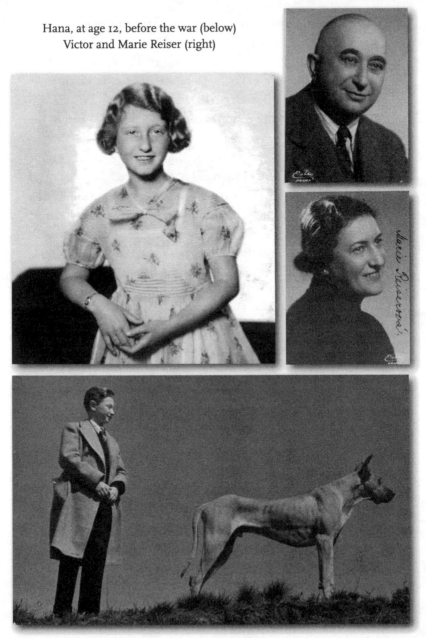

Hana, at age 12, before the war (below)
Victor and Marie Reiser (right)

Karl in Rakovník with his dog, Lord.

CHAPTER TWO

Rakovník, September 1937

WHEN KARL RETURNED to school that fall, it was as if nothing had happened. If his classmates knew about the anti-Semitic graffiti that had defaced the front of his home, no one commented on it. In truth, no one, other than Karl's family, seemed to care.

Karl stood to one side of the front lawn of the one-hundred-year-old public high school, watching students enter the building. He smiled and waved at George Popper, who returned the greeting. It was a pity that George was a year ahead of him in school. He could have used the solidarity of another Jewish boy in his class. Besides, no one touched George, not even the thugs who had it in for Karl. As a star pupil, George's quiet intelligence had gained the respect of students and teachers alike, religion notwithstanding.

Another student walked by and nodded at Karl. It was Rudolf Puchold, the son of Karl's art teacher. Mr. Puchold was one of the few teachers whom Karl actually liked and admired. Though Karl was not strongly academically inclined, he thrived in Mr. Puchold's art class. But Mr. Puchold taught more than just art; he also taught graphics and drafting, technical skills that Karl was drawn to, that called on his creativity and attention to detail. Though Mr. Puchold's son, Rudolf, was also several years older than Karl, they had formed an odd friendship, born from their common love of photography.

As a bar mitzvah gift on his thirteenth birthday, Karl had received a Leica camera from close family friends. He had known nothing of cameras or photography before that, but took an immediate interest in the craft, snapping pictures of anything and everything in his path. He took shots of the scenery in and around his home, posing agreeable family members and taking candid snaps of those who weren't interested in posing. His dog, Lord, was a frequent, albeit uncooperative, model.

The camera became Karl's best friend, helping him cope with his shyness. In his photographs, he could be bold and daring, capturing anything from grand landscapes to intimate portrayals of individuals and events. His photographs reflected an emotional connection with people and land, a keen eye for detail, and an expressive curiosity about the world around him. He felt alone without his camera; he felt complete with it. The camera had become his voice, and when he held it to his eye, he could step into conversations and respond to what he saw, heard, and felt.

Rudolf Puchold Senior and Victor Reiser were acquaintances. In fact, Mr. Puchold had done several oil paintings that hung in the Reiser home, one of which was a full-length portrait of Victor. It was a formal painting – Victor in a gray suit and fedora, seated in a chair, staring confidently through dark-rimmed glasses. The portrait now graced one wall of the Reiser family's home. When the two men discovered their sons' mutual interest in photography, they arranged for the boys to go on a hiking and photography vacation together.

Victor was keen for Karl to have a holiday different from the family's usual chauffeur-driven tours of Switzerland, or Karl's stays at Swiss camps to improve his French. This adventure with Rudolf was nothing like those vacations. The boys spent two weeks together, hiking and camping in the Tatra Mountains. They slept in tents and cooked on an open fire. They snapped pictures of mountaintops that emerged from shadowy clouds, fields that overflowed with sunflowers and daisies, and rivers that rushed from the mountains to fill the ponds and streams below. Rudolf owned a Leica just like Karl's, and Karl learned much about photography from the mentorship that Rudolf provided on that trip. But it was a one-time experience. When the boys returned to Rakovník, they retreated to their separate lives and, except for nodding in acknowledgment as they had done this morning on the first day of school, they rarely spoke to one another.

"Where did you disappear to all summer?" Karl heard Miloš Nigrin's voice and turned around to greet his friend, shaking hands with him and smiling broadly. "Were you locked up in your darkroom?"

Shortly after returning from the camping holiday with Rudolf, Karl had convinced his father to construct a darkroom for him on the main floor of Victor's office in a back room where Lord usually slept. Several of Victor's employees had knocked together some two-by-fours to create a frame for the enclosure, and hung heavy burlap curtains to darken it. Karl spent endless hours inside, learning the art of developing film mostly by trial and error, but also with the help of some instruction books. The first rolls that he worked on were a disaster. He emerged from the dark with sheets of blank pages, having immersed the film for either too long or too little time in the chemicals. But over time, and with continued practice, his skills had improved. The darkroom was another convenient place that Karl could retreat to when he wished to avoid the company of others.

"Sorry to hear what happened to your house," Miloš continued.

Karl nodded, grateful for the support. He often wondered how it was that his friend could remain so untainted by the anti-Semitism that lurked around every corner of town. It would have been so easy for Miloš to be drawn into that club that treated Jews like second-class citizens. But the fact that Karl was Jewish was a non-issue as far as Miloš was concerned. He never joined in with the taunting that plagued Karl, and in fact culti-vated their friendship with no concern for any consequences for himself. The two boys swam together at the pond, talked openly, and visited one another's homes. Yet after the vandalism of his house, Karl had withdrawn even from Miloš, and this was the first opportunity the boys had had to talk since then.

"My parents were upset about it, too," Miloš added. "You must have been so angry."

Karl nodded again. He was not much inclined to talk about the incident anymore. But Miloš was not about to give up.

"Do you know who did it?" he asked.

Karl shrugged. "Could be anybody." He pointed at a group of nasty-looking boys standing off to one side, leaning against the school building as if they were its keepers.

Miloš stared along with him. "Well," he finally said, "I think it was sickening." He turned back to Karl. "Let's go bicycling later today. I haven't seen you in a long time."

Karl nodded his assent and the two boys shook hands again just as the bell started ringing. Then they lined up to join the throng of young students marching up the stairs of the school and into the main auditorium.

The headmaster stood at the podium at the front of the hall eyeing the class with a severity that never seemed to leave his face. He quieted the room with one look and welcomed everyone, reminding the students that the coming year would be challenging. He then proceeded to conduct the census that always marked the beginning of the school year. On the first day of the fall semester, each student was required to stand and proclaim his religion out loud. In addition to academic subjects, one hour a week was set aside for religious studies, and this vocal declaration of religious affiliation would determine the students that would be assigned to the various classes. Karl shuddered as, one by one, the students rose and spoke aloud. The majority of students were part of the *České Bratři*, or Czech Brothers, the national religion of Czechoslovakia at the time. Many were Protestant, and some were Catholic. A few stood and declared, "*Bez vyznání*" – without affiliation. When it was his turn, Karl stumbled to his feet, lifted his chin, and proclaimed, "*Hebrejský*" – Hebrew – in front of the entire school body. Then he quickly sank down, hoping that the burning in his stomach and chest did not show on his face.

The religious affiliation of each student in this school was a foregone conclusion; the oral declaration merely confirmed what the headmaster and entire student body already knew. So why conduct this public spectacle? There was no question for Karl that the sole purpose of this exercise was to further humiliate and alienate him from this community. But this year, the feeling of estrangement was worse. Perhaps the attack on his home that summer had affected him more than he had been willing to admit. Maybe the growing unrest in countries around Czechoslovakia was more serious than he had realized. Or maybe his mother's heightened anxiety and dire predictions of the future of the Jewish community in Czechoslovakia had penetrated his thinking more deeply. Whatever it was, Karl knew that when he stood to declare himself as a Jew that day on the start of a new academic year, he was making himself vulnerable in a way that he had never experienced before.

CHAPTER THREE
Rakovník, March 1938

IT WAS DIFFICULT AT TIMES for Hana and Karl to reconcile what was happening outside Czechoslovakia's borders with the daily life they lived in Rakovník. School continued as if there were no difficulties elsewhere. They were in different grades and attended separate public high schools, both of which were known for their high academic standards and strict discipline. Hana and Karl learned Latin, French, and German, along with mathematics, history, geography, and other subjects. Their German teacher did mysteriously disappear at one point, and no one seemed to know where he had gone or why. But Leila continued to speak German to the children, as she had been doing for years, and they became more and more fluent in her native language.

And then, events in Germany took a new and terrifying turn. It was a particularly cold and blustery evening in March 1938 when Hana and Karl returned home from the cinema. As they entered the house, they were still in an animated discussion about the American film actress, Jeanette MacDonald. Their cheeks were flushed from the damp wind that had blown through the streets, whipping leaves and debris up into their faces.

Hana unwound her woolen scarf and cap and shook her curly red hair free. Lord and Dolinka were there to greet their masters, barking and jumping up and down enthusiastically. But when Karl and Hana walked into the salon, the stone faces of their parents instantly quieted them and their pets. At first, no one spoke. The only noise in the room was the sound of people cheering from the radio behind the heads of their parents. And the voice that shrieked loudest of all was unmistakably that of Adolf Hitler.

"What's going on?" Karl began. The looks on the faces of his parents alarmed him.

"Shh!" his father barked, further disquieting Karl.

This was not the first time he had heard Hitler's voice on the radio. On each previous occasion, the members of the household would stop whatever they were doing, nearly hypnotized by this man's fanatical pronouncements, each one ending predictably with an anti-Semitic tirade.

"They've taken over Austria." When his mother finally spoke, there was both rage and alarm in her shaky voice. "The Nazis marched into Vienna today. No one stopped them," she added bitterly.

"Listen to the crowd cheering," her husband added. "No one stopped them because they welcomed it. That maniac is being treated like a hero in Vienna."

Hitler's voice rose from the radio as he declared, "I have in the course of my political struggle won much love from my people, but when I crossed the former frontier, there met me such a stream of love as I have never experienced. Not as tyrants have we come, but as liberators."[1] And sure enough, the voices of the masses shouted in return, *"Sieg Heil! Sieg Heil!"*

"I knew this would happen," Marie stated somberly. She had the same stricken look she had worn the day the house had been vandalized.

In the weeks to come, she continued to hold fast to her belief that it was only a matter of time before Czech Jews would be targeted by Hitler. The details of the *Anschluss* were particularly shocking and depressing for Victor, who continued to insist that the family was still safe while declaring his contempt for the international events. But eventually even he had to acknowledge that the situation was deteriorating. Under pressure from his wife, Victor also began to buy up foreign currency to safeguard the family's funds.

George Popper's family came for dinner several weeks later, but food took second place to the animated conversation between George's parents and Karl's.

"I've been telling Victor for months now that we should ready ourselves in case we need to leave here," Marie declared. "The occupation of Austria is just the beginning of Hitler's crusade. But my husband doesn't see things my way."

"Don't be silly," said Mr. Popper gently. "We aren't in danger here. Great Britain will always guarantee our independence and integrity against any forceful aggression from outside." George's father sounded exactly like his own, Karl thought. Zigmund Popper was a gregarious man who believed in his family's assimilation into the country as much as Victor did.

"That's what I keep telling Marie, but she doesn't seem to want to believe me," Victor said. "She seems bent on leaving Rakovník, whereas I believe we are safest staying right here."

Also seated at the table was Rita Popper, George's sister and Hana's best friend. Rita was a pretty girl with straight brown hair. Her serious disposition was an interesting match for Hana's usual sense of fun. But both girls were silent that night, seemingly glued to the conversation.

"I saw one of our neighbors the other day, and she told me that her children have left for Palestine," said Mrs. Popper. "That poor woman. She seemed so bereft without them. Can you imagine separating your family like that?" Irena Popper was quieter than her husband in these social situations, but in her work, she was a force to be reckoned with. She ran the clothing business that she owned with her husband virtually single-handedly.

"Never!" declared Marie. "If we must go, we'll go together."

"Let me remind you that those children left for religious reasons," Victor replied. "They are the most observant family in town and their children wanted to pursue a more Jewish life in Palestine. That's not the case for any of us."

"I agree," added Mr. Popper. "We're Czechs first and Czechs we will always be. There will be no restrictions on us here in our homeland."

By now Karl had tired of this conversation. He excused himself from the table, motioned George to follow him, and the two boys made their way up onto the roof of the house where they could have their own discussion away from the adults.

"They say that we might be barred from attending school here," Karl said, pulling his jacket tighter around his body and flipping the collar up to protect his neck. The night air was brisk, though the sky was clear and overflowing with stars. "Can you imagine if they close our school to Jews?"

George pushed his glasses up on his nose and nodded. He was a tall, stout young man, with a bookwormish look that matched his exceptional intellect. "I'll be leaving at the end of this term to go to university in Prague. I think that, with everything happening in Austria, it'll be a relief to get out of Rakovník and into the big city. It's killing my mother to see me go," he added. "But at least it's close by. I'm sure I'll be back frequently."

"What about the rest of your family?" Karl asked.

"They'll stay here," replied George.

Karl nodded and said nothing. He knew he would miss his good friend – and he feared that when George left and Karl became the only Jewish student at the school, he would become even more of a target.

The ensuing days were uneventful. Everyone returned to their work or business, putting the events in Austria into the background, lulled into a false sense of confidence that no news was a sign of stability. And then one day Hana returned home from school anxious and distracted. Without pausing to say hello to her mother, she stormed up the staircase and pounded on Karl's bedroom door.

"What is it?" he asked as soon as he saw her face.

"Listen," she replied, dead serious. "I have to tell you what happened on the way home today."

She had been riding her bicycle home from school as she often did. The streets were quiet. "I was passing the photography shop and I saw that there were lots of pictures displayed in the store window. So I stopped to look at them."

The previous year, Hana, Karl, and their parents had gone to this studio for a family portrait. It had taken forever for the photographer to compose the family and snap his picture, long tedious hours during which Karl and Hana had wished they were outdoors with their friends, or reading a book, anything rather than being forced to primp and pose for a camera lens. But everyone had to admit that the final result was well worth the effort. The family portrait that hung in the living room was attractive and expertly done.

"I was thinking about our portrait and I was curious to see the other family photographs that the shopkeeper had lined up in the window." Hana paced in Karl's room as she recounted her story. "And that's when I saw it."

In the center of this gallery, proudly displayed, was one large framed picture that made Hana's blood run cold. It was an SS officer, no one that Hana recognized, but his uniform was unmistakable – particularly the swastika on his armband that radiated from the portrait.

"I couldn't believe my eyes," continued Hana. "He was smiling in the picture, but all I saw was the Nazi insignia on his arm. I just glared at his face." She stopped and faced her brother. "What are they doing proudly displaying this picture of a Nazi? Don't they know what he is?"

"What did you do?" asked Karl. He felt his own blood boil.

Hana gazed calmly at her brother. "I looked around her to see if anyone was close by. Then I looked back at the photo of the SS officer and I spat directly at the shop window." Hana finished her story. "That's what I did!"

Karl returned her gaze evenly and nodded his approval. "If I had been there, I would have done exactly the same thing, Hana," he said.

Meanwhile, in the Reiser household, more plans were being developed that would provide some safety for its members. Father Ferdinand Hrouda was a sympathetic priest in town. Victor knew this when he approached him to arrange for the priest to perform a Catholic marriage ceremony for Marie and himself. Notwithstanding his ongoing belief that Czech Jews were safe, Victor felt that Catholic marriage papers might provide some added protection in the event that they were targeted in any way. Father Hrouda obliged. He agreed to witness Victor and Marie's vows in a private ceremony. He signed the marriage certificate and provided the family with false baptismal certificates. Armed with these papers, Victor and Marie returned home to show their children.

"I always wanted to show your mother how much I loved her," teased Victor. "I never imagined I would do it in a Catholic service. What would our rabbi think of this?"

It's so easy for father to joke, thought Karl. But he wondered if these papers would really do anything to protect the family. Were they being naive to think that a piece of paper would separate them from other Jewish families in Rakovník if the Nazis came looking? Sometimes, Karl dismissed these negative thoughts and, like his father, held fast to his belief that all would be well. But these moments of calm were followed by moments of utter anxiety. More and more, he was beginning to fear that Jewish identity was not merely about religious observance. He could no more divorce himself from his Jewish heritage than he could deny his red hair and freckles. His father could pretend that being Jewish was of lesser importance. He could proclaim their Czech nationalism; he could try to hide his family behind Catholic documents. But, at the end of the day, they were being targeted for their roots – their genetics – and theirs were clearly Jewish.

Mother was not nearly as good-humored as Father. "There's one more thing that I want you to do," she insisted. "That villa in Prague that is owned by our friends, the Zelenkas – I want you to rent the downstairs flat from them." Victor looked puzzled. "It will be a place to go if we need it," she continued. "It will be easier for us to hide our identities in Prague amongst the masses."

Even with the Catholic papers in their possession, Marie's mind was still focused on leaving Rakovník. She had not abandoned the plan of getting out of the country, but Prague would be the first step in her exit strategy.

Victor shrugged. "What if people suspect that we are trying to run away?"

"Your business takes you to Prague every week," Marie replied quickly. It was true that Victor traveled to the capital city every Tuesday to sell his grain crops on the commodity exchange. "If anyone asks, we'll say that you are tired of staying in hotels," she continued, detailing an explanation that sounded as if it was already well rehearsed. "People will understand that a flat is a more comfortable place to stay."

Victor finally relented and, with his consent, it appeared as if the family might actually abandon their home and flee to a safer place.

No one in Karl's hometown suspected that his family was fashioning an escape plan. They shared no information with friends or other family members. Marie in particular did not want to implicate anyone else in their arrangements; she did not trust that anyone would be able to keep their plans a secret. As for Karl, he said nothing to any of his classmates. No one in any case would have cared about the intentions of the only Jewish boy in class. Besides, this was the *septima*, the last year of high school, and Karl's *matura*, the final exams, were fast approaching. They would be tough, a long set of oral and written tests that would determine his readiness for university. This should have been the most important time in Karl's academic life. He should have been solely focused on his studies, day and night, analyzing mathematical problems, memorizing historical dates, conjugating verbs in Latin and French. But Karl was thinking of none of this. The unrest that had begun in Austria was finally and inevitably moving inside the borders of Czechoslovakia.

The three million German-speaking citizens living in Sudetenland continued to claim that they were oppressed under the control of the Czech government. The reports that appeared in the local newspaper told of increasing clashes on the northern border between Sudeten Germans and Czechs. The leader of the Sudeten German Party was Konrad Henlein who had come to power in 1935 in an election that had been largely financed with Nazi money. On March 28, 1938, Hitler instructed Henlein to increase Sudetenland's demands for autonomy and its union with Nazi Germany. If the Czech government did not accede to these demands and turn over this part of Czechoslovakia to Germany, Hitler was threatening to support the Sudeten Germans with military force. The Czech government led by President Edvard Beneš turned to Britain and France, hoping that these powers would come to his country's aid. But this was to no avail. Britain and France were determined to avoid war at all costs. Britain's Prime Minister Neville Chamberlain said, "How horrible, fantastic, incredible it is that we should be digging trenches and trying on gas masks here because of a quarrel in a faraway country between people of whom we know nothing.... However much we may sympathize where a small nation is confronted by a big and powerful neighbor, we cannot in all circumstances undertake to involve the whole British empire in war simply on her account."[2]

In the end, Czechoslovakia's allies did not stand up for her at all. The Munich Agreement, signed by Germany, Italy, France, and the United Kingdom, stipulated that Czechoslovakia must cede the Sudeten territory to Germany. In exchange, the understanding was that Hitler would not make any further demands for land. Chamberlain held the signed document in his hand, waving it above his head as he addressed the British public and read aloud the details of the accord. "We regard the agreement signed last night as symbolic of the desire of our two peoples never to go to war with one another again.... My good friends this is the second time in our history that there has come back from Germany to Downing Street peace with honor. I believe it is peace in our time."[3] This could not have been further from the truth.

On October 5, 1938, as German troops were marching unopposed into Sudetenland, Beneš resigned as president, realizing that the fall of his country was inevitable. Almost a third of Czechoslovakia would now be subsumed into the growing Third Reich. The realization that the country was being pulled apart was hitting everyone in town with equal force.

Karl arrived at school on that day with his friend George. All around them, students were huddled in small groups, some talking frantically about the impact of these new developments in the north. Others stood in muted silence, absorbing the news and barely able to comprehend the impact on themselves and their country.

"Everyone looks as if they're at a funeral," George commented as the two boys pushed their way past their classmates and climbed the steps of the school building. "The country should have seen this one coming. Sudeten Germans have been clashing with the government forever."

"No one could have imagined this," replied Karl. "Countries are simply not carved up like this."

"Then you're blind, too," said George bitterly. There was a long pause and then he added, "Hitler's not going to stop. He's got Austria, and now he's got a part of this country. It's only the beginning."

"Stop it!" demanded Karl. "You're starting to sound more and more like my mother."

"I think she may be the one who's got it right after all," George replied, breathing deeply. "If Hitler can take over a third of our country just like that, who knows what else he's capable of doing. The man is hungry for more. He's like a bear that smells blood – he'll stalk his prey until he devours it all."

Karl had never heard his friend sound so cynical or contemptuous. The two boys stood silently watching their fellow students begin to assemble for the start of classes. A strange stillness had settled on the school grounds – a sense of dark foreboding.

"There may be an advantage for us in all of this," said Karl, as the students began to enter the building. "As long as Czechs are focused on Germans, either here or in Germany, perhaps they'll be less likely to focus on us."

"I doubt it," replied George. "I suspect that Jewish families living in the north are going to be flooding into this part of the country. Why would Jews want to stay there knowing how much Hitler hates them – hates us? And if you think Jews are going to be welcomed here, then you're totally naive. I can't wait to get out of here," he added, "to get to Prague where at least it doesn't feel as if everyone knows you and is watching you. I just wish my family were coming with me. You need to get out, too."

Within the Reiser household, Leila was particularly distraught over the news of the annexation of Sudetenland. It was difficult for her to understand the bitter fragmentation of her country. Her roots were in Sudetenland, where she had been born and where she still had relatives. And yet, her heart was here with the family she had been with for almost two decades.

Later that day, Karl walked home with Leila after accompanying her to the market to pick up some groceries.

"What would I do without your family?" Leila muttered as she struggled to keep up with Karl's long stride. "Yours is the only home I know."

Karl squeezed Leila's arm reassuringly. He glanced around to make sure no one was listening. Leila's Czech was extremely limited, and German was the only language she spoke in the Reiser home. But here in public, Karl was cautious about responding. These days, speaking German was probably as dangerous as acknowledging one's Judaism. He did not want to provoke anti-German sentiments any more than he wanted to incite anti-Semitic ones, and both were easily aroused. He nodded, and ushered Leila along. It was only once they were safely back home and Karl had deposited the groceries in the kitchen that he turned to face her.

"You're the mainstay of this family, Leila," he said in his near-fluent German. "We'd be lost without you." He hugged her lovingly, nearly smothering the tiny woman.

"And you and Hana are like my own." Leila returned the hug, sniffling loudly, and then shooed Karl out of the way so that she could begin to prepare that evening's meal.

But the news of the Sudeten takeover was still troubling Karl. He was overwhelmed by the growing fear that his mother and George Popper might be right, that this was only the beginning. There was a smell of war in the air, and it was settling over the country like a thick fog. It had been easy to dismiss the unrest when the events were taking place elsewhere, across the borders. Karl, like many others, had tried to hold fast to the belief that his country was safe from conflict and that if circumstances escalated, other countries – more powerful and influential – would come to Czechoslovakia's aid. One by one, these beliefs were being eroded.

And the situation continued to spiral downward. That November, in Germany and Austria, Jewish shops and department stores had their windows smashed and contents destroyed in what was being called *Kristallnacht* – the night of broken glass. One hundred and nineteen synagogues had been set afire and another seventy-six burned down completely while local fire departments stood by. More than two hundred thousand Jews had been arrested. Many were beaten and even killed. Once again, Hitler's voice shrieked from the radio. Appearing before the Nazi parliament, Hitler made a speech commemorating the sixth anniversary of his coming to power. He publicly threatened Jews, declaring, "In the course of my life I have very often been a prophet, and have usually been ridiculed for it…. Today I will once more be a prophet: if the international Jewish financiers in and outside Europe should succeed in plunging the nations once more into a world war, then the result will not be the bolshevizing of the earth and thus the victory of Jewry, but the annihilation of the Jewish race in Europe!"[4]

That same month, Karl celebrated his seventeenth birthday. What should have been a memorable occasion passed as a non-event in the Reiser household. There was no possibility of festivities given the intense feelings that *Kristallnacht* had aroused in everyone in the family. As Marie became even more resolute in her urging to leave the country, Karl felt his resolve crumble once and for all. He joined his mother's camp, advocating for the family's immediate departure from their home. Meanwhile, Victor continued to pronounce that all was still well.

"It's different here," his father declared over and over again, when Karl pressed him to respond to the news of *Kristallnacht*. "We are not like the German Jews. We are Czechs first – everyone knows that – fully assimilated into Czech society and culture. Of course I'm worried about the country. But not about us."

How many times had Karl heard his father recite this mantra? It was losing its strength. And though the words that Victor spoke were strong, the voice behind them seemed more doubtful, and his eyes betrayed his uncertainty.

Karl at age 16 in Rakovník

Marie and Victor's Catholic marriage certificate, dated December 19, 1938.
Behind are Marie and Hana's false baptism certificates.

A letter from the Deputy Mayor of Rakovník (top) dated December 2, 1938, stating that the Reiser family is held in high esteem within the community. The translation (bottom) is notarized in Prague on June 14, 1939, suggesting that Marie must have had the translation done when the family fled there.

CHAPTER FOUR

Rakovník, Late 1938

BY LATE 1938, despite the fears arising from *Kristallnacht*, life went on as usual in Rakovník. There were still no laws enacted to discriminate against Jews in Czechoslovakia. Victor's work continued unchanged. The family lived in their home and could come and go as they wished. The synagogue was open and functioning. Karl still went to the theater and cinema, played sports, and socialized with his few friends. School exams were still approaching.

Victor noted the passing of time with satisfaction. "You see," he said. "I told you things would be fine here."

And while Marie shook her head in response, pursing her lips in a grim line, it was true that, while war and the loss of freedom threatened at Czechoslovakia's doorstep, that door had so far remained shut.

One day in February 1939, Karl arrived home to some unfamiliar voices coming from the sitting room. He closed the front door behind him and removed his jacket, which was still wet from the rain and snow falling outside. Shivering, he walked toward the noise in the salon. It was difficult to keep the house warm even for a family with enough money to heat the wood stoves and fireplaces.

"Ah, Karl," his mother said as he stood in the archway of the salon. "Come in."

Karl entered and greeted his parents. There was another man in the living room, someone Karl didn't know, and he waited expectantly.

"This is Mr. Schmahl. He owns an art gallery in the next town," Mother announced. "Our son, Karl."

Karl reached out to shake hands with the stranger. He was in his thirties, a dumpling of a man, dressed in a well-tailored, dark silk suit. He shook hands with Karl and bowed formally. Karl noted the large gold ring on his finger. A second stranger, similarly dressed, hovered in the back of the sitting room. No one moved to introduce him.

"Mr. Schmahl married our cousin, Irene," his father said. Karl glanced at his father, surprised by the disdainful tone in his voice. His dislike for this gentleman was obvious, and this puzzled Karl. Mr. Schmahl was talking and Karl stepped to one side of the room to listen in on the conversation.

"As I was saying, my business has not gone as I would have hoped. People simply do not appreciate fine art anymore. All this talk of war has scared many off from purchasing art. Besides, who would have suspected a Nazi occupation when we opened our gallery in Karlovy Vary? Certainly not us." Karlovy Vary was located in the Sudeten region. "I have been forced to close my gallery, despite my best efforts." Mr. Schmahl shook his head and tugged nervously at his tie.

"Perhaps your extravagant lifestyle has something to do with the failure of your business," Victor commented curtly. This set Mr. Schmahl on another round of tugging and twitching.

"Not at all," he stammered. "In the art business, one must look the part if one is to succeed."

Karl was beginning to understand his father's reaction to Mr. Schmahl. Despite their family's wealth, Victor was a modest man. He was unassuming and reserved when it came to outward shows of prosperity. In contrast, Schmahl flaunted his wealth, from his gold cufflinks, silk tie, and fine leather shoes to his affected speech. Even Karl knew that parading one's wealth was not recommended in a country that needed little provocation to target Jews.

Mr. Schmahl struggled to compose himself. He hesitated, then stumbled on. "At any rate, the loan which you so graciously gave me – I'm…I'm afraid that I will have trouble paying it back."

Victor said nothing. It appeared that this news did not surprise him. Marie stood next to her husband, silently watching the exchange.

"But I am an honest man, I assure you. And I honor my debts. I've simply fallen on hard times," lamented Mr. Schmahl, "like so many others these days. Surely you as an astute business man will understand this." By now, he was practically convulsing in front of Victor, who continued to stare in silence. "In this case," continued Mr. Schmahl, trying to compose himself, "in lieu of the money, I have brought you these."

With that, he gestured behind him to a tall mound, draped in heavy cloth. He snapped his fingers at the other man in the room who rushed forward to help. Ceremoniously, the two men grabbed either end of the cloth and pulled it downward, revealing a stack of paintings. With the help of his assistant, Mr. Schmahl lined the paintings up across the salon for everyone to see. They were heavy, even for two men. Karl and his parents leaned forward to inspect the artwork.

There were four canvases – large, wall-sized oil paintings, mounted in ornately sculpted gold frames. The first and perhaps most imposing of the paintings was entitled *Forest Fire*. "You may be interested to know that this is nothing like the artist's other works," Schmahl said. Karl squinted to see the artist's name: Rudolf Swoboda. "The painter was a well-known Orientalist," Schmahl continued. "In 1886, Queen Victoria commissioned him to paint a portrait of a group of Indian artisans who had come to Windsor to celebrate her Golden Jubilee. She was so impressed with his work that she paid his way to India so that he could produce more paintings of her subjects. Many of his paintings of the 'ordinary people of India' are hung in what was once Queen Victoria's residence, Osborne House on the Isle of Wight."

Karl looked closely at the canvas. He had taken enough photographs

Le lavabo à l'école maternelle by Henri Jules Jean Geoffroy (top)
Forest Fire by Rudolf Swoboda (bottom)

Ready for the Ball
by Antonio
Ermolao Paoletti

Die Hausfrau
by Hugo Vogel

of the countryside around his home to appreciate the artistic details of the painting in front of him. It depicted a darkly lit forest engulfed in deep red and orange flames, creeping upward and choking the life out of the forest trees. The gray smoke appeared to almost lift off the oil; the foliage all but disappeared behind the advancing fire. Karl was mesmerized by how lifelike the fire appeared.

Mr. Schmahl was talking again. "Take a look at these two vertical paintings," he said. "This one is called *Die Hausfrau*." Karl glanced over at the artist's signature: Hugo Vogel, a German name. This painting was of a young woman standing in front of a draped harpsichord, her head tilted slightly to one side, absently flipping through pages of sheet music with one hand. Her other hand held a feather duster and rested carelessly on her hip. Light poured in from the window beside her, illuminating her face and the music in front of her.

Karl's mother joined him next to the painting. "Look at how the light falls here on the manuscript pages and how her hair glows through the cap she is wearing," she said. "She appears to be daydreaming."

"Perhaps she wishes to abandon the tediousness of everyday chores for a musical interlude," Mr. Schmahl replied. He may have been gaudy in his manner and dress, but he certainly did know art. Sensing that he had captured the attention of at least two people in the room, Schmahl continued. "Note how whimsical the painting is. It's the portrait of a woman longing for something more, something beyond the life that she has been leading."

The other vertical painting told a different story of a young woman. This one was called *Ready for the Ball*. The woman depicted here was dressed for a party, in a deep red and green Spanish-style gown and an ornamental black mantilla. Her sleeves were adorned with fine lace, and she held a closed fan up against her face. Her eyes gazed longingly to one side, as if she were dreaming of a night of music and merriment.

"The artist is Antonio Ermolao Paoletti, an Italian," said Mr. Schmahl. "He was known for painting the ceiling of one of the finest gothic churches of Europe, the Madonna dell'Orto. Mrs. Reiser, I can see that you recognize that the artist has painted a woman of aristocracy. She is attractive, alluring, and perhaps a bit mysterious." Mr. Schmahl was now in his element, expounding on the virtues of the art that he had brought, gesturing in the air like a conductor leading a large orchestra. Karl's father remained silent, though even he had approached the paintings to examine them more closely.

"Take a look at this one." Marie gasped as she paused in front of the last of the paintings.

"Ah yes, perhaps I've saved the best for last," smiled Mr. Schmahl. "*Le lavabo à l'école maternelle,* by the French artist Henri Jules Jean Geoffroy. One has to look carefully to see and enjoy the many fine details of this work of art."

The last painting was indeed special. Here, more than two dozen nursery school children were gathered in a bathroom along with two teachers or nannies who were attending to them. Several children were standing around a large tub scrubbing their faces. One little boy, off to one side, was bent over, trying to tie his shoelaces. A piece of bread lay on the ground in front of him. Another little boy was tugging at the skirt of the attendant. Several others were standing, arm in arm, waiting to scrub or to leave. In the background, more children were filing in through the open door.

"Yes," Marie murmured. "It's particularly lovely."

"And worth a lot of money," added Mr. Schmahl, looking over at Karl's father. "I believe that these paintings more than make up for the money that you loaned me, Mr. Reiser." Once more, Mr. Schmahl tugged at his tie, waiting for Victor's reply.

Father shrugged his shoulders and Karl couldn't help but smile again. Art was not new to the Reisers. Paintings hung throughout the house. His father admired fine art and often bought paintings abroad. In fact, art was the one place where Victor permitted himself to display his wealth, knowing it would not be obvious to those outside the home. But the truth was that Karl's father would help out anyone in need, and rarely took notice of the bill. He had assisted other merchants in other ways in the past — those who couldn't make ends meet, those who owed money. He could see that Schmahl was doing the honorable thing by paying off the loan in the only way he could. Karl knew even before his father answered that this exchange – art for the release of the debt – would suffice. The two men shook hands and Mr. Schmahl left the house soon after.

That night at dinner, Marie continued to elaborate on the merits of the paintings. "I've been doing some reading about them. I dare say they may be the most valuable paintings we have in our home – certainly the largest!" There were many art books in the family library and Marie loved to pore over them. "I'm simply riveted by these paintings, all four of them. The details are marvelous and they are so different from one another. Each one tells a unique story. I could stare at them forever."

A guest had joined them that evening, an army officer who had command of the district in which Rakovník was located and who was staying in the Reiser home's guest quarters. It was common practice that the highest ranking military officer would be billeted in the best accommodation in the area, which, of course, was Karl's home. This was not the first time that this commander had stayed with them.

"Are you fond of art, *Plukovník?*" asked Marie, addressing the officer by his military rank.

The colonel smiled. "I'm afraid I have not had many opportunities to go to the galleries, though I am certainly enjoying the fine works here in your home." He turned back to the platter of chicken and rice that one of the servants had placed before him.

"Hana, have you had a chance to see the paintings?" Mother asked. "Did you see the one of the small children? I know this artist, Geoffroy; I've seen his moniker, GEO, on other portraits of children. The faces that he paints are truly delightful."

Hana shook her head and said nothing. She often became quiet when there were guests in the house. She preferred the family to be alone, just the four of them, and Leila of course, without all of those extra people occupying her parents' attention.

"Well you must go and look at them, Hana," Marie continued. "They are really quite special, the most extraordinary paintings we've ever had.

Victor, I think we are lucky to have received them, despite the particular circumstances under which they arrived."

Victor glanced at his wife. "I'm glad you are enjoying them, my dear," he said, and turned his attention to the officer. "Commander, please tell us what you can of the military operations that are going on. Surely we won't let that bastard, Hitler, get any more of this country than he already has."

Karl leaned forward to catch this exchange.

The officer shrugged his shoulders, choosing his words carefully. "We are readying ourselves, just in case the Nazis decide to do anything else." It was common knowledge that Czechoslovakia was in a state of military mobilization. Battalions of armies were being shifted and moved to border regions. The Colonel wasn't telling them anything they didn't already know.

"And a good thing that the army is preparing itself," Marie interjected. "That man can't be trusted. I hope our government knows that."

"My wife is a skeptic, as you no doubt can see," said Victor.

"There is talk of an escalation in the conflict," the officer continued, cautiously. "We are all waiting to see how the new president will handle the situation."

Emil Hácha, the newly elected president of what was being called the Second Republic of Czechoslovakia, was facing huge challenges, particularly as the Sudetens, following the annexation of their part of the country, were continuing to agitate for more – for a completely independent state.

"Hácha!" sneered Marie. "That man is sixty-six years old, inexperienced, and has a bad heart condition. I am not certain that he is capable of dealing with this mess."

"Nonsense," countered Victor. "Hácha's sense of justice will prevail, just as it did for his predecessors. No harm will come to Czechoslovakia, or to us."

The commander's face was grim. "The next weeks and months will be a critical time. I can't say much more than that. But we mustn't lose hope."

Karl sat back. His hope was fading on a daily basis, and this officer was doing little to revive it. The country was being pulled into a powerful current, heading toward a precipice where there would be tragic consequences, and not even the army had answers for how to rescue it. On top of that was still the nagging uncertainty of what would happen to Jewish families if there were an invasion. There was no discussion about the situation for Jews with this commander. It was uncertain whether or not he even knew that Karl's family was Jewish. But it was better these days not to raise the issue. One never knew how someone, particularly a member of the military, might respond – it was hard to tell who was a friend, and who was not.

The commander thanked Marie for the meal, rose, and bowed to the family. "I would like to have a look at those paintings. Would you mind showing them to me?"

Marie led the officer into the salon, leaving Karl, his father, and Hana to finish their dinner in silence. Days later, Marie arranged to have the paintings hung in the salon. Though Karl passed them virtually every day, he rarely took much notice of them. They simply became part of the house and part of the family.

CHAPTER FIVE

Toronto, February 19, 1990

THEO ENTERED HIS OFFICE at the back of the small gallery in an affluent part of Toronto and switched on the light, sinking into a plush swivel chair behind a large mahogany desk. The desk was piled high with art books, file folders stacked into colorful towers, unanswered telephone message slips, and a number of unwashed coffee mugs. A half-empty glass of wine and several old newspapers added to the clutter. He placed the files on the floor, pushed the dishes and papers aside, and reached into his briefcase, extracting the photographs of the four paintings. Spreading them out in front of him, he leaned in so that he could study them with a critical eye.

Theo picked up the photo of the Spanish dancer first and brought it up to the light. It was probably a commissioned portrait of someone's daughter, he thought. He recognized it immediately as late nineteenth century, the end of an era, the last hoorah for that kind of painting of a young courtesan. The artist had achieved a beautiful lightness in the hands, the tilted head, and the eyes that almost moved. Yes, the eyes were certainly most appealing. But for the most part, the painting was heavy – a black dress, black hair. The young woman's body all but disappeared in the weight and color of her clothing.

He reached for the photo of the housewife next. It was probably the best executed of the four, he thought, simply because of the light that swept across the scene, creating a warm glow that almost lifted off the canvas. The woman was picking up a corner of some sheet music, and you could almost see the page move beneath her hand. Theo recognized the complexity of the artist's rendering in this painting; the background was intricate, from the window, with its complex wrought-iron design, to the rich, textured tapestry. The young woman's face was full of delight and curiosity. And, unlike the Spanish dancer, you could almost see this young woman's body underneath her dress, her full breasts, hips, and delicate neck.

The painting of the forest fire would probably be the least attractive to most people, though most would have to concede that it was well executed. It moved. The flames crept horizontally, while smoke drifted across the canvas in one direction and trees fell in the opposite direction. Theo was drawn to the sense of destruction and devastation it depicted; it was almost like a war painting. It must have been done from memory, as it would be unlikely for the artist to have been present for a fire of this magnitude. Perhaps the inferno had been personally significant for the painter; maybe someone he knew had died in the flames.

Finally, Theo reached for the photo of the children. This was certainly the most appealing of the four works of art, and it, too, was superbly painted. Theo noted that no two of the youngsters' faces were alike. That alone was an incredible feat. Typically, an artist would have used two or three models for a painting of this kind, and simply moved the faces around the canvas. But here, each child was unique: this one melancholy, this one a bully, this one a demure little girl with her eyes cast downward. Theo imagined that the artist would have painted the background first, and then placed each child into it. This painting would be extremely valuable, Theo surmised, both for its complexity and for its joyful nature.

He sighed and lay the photos down again, lining them up in a row in front of him. Two verticals and two horizontals. *Ready for the Ball* was the smallest of the four at 116 by 88 centimeters; *Forest Fire*, at 104 by 157 centimeters, the largest, though, in truth, the difference was trivial. Once framed, each one would fill half a wall.

Theo leaned back and questioned himself. What was it that was driving him to think about risking his own safety to liberate valuable property that he did not even own, for someone he barely knew? Was it fame – the notoriety that might come from duping the corrupt Czech government of the day and completing a rescue mission of this kind? It was no secret that Theo loved the spotlight, reveled in being the center of attention in a crowd of admirers. But it was unlikely that anyone beyond this particular family would ever know of his efforts here.

Was it monetary reward? The payment he would receive for this assignment was certainly respectable, though it didn't come close to equaling the real value of the paintings, and most of it would be used to fund this undertaking. Besides, money was not really a worry for him. He lived the same entitled and affluent lifestyle whether he had the means or not. And when he didn't have the money, he borrowed it, often burning the bridges of friendship when he failed to return the loan.

Was he tempted to simply steal the paintings for himself? He was after all, a self-proclaimed smuggler, one who had been moving valuable art out of Czechoslovakia for some years, even if this was merely a sideline to his legitimate deals. Why be altruistic now? The paintings were valuable – Karl had said that they could be worth in excess of half a million dollars. The opportunity to get his hands on artwork of this caliber and significance would be a tremendous coup for Theo.

But the truth was that there was something else that was drawing him to this journey. Like wrongly accused prisoners of war, the paintings were being held captive in Czechoslovakia – they were calling out to be rescued. And he was the one who had been summoned to respond. He envisioned himself swooping into Prague, liberating these paintings from captivity, and restoring them to their rightful owner. Theo chuckled at his theatrical fantasy and at having cast himself as such a hero in the adventure. Those who knew him well understood that he was all about pleasure and conquest, and this was an assignment he could not resist. The challenge of retrieving these paintings had already ignited a spark of excitement in him that was beginning to smolder. The operation itself – the thrill of the heist – was his driving inspiration.

Besides, he liked the man who had asked him to take on this job. Theo could see that Karl was decent and trustworthy. In introducing Theo to the paintings, Karl had first talked extensively about his family's past. At the thought of Karl's story, Theo lifted his eyes from the photographs, swiveled in his chair, and stared out the window behind him. The history behind these paintings, lovely as they were, intrigued him – a family's escape from the grip of Hitler's campaign of hatred, and the property they were forced to leave behind. Theo had been born in Prague in 1952, years after the end of the Second World War, and raised in a country firmly entrenched in the dogma of Communism. What did he know of those who had suffered in the Holocaust? In truth, not much. An adored son of a wealthy family, there had been little deprivation or discipline in his upbringing. It mattered little to Theo that Czechoslovakia was an oppressive and authoritarian state. He knew how to work and move within the system. Even his name elevated him above others. Theofil Král – "Theofil" was Latin for "loved by God"; "Král" was the Czech word for "the king." Theofil Král. His name said it all, a combination of deity and monarchy joining forces in the growth and development of this confident, and at times arrogant, young man.

It certainly helped that members of his extended family had risen to senior positions within the Communist party. He himself had been a member and his brother-in-law was second in the chain of command within the government, which meant that Theo and his family were protected and assisted in all aspects of their lives. Theo took advantage of the family patronage, even going so far as to use his brother-in-law's influence to avoid being drafted into the army. Theo had decided to go to university and had chosen the prestigious Film Academy of Prague as the place he wished to attend. Everyone knew that the Academy accepted only twenty students a year, and only the top elite of the Communist party were considered. Placement in the school was seen as a reward for loyal service. The class had already been picked in the year that Theo decided to apply. Undaunted, he called on the assistance of his family to make the necessary arrangements and walked into the office of admissions. When he walked out a couple of hours later, he had been admitted. He knew nothing of film or art at the time and spent the next month preparing for the program by reading introductory books on the history of art.

Theo smiled at the memory of those days at the Academy and turned back to his desk. He had learned much about fine art in those years, had nurtured his natural creativity, and had developed a keen eye for oils. He couldn't paint, but he knew what was good. And Karl's four paintings were wonderful, as amazing as the story behind their acquisition and subsequent existence. He stared again at the photographs lined up in front of him. If they could speak, what stories would they tell? This artwork had been hidden away for more than fifty years. The paintings deserved to be set free, he thought. It was time to bring them out of hiding, to return them to their rightful owners, extricate them from the captivity of a previous war and an overly zealous totalitarian government. And Theo knew that he was the perfect man – perhaps the *only* man for the job.

CHAPTER SIX

Rakovník, March 15, 1939

BEING WOKEN in the middle of the night was never a good thing, Karl knew. You were roused in the middle of the night when someone died, like his grandmother had years earlier, or when someone was sick and about to die. No one woke you at that hour to tell you all was well. So when Karl's mother shook his arm to awaken him from a deep sleep at the crack of dawn on March 15, 1939, Karl was instantly alert.

"What is it? Is someone sick?" Karl asked, sitting up in bed and squinting into the darkness.

"Get up, Karl. Get dressed at once." His mother's face moved in and out of the early morning shadows, an eerie silhouette fading and reappearing. "I'll tell you everything once we're all downstairs."

She turned and left the room. Karl paused, rubbing the sleep from his eyes. A second later, he threw back the covers and leaped out of bed, shuddering as he crossed the room to get his clothes. It was cold in the house, but it was apprehension that made him tremble. He dressed quickly, ran down the stairs, and joined his mother in the salon. Hana and Leila were already there. Hana looked pale and she glanced nervously from her mother to Karl and back. Marie was pacing across the floor, looking more distressed than Karl could ever remember. Karl stood silently in the center of the room waiting for his mother to speak. Finally, she turned to face her children.

"Hitler is going to invade," she said. "His troops will march into Prague today."

The unthinkable was about to happen. In recent days, President Hácha had been ordered to Berlin and given an ultimatum by Hitler: surrender Prague or it will be bombed. In the end, Hitler had not lived up to the commitments he made at the Munich conference. Appeasement had failed.

"It was the *plukovník* who told me," continued Mother. The colonel had returned to Rakovník a week earlier, and once again he had been staying in the Reiser home. "The commander was called away in the middle of the night. Before he left, he informed me that the army had been ordered to lay down its arms. There will be no resistance." Mother's face was drawn and tight. She looked as if she had aged years overnight.

Karl was shocked and his mind was racing, trying to grasp the magnitude of what his mother was saying. After all the conversations with his parents, after all the newspaper and radio reports, after all the debates back and forth about what to expect and what might possibly happen, this was the end result. Hitler had once again deceived the world, laughing off his promises to respect established borders. And Czechoslovakia was about to become the next casualty in his campaign.

"We're leaving," Mother announced to the stunned room. "Children, pack some clothing – nothing else. We don't want to arouse suspicion. Leila, gather your things along with some essentials from the house. Tell Kalina to bring the car around in an hour."

Karl struggled to understand what his mother was saying. "What do you mean?"

"We have to get out of here immediately," she said. "Before he left, the commander advised me that it would be better for all of us if we left Rakovník as quickly as possible. He told me that directly. I know what that means, Karl. It means that as Jews we are no longer safe here."

Karl nodded and looked away. The officer had given them a warning that was meant to save them. He must have known they were Jews all along, though he never acknowledged it explicitly.

"With the Nazis on our doorstep, who knows what will happen to us," continued Mother. "We're going to Prague and from there we'll find a way to get out of the country. I don't know how, but I do know that we can't delay. Once we're in Prague, I will contact your father."

At the mention of his father's name, Karl glanced up at his mother. Victor was away on business, traveling in Holland and France. He was due to return in a few days. Two weeks earlier Karl and Hana had returned home from school to find another stranger in their home meeting with their father. When Hana and Karl had entered the dining room, Father was deep in conversation. This was not unusual. Father frequently entertained business associates in their home. Mixing business with family life was a way of life for him, particularly as his office was only steps away from his living quarters.

"Hana, Karl, come in." Father gestured to his children to enter the dining room. Karl walked in to meet the gentleman who rose from a chair to face him. Hana, always more tentative with strangers, hung back awkwardly. "This is a colleague of mine – Alois Jirák," continued Father. "And these are my children."

Introductions done, Karl sat down at the table, curious about the purpose of this business meeting, while Hana continued to hover at the entrance to the dining room.

"Mr. Jirák and I were discussing my upcoming business trip to Paris and Amsterdam."

Alois Jirák was tall and well dressed. He was older than Victor by about a dozen years, and though he had little hair left on his scalp, he appeared vigorous and sharp. "I'm confident the meetings in Paris will go well," Mr. Jirák said. "The market is strong these days, notwithstanding the political unrest here and abroad."

At that time, a grain monopoly existed in Czechoslovakia, and Victor sat on the board of the organization that controlled the export of agricultural products. This board set grain prices and established the regulated schedules by which farmers would deliver their produce; it was in effect a forced pooled selling system. Victor's role abroad was to represent the board as he met with other businessmen like himself.

"Will you be gone long, Father?" asked Karl.

Victor shook his head. "Several weeks at the most. Hana," he added. "I believe you know Mr. Jirák's grandson. He attends your school and is in your grade, a boy named Jan Pekárek?"

Hana thought a moment and nodded but did not reply.

"Children, tell your mother that we will have a guest for dinner. Alois, you will join us, of course."

Mr. Jirák nodded. "Thank you, Victor. I'd be delighted. You can tell me how my grandson does in school," he added, bowing slightly to Hana. "His father, my son-in-law, does not give me much information." Mr. Jirák smiled, trying to engage Hana in conversation, but she would have none of it.

As they left the room, Hana turned to her brother. "Why do we always have to have strangers at our dining room table?" she asked.

Karl shrugged. "I like having company in the house. It's less boring that way." Besides, he was truly interested in this man – Alois Jirák. His father clearly trusted him, so that was enough for Karl. "Do you know who his grandson is?"

Hana nodded. "Jan Pekárek. He's one of those *přespolní*.* He lives in Krušovice, I think, and he's bussed in every day. I don't have too much to do with him, but he's a good student."

The events of that evening returned to Karl's mind now as he sat listening to his mother talk. Shortly after that dinner with Alois Jirák, his father had departed for his business trip. Karl stared at his mother and she returned his look evenly.

---

* The literal translation is "someone from over the fields." It refers to someone who is from the country.

"It's my decision to leave, not your father's," she said, reading her son's mind. "I know what I'm doing. I know what's best."

Karl looked away. He knew that if his father were here they would not be leaving so quickly. But in Father's absence, Mother was taking charge.

"Where are we going to live?" Karl asked. It was one thing to run from their home, but where would the family run to?

"We'll go to the flat that your father rented in Prague, the one owned by the Zelenkas. At least we have a place to go to."

"But, Mother," continued Karl, "do you think it's wise for us to go to Prague? Isn't that where all the trouble is going to be?" Karl couldn't help but recall the radio report of the annexation of Austria, when hundreds of thousands had come out to support Hitler. The Jews in Vienna had been targeted almost immediately.

"I have to believe that we'll be safer in the big city," she explained. "Few people know us there, and fewer still know that we are Jews. We will lose ourselves in the midst of that large population." Clearly, Marie believed that neither the Catholic marriage certificate that she and her husband had in their possession nor their false baptismal documents would help conceal who they were in Rakovník. "It won't be for long," she added. "This is only the first step, but it's the best option we have for the time being."

For the first time, Hana spoke. Her voice was small and uncertain. "But, Mother, what about the house? All of our things?"

Karl glanced around the room at the furnishings, the carpets, the grand piano, and the books on the shelves. The four paintings that Mr. Schmahl had given the family hung on the walls of the salon. *What about the paintings?* wondered Karl. His mother had said that they were the most valuable works of art that they owned.

Mother was visibly shaken. "We can't worry about any of that right now," she stammered. "We'll worry about that later. Go! Get ready. There isn't much time."

Mother left the room with Leila following close behind. Leila had not spoken a word during Marie's announcement, though her face spoke volumes, lined, broken, and etched in grief. With the fall of Sudetenland, she had already lost her country once. Now it appeared that she was losing her home for a second time. At least she was going with the family to Prague. Their fate would be her fate. She would not be left behind.

Karl turned to Hana who had sat motionless during the entire discussion with their mother. "What do you think?" he now asked as Hana stood to go to her room.

She shrugged. "It will be an adventure," she said. "That's the way I'm going to think about this. Besides, we've done nothing wrong. So what could anyone do to us?"

Karl sighed. At thirteen, perhaps Hana was still too young to appreciate the enormity of what was happening to their country and what was about to happen to their family. He envied her this detached, seemingly unconcerned attitude. As for Karl, he was anything but relaxed. He climbed the stairs to his room, moving slower now, struggling to comprehend what was about to happen. They were leaving their home – the home in which he had lived for his entire life. They were leaving everything behind and fleeing, perhaps for their lives, or so his mother was suggesting. And they were heading straight for Prague, the eye of the hurricane, the site of the impending invasion.

Karl entered his bedroom and glanced around. What to pack? His mother had said to bring only clothing, but that meant that everything of personal importance and value would be left behind. The camera was a must, he thought, throwing it into a bag, though he wondered what if anything he would be able to photograph. His books lay open on his desk and he suddenly realized that he had only two more months left of school. His *matura*, the final exams for which he had been studying for months, would now be abandoned as well. He would not complete high school. There would be no graduation.

With his bags packed, Karl descended the staircase, walking slowly this time, taking in the details of his home as if he were seeing them for the first time. At the bottom of the stairs, he turned to go to the front door when something in the salon caught his eye. It was his mother. She was circling the room, stopping in front of each of the four large paintings that had graced the walls for months now. As Karl watched, she reached out to touch the painting of the young housewife, her face almost as pensive and distracted as the model's.

"Mother?" Karl whispered.

Startled, Marie withdrew her hand and turned around. "Are you packed, Karl?"

He nodded and glanced up at the painting behind her. She followed his gaze.

"It seems silly, doesn't it?" she asked. "To be so attracted to these paintings and to be so sad about leaving them. They're just things after all, so unimportant compared to our lives. And yet...." She paused, looking back at Karl and then again at the painting. "I can't help this feeling," she continued. "I wanted to have something to pass on to you and Hana one day. And now, I'm not sure if we'll have any of it."

Karl stared, unable to respond.

"Come," she finally said. "It's time to go."

When all the bags had been loaded into the car, Marie, Hana, Karl, and Leila climbed in, squeezing next to one another and next to the dogs that were also accompanying them. There had been one final discussion with Mother about the fate of their beloved pets and in a moment of weakness she had acquiesced to the pleas of Karl and Hana.

The sun was just beginning to rise over Rakovník. A layer of frost covered the town and Karl's breath formed a steamy circle over the window as he gazed out. It cast his town in a white, hazy shroud. Once more he shuddered. War was on the horizon, but here it was eerily quiet, a kind of peacefulness that was a complete antithesis to what the country was facing. He breathed in deeply, trying to savor the calm.

"Let's go, Kalina," ordered Mother, and the car began to inch forward, driving the family eastward toward Prague. Karl did not look back.

CHAPTER SEVEN

Prague 1939

THE WEATHER HAD TURNED quite miserable by the time the Reiser automobile rolled through the streets of Prague. Snow was falling in a steady cascade in one of the worst storms of the season, blanketing a city that lay in wait for its opponents to strike. Few people were outside and those who walked had their heads and eyes down, keeping the business of the world at bay.

The family car headed straight for the villa in the Vinohrady suburb of Prague at 20 Benešova ulice, a beautiful section of the city with tree-lined streets and impressive private homes. It did not take long to unload their luggage and settle into the spacious apartment.

Within hours, just before noon, a gray column of soldiers, tanks, and motorcycles began to roll through the streets. Hitler's army had arrived and his limousine led the military parade. Generals came next, followed by marching soldiers, their faces set and staring ahead, their boots clomping through the snow in perfect synchronicity.

In the hundreds and thousands, the citizens of Prague came out to witness the arrival of Hitler's victorious army. They emerged slowly from their homes, shops, and businesses to line the streets and watch the take-over of their country. But there was little cheering, no chanting of slogans, and few sounds of adulation. They would accept their fate, but would not welcome it. Unlike their neighbors in Austria, the people of Prague were not pleased by Hitler's appearance. Many wept and openly jeered at him. For others, his invasion was met with stunned and stony silence.

Karl and his family remained indoors during the army's arrival. They stayed out of sight and listened to the distant sounds of marching, wondering what would happen next. During this time, Karl's mother paced frantically in their new living room. She was anxious to find a way to contact her husband.

"I can't imagine what your father must be thinking," she said as she approached the window to glance outside. As she turned away, the satin drapes fluttered closed behind her, blocking the view of the city as the snow continued to fall. "I'm sure he's been trying to call the house all morning. He'll be beside himself worrying about what's become of us."

Marie was reluctant to use the telephone in the villa to contact her husband. She feared that police or censors might be tapping phones, listening in on conversations. The family's goal was to be as invisible as possible – no overt contact with the outside world, nothing to draw attention to themselves, particularly as Jews. But by mid-afternoon, Marie could not stand it any longer. She announced to her children that she was going out to find a public telephone.

"I'm terrified that he's going to make the mistake of returning and I can't let him do that," she said. "At least one member of this family is safe outside Czech territory. He'll be more help to us from France right now than he could ever be here." She pulled on a heavy wool coat, wrapped a scarf around her head and neck, and headed out into the streets.

While his mother was gone, Karl wandered through the villa from room to room, inspecting this new, temporary home. It reminded him of his home in Rakovník with its tall ceilings, grand chandeliers, and fine Oriental carpets. There was a spacious garden in the courtyard at the back, now covered with snow and looking rather bleak.

Karl longed to watch the activity surrounding Hitler's arrival. He imagined the dictator crossing the Charles Bridge and emerging from his limousine at Hradčany castle, ready to inspect his troops on this historic occasion. Unbeknownst to Karl, Hitler would make a speech that day, declaring the entire western region of Czechoslovakia to be a German territory called the Protectorate of Bohemia and Moravia and under the rule of German-appointed Reich protector Konstantin von Neurath. In reality, this part of the country would be totally subjugated to Germany. Slovakia in the east would be declared an independent state under its president, Jozef Tiso, another of Hitler's pawns. Karl knew none of these details then, but he envisioned the Czech flag that flew over the Prague castle being lowered, and replaced with the swastika. And as he pictured the takeover of his country, a vile taste rose in his throat. He wanted to spit in Hitler's face, just as Hana had spat at the photograph of the SS officer in the photography shop window.

When Marie returned, Karl rushed to the door to greet her and hear the details of her call to his father. As expected, Victor had been frantic with worry over his family's whereabouts. When news of Hitler's invasion had reached him in Paris, he had called the house in Rakovník repeatedly but no one knew what had become of his wife and children. The family had left early in the morning and had told no one where they were going. For Victor, it was as if his family had disappeared into thin air, and he feared the worst. And, just as Marie had anticipated, Victor wanted to join them in Prague.

"It took everything in me to convince your father not to come back here," Marie explained, rubbing her tired eyes. She pulled a lace hankie from her sleeve and wiped her brow.

"How is Father?" asked Karl.

"A nervous wreck," his mother replied. Marie looked so distraught that Karl could only imagine just how difficult it must have been for her to persuade her husband not to rush to his family's side. "But now it's up to him to find a way to get us out of here. And it's up to us to stay out of the clutches of the Nazis."

It still felt somewhat unreal to Karl that the danger could be so imminent. But he was becoming increasingly impressed by the accuracy of his mother's assessments. Karl barely recognized his mother these days. The woman who had quietly stood behind her husband's authority all the time that Karl was growing up was emerging as a person in charge. Were it not for her, they would certainly never have left Rakovník so quickly.

Three days after Karl and his family arrived in Prague, Victor traveled to Zurich to finish off the business that had taken him out of Czechoslovakia in the first place. While he was there, he met with a notary to have his power of attorney turned over to Marie in Prague. Thanks once again to his wife's foresight, Victor had at his disposal a sizeable amount of family money that had already been transferred to the Crédit Lyonnais in Paris. Marie would now be in control of what was left of the family's estate and fortune in Czechoslovakia.

A few days later, Marie met with a notary in Prague and arranged to have her power of attorney assigned to Alois Jirák, the same colleague of their father's whom Hana and Karl had met in their home weeks earlier. Not only was Jirák a trusted business associate of Victor's, but, more importantly, he was Christian. Marie and Victor feared that the Nazis might freeze the bank accounts of all wealthy Jews, and hoped that placing their estate in the hands of a non-Jew would protect it from confiscation. In Germany it was already illegal for non-Jews to help Jews hide their holdings. But those laws had not yet arrived in Czechoslovakia.

The discussions for how to proceed with these arrangements were all done by telephone. Marie had found a payphone at the Hotel Paris in the center of Prague. There, she could talk with her husband uninterrupted, and she spoke frequently with him, awaiting his calls at preappointed times, and then returning to relay information to Karl and Hana. Once these financial plans were in place, Marie arranged to meet with Jirák in Prague to seal the agreement.

When she did, she had one more important request. "There are four paintings that we left behind in Rakovník," Marie said, describing the artwork. "They are the largest paintings we own, wall-sized oil paintings that are hung in the salon. You can't miss them. I would be devastated to see them destroyed, or worse, to think they had been taken by some Nazi thief. So I want you to take personal custody of them. Do whatever you must do to keep them safe."

Jirák nodded. "I understand," he said. "And if the Nazis search your house, I don't want them taken either. To be on the safe side, I will hide the paintings at my son-in-law's estate. He lives in the village of Krušovice, close to Rakovník. His name is Václav Pekárek. As you will recall, his son, Jan, attended school with your daughter. The paintings will be safe there. You can be confident of that."

Marie nodded. Jirák was so sincere, and appeared so earnest, that her fears about losing the works were immediately laid to rest. Her husband had trusted this man and she would do the same. With these arrangements in place, her mind was temporarily eased.

After Marie outlined her agreement with Jirák to him Karl asked, "Will we ever see our home again?"

Marie had difficulty answering her son, and she looked away. After several minutes, she turned back to him. "We can't worry about that right now," she said. "For the time being, we're safe and our belongings will be safe. The most important thing now is to get out of the country and to do it quickly."

Marie was right. This was not the time to worry about other things. The immediate order of business was to find a way to get out of the country, and do it while conditions were still relatively stable. The Nazis had predicted they would receive the same kind of reception in Czechoslovakia that had met them in Austria. Expecting the support of the masses, they anticipated moving quickly with new laws, including anti-Jewish measures. But because the citizens of Prague did not flock to show their adulation for the conquering army, few restrictions were imposed on Jews in the early days of the takeover, and Karl and his family were able to blend easily and quietly into life in the country's capital.

Almost immediately, Marie had arranged for Hana to go to school

at a local public high school. Hana, bored by the inactivity and confine-
ment of their villa, had been only too delighted to begin attending classes.

"I told you it would be a new adventure," she told Karl confidently
as she headed out for classes one bright morning. The snow and cold had
left Prague almost as quickly as it had arrived, and while it was still rather
gray and bleak outside, the assault of winter was retreating.

"Just be careful, Hana," warned Karl. He did not want to jolt his
younger sister out of her easy state of mind, but Karl had listened to his
mother's dire predictions about the fate of Czech Jews for too long. For
him, it felt as if the country was waiting for the guillotine to fall. Still,
Hana laughed easily as she walked out the door.

School was not an option for Karl. He had already missed his final
examinations in Rakovník, and it would be impossible to find a place
where he could register for exams in Prague without drawing too much
attention to himself. He imagined the conversations with school officials;
"Why did you leave your home town just as your *matura* was taking place?
Why did you have to leave so quickly? Why could you not wait a few more
days – a few more weeks?" These were questions that Karl was not prepared
to answer. Although school had never occupied the most important place
in his life, he mourned the loss of the completion of his education just as
he mourned the loss of his home. He often wondered if their house had
been plundered, either by Nazi soldiers or by greedy natives of Rakovník
who couldn't wait to be rid of their Jewish neighbors. Was everything they
had once owned now gone?

When his mother found a tutor for him in the city, and he began
taking private lessons in Spanish and English, Karl's days were occupied
and he found that he worried less. He also managed to locate his friend,
George Popper, who had been attending university in Prague for almost
a year. The two young men easily picked up their friendship.

"I'm concerned about my family," George said one afternoon as he
and Karl stood waiting in line at one of the many financial institutions
in Prague. Each day, Marie sent Karl to one of the banks to withdraw the
legally controlled limit of funds allowable on a daily basis – fifty Czech

crowns. Through Alois Jirák, Marie had access to larger sums of money in their estate. However, some of the family's funds were here in regular bank accounts. "I don't want the government to have any of it," Marie insisted. "We'll get it out of the bank, bit by bit if we have to."

"Your mother was smart to get you out of Rakovník when she did. I told you that she knew what she was talking about when we were still there," continued George. "Mine refused to leave. I haven't heard from my parents in weeks." Karl nodded sympathetically. He didn't even want to mention this news to Hana, knowing how she would worry about George's sister, Rita. It was difficult enough for Karl and his family to be separated from his father, but at least they knew where he was. There were too many rumors that Jews in smaller towns were being arrested. Karl's mind often wandered to thoughts of the Jewish families in Rakovník. He wondered if they had had the foresight to get out as Marie had.

The line in front of the bank wound its way down the street and around a corner. Now it inched forward ever so slightly. Hundreds of citizens lined up here on a daily basis to try to retrieve their savings. Along with a growing tension in the air was a sense that the market in Prague might collapse, leaving many without financial resources. Karl and George spent long hours here on a daily basis. Still, it passed the time when there was little else for Karl to do.

As for Marie, she was working furiously to get her family out of Czechoslovakia. Through conversations with Victor and various friends and officials in Prague, the family learned that to get out of the country, three key documents were required. The first was Czech passports. They were fortunate that they had these in their possession. The two remaining requirements were a permit from the Gestapo allowing the family to leave and cross the border, and a visa from a country willing to accept them. Victor was trying to acquire the latter. Marie was in charge of the exit permits. But the acquisition of these two key documents was proving to be a daunting task.

"Even if we are able to get out of Prague, what country will take us in?" Marie voiced this concern as she sat with her children in the evenings, discussing her ongoing telephone conversations with her husband and their efforts to obtain the necessary papers. The simple truth was that not many countries were willing to open their doors to Jewish refugees, and more and more were desperate to escape their countries. Many nations thought that by accepting Jews they would be bringing the wrath of Hitler upon themselves. Besides, many refugees had no jobs and no money, and could prove economically burdensome to countries dealing with their own unemployment and poverty. Instead of refusing entry to Jewish refugees outright, many countries made the conditions for entry so difficult that it was nearly impossible to comply. Stringent quota systems on the number of Jews admissible were put into place, adding to the list of obstacles facing Jews who wanted to leave their homelands. All of this conspired to keep Karl and his family in Prague as Hitler's noose tightened ever so slowly around their necks.

By early June, prominent Czech Jews began to disappear mysteriously. Jewish synagogues across the country were burned down and Jews rounded up and beaten on the streets. Jews were barred from owning businesses and Jewish property was seized across the protectorate. On June 21, von Neurath, the new Reich protector, issued a long list of anti-Jewish decrees, not unlike those already enacted in Germany, all designed to destroy the economic viability of the Jewish population. The seizure of Jewish property became commonplace. And while some Jews were still offered the opportunity to get their exit permits and leave the country, doing so meant that they would have to transfer their capital and property to the Nazis, thus forfeiting all of their belongings.

With their family fortune in the legal hands of Alois Jirák, Marie hoped to avoid surrendering their assets to the Nazi government. She searched the city, spoke to some trusted contacts, and managed to locate a lawyer who said he was willing to help with the exit permits. Marie returned home optimistic after her first meeting with the solicitor.

"He's charming, and so reassuring," she said. "I really think he'll be able to help us."

Trusting him, she turned over their passports and a large sum of money. She believed that within days, the family would have the necessary papers to leave. Each morning after that, she awoke, ready for the call that would summon her to the lawyer's office to pick up the documents, and each day there was no such call. Eventually, the lawyer contacted Marie, stating that he was having difficulty securing the necessary papers. He declared that he would need more money if he were to be successful in this task. More hesitantly now, Marie complied and turned over an additional large amount of cash. Still the lawyer did not come through. Reluctantly, Marie began to suspect that she was being extorted by an unscrupulous man. Karl accompanied her on the day she went to his law office.

"I insist that you return our passports," Marie said firmly when she and Karl were finally ushered in to face the lawyer. She stared evenly at him as she sat on the edge of a large armchair.

Karl stared at the lawyer who was trying to take advantage of his family. He was tall and gaunt, a humorless man with a permanent sneer on his face, so different from the "charming" person that Marie had at first described. He wore an ill-fitting black suit and eyed Marie quietly through thick glasses, returning her stare with one equally cool and detached. "Perhaps if you give me more money, I could do more for you. Money talks, you know."

Marie rose taller in her seat. "I will not give you one more crown."

The lawyer raised his eyebrows above his spectacles in a gesture that indicated his complete disdain for Marie. He shook his head. "That's a great pity," he replied, ice cold. He then went on to say that he had turned the passports over to his contact at the Gestapo. "Perhaps you'd like to deal with them as opposed to me."

Karl gulped. *This man had them*, he thought. *There would be no escape after all. Their belongings would be confiscated and his family would simply be fed into the jaws of the Nazis.* Karl watched his mother. What could she possibly do in the face of this threat?

Marie paused a moment, and then slowly rose out of her chair to face the lawyer. "I have nothing to lose here," she said, so quietly that Karl and the lawyer had to lean forward to catch every word. "I have reached the end of my rope and I will do anything to get my family to safety. Unless you return the passports to me immediately, I will go to the Gestapo myself and report you."

Karl was dumbfounded. This was an incredible and perhaps reckless display of bravado. What influence could Marie possibly have with the Gestapo, and why would they even care if one more Jew was being defrauded? But Marie was calling this man's bluff, hoping that he would not want any kind of attention brought to himself. How would he respond? He and Marie faced off against each other, staring one another in the eyes, waiting to see who would blink first. The lawyer's nostrils flared and his breathing made a high-pitched whistling sound. Minutes passed – an eternity. Finally, he rose, turned, and walked over to a large safe behind him. He opened it and reached inside. When he turned around he was holding the family's passports in his hands. He handed these precious identification papers over to Marie and motioned for her to leave with a wave of his hand, as if he were shooing away an annoying fly. Without uttering another word, Karl and his mother turned and left the office.

Once on the sidewalk they both breathed a deep sigh of relief. But Karl could see that, for all of his mother's daring, her hands were shaking as she placed the passports securely back inside her purse. She smiled weakly up at her son.

"We won that round, didn't we, Karl?"

Karl nodded admiringly. But, in the next moment, his heart sank and the sense of victory was replaced with one of despair. They were back to square one. They had no travel documents, no visa, and no means to leave the country.

In this first of a three-page document, Victor transfers to Marie full power to deal with all assets, and power to take whatever action in relation to those assets that she deems necessary.

Já podepsaná Marie Reiserová, bytem Praha XII., Benešovská ul. čís. 20 přenáším tuto plnou moc, mně udě-
lenou mým manželem Viktorem Reiserem na pana Aloise
Jiráka, profesora Praha VII., čp. 854, kterého sou-
časně i vlastním jménem zmocňuji a ustanovuji jako
správce svého celého jmění jak movitého, tak nemovi-
tého.

V Praze, dne 22. března 1939.

Marie Reiserová v.r.

Tuto plnou moc přijímám.
V Praze, dne 22. března 1939.

Alois Jirák v.r.   Marie Reiserová v.r.

Kolek 3 K   Číslo jednací 82.873.

Osvědčuji, že paní Marie Reiserová, bytem v Praze
XII., Benešovská ul.20, doznala dnes přede mnou,
že tuto listinu vlastnoručně podepsala. Její osobní
totožnost potvrdili mi osobně mi známí: pan Dr.
Josef Schwarz, advokát v Praze I., Skořepka 2, a
sl. Blažena Kašparová, úřednice tamtéž, co svědci
totožnosti.-V Praze dne dvacátého druhého března
roku tisícího devítistého třicátého devátého.-----
                    Dekretem notářské komory v
Popl. kol. a daň K 12.35 Praze ze dne 28. ledna 1939
              čj. 2468 n.k. podle § 3 půst.
              3 opatření Stálého výboru ze dne 16.
              listopadu 1938 čís. 285 Sb. z. a nař.
              zmocněný zástupce notáře JUDr.
L.S.   Aloise Frenzla v Praze.

              D.S. Dr. Karel Frenzl v.r.

In response to assuming power of attorney from Victor, Marie transfers this power to Mr. Alois Jirák, "professor whom I...empower as an adminstrator of our assets, real estate or other..." At the bottom of the document is a statement by Jirák saying that he accepts this power of attorney.

CHAPTER EIGHT

Prague, July 1939

AFTER THE FIASCO with the lawyer, Marie began to proceed more cautiously to obtain exit visas from the Gestapo. It was becoming increasingly clear that few people in Prague could be trusted to help. Swindlers were everywhere, looking for opportunities to take advantage of desperate Jews who were trying every avenue to get out of the country. As hard as his mother was working to secure the exit documents, Karl knew that his father was working equally hard to find a country willing to accept them, and to obtain the necessary entry permits. And by July 1939, it appeared that Victor might be having some luck.

As Karl was returning home from his English lessons one afternoon, the streets were busy with people rushing about at the end of the workday. At first glance, all appeared normal. But a second look told a different story. On every corner and in front of many shops and stalls, there were Nazi soldiers and Czech police patrolling side by side. Their rifles were slung over their shoulders in an almost casual manner. But their eyes were trained on the faces of the people as they passed by. *What are they looking for?* Karl wondered as he kept his head down and walked quickly toward his home.

Were they searching for Jews? And would they recognize him as one if they had a good look? Signs and placards in stores and cafés warned that Jews were not permitted to shop or sit. The flag bearing the swastika flew at every street intersection and draped the tallest buildings. Karl resisted the burning urge to document the pillage of this city with his camera. It had remained tucked away in his suitcase at the flat. A young red-haired man snapping photographs of Nazi soldiers would be a beacon and he was smart enough not to risk this exposure.

As soon as Karl pushed open the front door of their apartment, he was greeted by the most intoxicating smells coming from the kitchen. There was the familiar aroma of caraway, paprika, and dill combining with garlic and onions. He closed his eyes and felt himself transported back home where these smells at the end of the day meant only one thing – a banquet in the dining room and guests for dinner.

Karl followed the smells into the formal dining room at the back of the flat where he was startled to see Leila setting the table with the fine china, silverware, and crystal wine glasses that had been there in the villa when they had arrived. This ceremonial dining ware had seldom been used by Karl's family. It seemed pointless to dine formally when it was only Karl, his mother, and sister.

Marie was directing Leila from one side of the room but stopped when her son entered. "Karl," she said brightly, her face more alive than he had seen in weeks. Strands of hair had escaped from her bun and flew about the top of her head. She had a schoolgirl excitement about her. "How were the lessons today?"

Karl nodded. "They were fine. I'm actually enjoying the classes. My English and Spanish are becoming almost as good as my French, Latin, and German." With his strong aptitude for languages, the classes were proving to be a gratifying challenge.

"Good," his mother replied, "because English may come in quite handy for you." She paused and smiled at the puzzled expression on her son's face. "Let me tell you about my telephone conversation with your father today."

Marie went on to explain that Victor had made an important contact in Paris earlier that week. He had been working feverishly, desperate to find a country willing to accept them. Rumors were rampant about where to go and which country might be offering visas. As everyone was discovering, there were fewer and fewer legal avenues open. But two countries in particular, Canada and Cuba, had the reputation of having immigration officials who might be willing to accept bribes in exchange for providing those all-important entry documents.

"Your father is worried that the Cuban visas might turn out to be forgeries. That's what people are telling him. Can you imagine arriving in a country only to be turned back because the papers are counterfeit!" Marie exclaimed as she inspected the placement of the last of the dishes on the dining room table. She turned again to face Karl, her face shining. "But Canada! Your father believes that we have a chance to get genuine entry papers to go there. He's met a man who's willing to help us."

The man was George Harwood, a Canadian official stationed in Paris, working as an agent of the Canadian Pacific Railway in a section known as the Department of Colonization and Immigration. His job was to find and recruit suitable employees to work for the CPR in Canada and to find immigrants who could work the land. "These immigrants are not necessarily meant to be Jews," continued Marie, "though I imagine there are many, like your father, who are trying to get hired on just to be able to get the papers. But, more importantly, your father has learned that Mr. Harwood is a man who will take money under the table. And that's what we're counting on. Remember, money talks, Karl." She was quoting what the corrupt lawyer had said before he had swindled them out of a large amount, and Karl wondered if Mr. Harwood's intentions were any more legitimate.

"Mr. Harwood is here in Prague; he's come to meet some prospective recruits. And I've invited him to dinner here tonight!" Marie turned to face her son. "Oh, Karl, we must remain hopeful that this plan will work, and we must impress Mr. Harwood, no matter what. Now, I have so much to do." With that, she flew out of the dining room, calling instructions to Leila.

George Harwood was a charming and talkative man, who happily accepted Marie's hospitality as if he were a long-lost friend. "It's so lovely to enjoy a home-cooked meal, Mrs. Reiser," he said patting his rather large stomach. He finished off his third plate of food and washed it down with another glass of red wine. From his portly stature he looked as if he had enjoyed many a good meal. "I can't tell you how tedious it has been to dine in those hotel restaurants night after night."

Marie, ever the gracious hostess, smiled warmly. "We're pleased to welcome you, Mr. Harwood. As you can imagine, I haven't had many opportunities to entertain lately. I miss the dinner parties we used to have. This is a treat for me as well."

Marie had gone out of her way to prepare a banquet. All of Karl's favorites were there: *česneková polévka* – garlic soup – to start, followed by *hovězí* with *opekané brambory* – beef with roasted potatoes – for the main course. Dessert was the best surprise – *borůvkové knedlíky*, dumplings with blueberries hidden inside mounds of delicately chewy dough. With restrictions on shopping for Jews, it was difficult to know how she had managed to acquire all of these delicacies. Leila must certainly have helped.

There were other guests for dinner that evening: Mr. and Mrs. Zelenka, the couple that owned the flat that Karl and his family were renting. They also wanted entry visas to Canada, and hoped that Mr. Harwood would be willing to help.

"You have a lovely home here," Mr. Harwood said, finally pushing away from the table and leaning back in his chair.

"We are very comfortable," said Marie. "And lucky, thanks to the Zelenkas. But I wish you could see what we left behind, Mr. Harwood. Our books, music, furniture, artwork." She went on to describe the four large paintings. "They were really quite special. I think I miss those most of all."

"I love the arts, too," said Mr. Harwood. "My family owned a music store in Winnipeg, where I grew up."

"My son, Karl, has been studying English," said Marie. "I hope he gets to use it in your country."

Karl and Hana watched and listened from their spot at one end of the dining room table. They had been told to dress for the evening. Karl wore his best suit, while Hana had on a silk dress in the softest shade of green. It set off her curly red hair and vibrant eyes, but she was quiet. The presence of these guests reminded her of those days in Rakovník when the house had been overrun with unfamiliar faces. The preceding couple of months in Prague had been a welcome opportunity to have her family to herself, notwithstanding the circumstances under which they were there. Karl was glued to the conversation, anxious to hear word of when the family might be leaving and when he would be reunited with his father.

"The country doesn't want us here anymore – that is becoming abundantly clear. But they're making it impossible for us to leave." Mr. Zelenka was speaking and his face was red as he gestured in the air angrily with his knife, hardly noticing the bits of food and gravy that flew in all directions.

"Perhaps things are not as bad as some would suggest." This statement came from Mrs. Zelenka, a thin woman dwarfed in size and personality by her outspoken husband. "My parents will never leave, no matter what, and I'm still not sure I can leave them behind. They believe that because they are elderly, no one will bother them. 'What would Hitler want with old Jews?' my father often asks." She smiled and others at the table joined her.

"We will all have to leave eventually. That's what I think," continued Mr. Zelenka. "Hitler's right-hand man, Eichmann, is here in Prague right now, trying to push all of us out. He's even established a branch of the *Zentralstelle für Jüdische Auswanderung*. They say that if you sign up with this Central Office for Jewish Emigration you'll receive an exit visa. Simple as that! But is it?"

"If Jewish families register with this organization, doesn't it mean that they have to transfer all of their capital and property into the hands of the Nazis?" Karl asked from his spot at the table, no longer able to resist contributing to the conversation. "That makes it impossible for most families to leave."

"Exactly my point!" Mr. Zelenka's head bobbed emphatically. "They want us out, but then they create all kinds of obstacles to our leaving.

Some are suggesting that this branch of the SS is merely a front. Jews register to leave and once they come forward, they are arrested and never heard from again."

Marie recounted the story of how the lawyer had swindled her out of a large amount of money. "Not only that, but he threatened to report us to the Gestapo."

Mr. Harwood nodded sympathetically. "It's no easier to get in anywhere, as I'm sure you all know. It was possible a few years ago. But now, Canada and many other countries are reluctant to take in Jewish refugees. There's a fear that we'll be flooded with families escaping Europe. Besides, few countries want to alienate Hitler these days."

"Not even Palestine," added Mr. Zelenka, shaking his head. "One would have thought that Jews could go there. But the British are worried that there might be another Arab uprising like the one in 1936. So those doors are closed as well." The Arab revolt against mass Jewish immigration had lasted off and on for three years and had prompted a renunciation of Britain's intent to create a Jewish national home in Palestine.

There was a moment of silence at the table. Then Mr. Harwood said, "Thankfully, for you and others, I'm able to bend the rules to allow selected immigrants into my country – not an easy task, I assure you." He stopped short of saying that it would cost these families dearly for the privilege of entering Canada. The details of that would come later.

"We are all so fearful of Hitler's plans," said Marie. "Here, there are more and more restrictions emerging on a daily basis. Now Jewish doctors and lawyers can't practice; professors and instructors can't teach."

"And what about those who are being arrested?" asked Mr. Zelenka. "They call it protective custody, whatever that means. Who's being protected? And where are they going? No one seems to know."

"First Austria, then Czechoslovakia. What next?" Marie lowered her head and closed her eyes.

"Poland!" declared Mr. Zelenka. "Hitler recognized a valuable prize when he took Czechoslovakia. Not only did he get this vast land, but also it paved the way for further conquests. He's already denounced the non-aggression pact with Poland and he's demanding the return of Danzig to Germany. Mark my words: Poland is next."

"Will no one come to Europe's aid?" Mrs. Zelenka whispered these words.

Mr. Harwood shook his head. "President Roosevelt has outlined a peace proposal for Europe, but it doesn't look like Hitler is going to listen to it. I'm afraid we're headed for all-out war."

There was silence at the table as each guest digested this pronouncement. Karl was angered by the discussion. How was it that they had become fugitives? They were being forced to leave their homes and were being treated like criminals for no reason. They weren't wanted in their home country, and they weren't wanted elsewhere. None of it made sense. Karl's family had barely acknowledged its Jewish background, but now it seemed to glow above their heads like a spotlight.

"Enough talk of war," said Marie, shaking her head wearily. "Please enjoy the wine, the meal, and our hospitality, Mr. Harwood. Let's talk of happier things. Let's talk of a future in your country." She raised her glass and said, "To Canada. And to peace!" The others joined her in the toast.

Shortly after that, the Zelenkas said their good-byes and went upstairs to their flat. Marie walked over to Mr. Harwood and extended her hands to him. "I know that you and my husband have discussed the terms under which we might be able to get into your country," she said, referring to the bribe that would buy them their precious entry visas. "We will complete our part of the agreement. Please fulfill yours. Do not let my family down." She spoke these last words fervently, staring Mr. Harwood in the eyes and clutching his hands in a forceful grip.

Mr. Harwood nodded. "I'll meet with your husband as soon as I get back to Paris. When the details are in place, I'll arrange your visas through the consulate there," he said, bowing slightly. "Thank you again for the lovely evening."

Within days, Victor called his wife at a prearranged time on a public telephone to report that the monetary transaction with George Harwood had been completed and the entry visas to Canada would be issued. Karl didn't know how much money had passed between his father and Mr. Harwood, though he believed it must have been a sizeable amount. What was important was that one more hurdle had been cleared to enable them to leave.

With the visas seemingly secured, Marie turned her attention once more to acquiring the exit permits, the final and perhaps most important documents standing in their way. It was dangerous to try to arrange a meeting with the Gestapo. Notwithstanding the power of attorney in the hands of Alois Jirák, Marie knew that she would risk having to disclose their family fortune if she were to meet with Nazi officials. And she worried that by concealing their wealth, she was jeopardizing the safety of her family. If the Nazis were to discover this deceit, not only would they confiscate the estate, but they would probably also arrest the Reisers. The Gestapo did not need a reason to take a Jew into custody. Marie could chance none of this.

But the pieces were falling into place, one by one. Once again, Marie cast out her net and pulled in contacts. She discovered that in the town of Zlin there was a Gestapo official who, like George Harwood, was known to take bribes. This was all she needed to know. She awoke early one morning and announced to her children that she would be traveling by train to Zlin, staying there overnight, and would return later the next day.

"I haven't even told your father these details," she said, before leaving the villa. "Better not to worry him too much more." Though Victor had remained in Paris as per his wife's wishes, the stress of being separated from his family was taking its toll. Marie knew this from their telephone conversations and she in turn worried about her husband's health. "I'll give him the good news tomorrow, after I've got the papers in my hand," she said brightly.

Karl wondered if her optimistic attitude was merely a front for the anxiety that she surely must have been feeling. He too was anxious for his mother's safety, though he could not state these concerns. He watched her, wondering how she was ever going to pull off this feat. What Gestapo official would agree to meet with a Jew, let alone a woman? But Karl knew that his mother had already proved herself capable of accomplishing the impossible, and Karl prayed that this journey to Zlin would be no exception. When he saw her striding confidently up the sidewalk toward their apartment the following evening, he knew that she had accomplished her mission.

"I've got them," she announced jubilantly as she entered the villa and grabbed her children in a fierce embrace. "Imagine! It only took a few minutes." She went on to describe the trip. The train ride to Zlin had been the most anxiety-provoking part of the journey. In every car, Nazis patrolled the aisles or mingled with passengers. Marie's greatest fear had been that she might be asked for her papers and questioned. It would have been difficult, under Nazi scrutiny, to hide her religion. But the trip passed uneventfully. Perhaps the guards had passed her by because she looked so refined. Several actually had nodded at her and she had forced herself to paste a smile on her face as she hid her trembling hands in her lap. In Zlin, she proceeded to Gestapo headquarters, and asked to speak to the official whose name she had obtained. He saw her immediately.

"Like being close to the devil himself," Marie described. "That's what it felt like in the room with that man staring at me." She breathed in deeply before continuing. "I took the envelope of cash from my purse and slid it across the table toward him. He would never have taken it from my hand – wouldn't dare touch me, a Jewess. But my money was certainly good enough for him. We barely spoke, we didn't need to. He knew why I was there. Look Karl, Hana, my hands are shaking even now as I think about it."

Karl could only imagine what it must have been like for his mother to face this Gestapo officer and ask for the exit papers. Her initiative and sheer guts were more impressive than ever. In exchange for payment, Marie had left the building with the exit permits in hand. Proudly, she displayed the documents to her children, one in her name and one in Karl's name. Hana would travel under her mother's passport. Everything was now in place, but Marie was still worried.

"What if these permits are invalid?" She voiced her apprehension that evening as they celebrated the acquisition of the documents. All the necessary papers lay on the table in front of them: passports, exit permits, even the false baptism papers and Catholic marriage certificate. This accumulation of documentation had more value to the family than their entire estate. And Karl knew that they were luckier than most to have collected them. There was the underlying sense of a near stampede in Prague as other Jewish families were desperately trying to acquire the very papers that the Reisers had lying in front of them. "What if the exit documents are forgeries, or stolen from someone else?" Marie continued. "What if that Gestapo official deceived me, just as that terrible lawyer did? Without proper papers, we could be stopped at the border and that would be that."

Chances were, with invalid papers, not only would they be turned back from the border, they would be arrested. Though sanctions against Jews had been slower to take effect in Prague, this infraction would no doubt lead to severe consequences.

"I do have one idea," Marie said, turning to Karl. "But you are going to have to agree to this."

What now? Karl wondered.

"I want you to test these documents for us." It seemed that Marie had already thought this plan through. "I want you to get on a train to Paris with your permit. If you can get through passport control at the border, then we will know that the papers are good." Once safely in France and reunited with his father, Karl would notify his mother and sister to come immediately.

The plan hung in the air as Karl digested its implications. "You're smart and quick, Karl," Marie added, reaching across the table to take her son's arm, as if to pass her strength to him. "You can manage any situation. I'm sure of that."

Karl swallowed and nodded. This had an ominous tone to it. But he knew what he had to do. He was being asked to put himself on the line, to test these waters for the family. And, in the absence of his father, he was the only one who could do it.

Durchlaßschein Nr. *3378*

Der — Die *Karl Reiser*

(Vorname, Familienname, Beruf)

aus *Zlin*

(ständiger Wohnort, Straße, Hausnummer)

ist berechtigt, unter Vorlage des Passes (Paßersatzes) ²)

Nr. *6174*,

ausgestellt von *Bez Beh Rakouniko*

in der Zeit vom *23. 6.* 1939 bis zum *31. 7.* 1939

einmal ¹) — wiederholt ¹) — über die an der Grenze des Protek=
torats Böhmen und Mähren amtlich zugelassenen Übergangs=
stellen das Gebiet des Protektorats zu verlassen und in dieses
Gebiet wieder einzureisen.

Zlin, den *23. 6.* 1939

Geheime Staatspolizei

Staat (Dienststelle)elle Brünn

Außendienststelle Zlin

(Unterschrift)

(Stempel)

¹) Nichtzutreffendes streichen.

²) Bei Reichsangehörigen ist nur ein Paß, bei Ausländern ein Paß oder Paßersatz
zulässig.

Karl's exit permit issued by the Gestapo in Zlin, June 23, 1939.

82

LÉGATION
DE LA RÉPUBLIQUE TCHÉCOSLOVAQUE
A PARIS
15, Avenue Charles-Floquet, 15
(7e arrt.)

18.278/39

    La Légation de la République Tchécoslovaque à Paris présente ses compliments empressés au Minis--tère de l'Intérieur -(Direction Générale de la Sûreté Nationale.)- et a l'honneur de recommander à son avis très favorable,la demande d'autorisation de séjourner à PARIS de Monsieur Karel Victor REISER ressortissant tchécoslovaque, très honorablement con--nu de cette Légation qui donne toutes garanties pour sa parfaite moralité.

    Monsieur REISER, se trouve dans l'impossibi-lité de rentrer en Tchécoslovaquie étant donné l'acti-vité qu'il y avait développée en tant que grand patri-te tchèque. Il dispose de moyens de fortune largement suffisants pour assurer son existence et celle de sa famille sans chercher d'occupation rénumérée.

    Monsieur REISER voulant se vouer aux oeuvres sociales s'occupant des réfugiés tchécoslova-

MINISTERE DE l'INTERIEUR

Direction Générale de la Sûrete Nationale

    P A R I S.

                                             ./.

A two-page document issued by the Czech Embassy in Paris.

This document enabled Victor to remain in Paris while trying to get his family out of Czechoslovakia. It provided support to him in his efforts to obtain his "carte d'identité," the official papers needed to remain in France during the war.

CHAPTER NINE

Prague, July 18, 1939

THE WILSON TRAIN STATION was bustling in the twilight of a warm Prague evening. No one paid too much attention to the attractive woman and her tall, pale son who stood together on the platform waiting for the departure of the Prague–Paris express. It was an overnight train, due to arrive in Paris early on the morning of July 19. Nazi officials patrolled the station, glancing casually at the passengers who were waiting to depart or awaiting the arrival of friends and loved ones. An uneasy calm prevailed as people went about their business and tried to avoid catching the eye of the guards. Karl and his mother were doing the same.

"I'm so proud of you, Karl," his mother whispered, reaching up to kiss her son on the cheek. When had he grown to be so much taller than she?

Karl returned her embrace, feeling the weight of responsibility on his shoulders for what he was about to do. His mind was galloping, reliving all that had transpired in the preceding twenty-four hours.

Packing had been simple. No one wanted to attract too much attention and a large quantity of luggage could draw unwanted questions from border officials, or those Nazi guards who continued to walk past on the platform. He had only brought clothing and a few books with him from Rakovník to Prague, and he would take the same belongings, plus his precious camera, to Paris. Perhaps he would have a chance to use the camera again once the family was in a place of safety. Karl's small brown suitcase rested next to him as he stood with his mother.

Saying good-bye to Leila that morning had been difficult. The truth was, if this escape were successful, it was possible that he might never see his nanny again. She had held on to Karl for a long time, sobbing quietly, and wishing him a safe journey and a good life. The memories of his childhood in her care welled up inside of Karl even now and he shook his head trying to regain his composure. Bidding farewell to his dog was also painful. He knew in his heart that it was unlikely he would ever see his pet again, and when he had buried his head in Lord's neck and clung to him, the Great Dane squirmed and barked loudly, perhaps sensing that something was different in this embrace with his master.

Just before leaving the villa, Karl had had one last, brief conversation with Hana. "Do you still think this is all an adventure?" he asked.

Hana had tilted her head to one side and eyed her brother thoughtfully. "We will all be together looking back on this one day, Karl. I'm sure of it. Besides, you're the one who always gets me out of trouble. So I'm counting on you to do that for all of us, now."

Karl recalled all that and more as he stood with his mother waiting to board the train. "I hope it's on time," he said, trying to make casual conversation.

"I'll see you in Paris in a few days," his mother replied, reaching up to straighten his starched shirt collar.

Karl nodded. His mother's words sounded calm and confident, but he knew her well enough to detect the worry in her eyes. This could not have been easy for Marie – to relinquish her son with no certainty that he would be safe. As for Karl, in truth he was feeling a bit like the sacrificial slave about to be thrown into the gladiator's ring. He was hopeful that all the papers were legitimate, as the Gestapo official had promised, and that he would make it safely across the border. But they were putting their lives into the hands of a Nazi, all of whom were deceitful as far as Karl was concerned.

The fear that things might go horribly wrong crept into his brain and threatened to destroy his resolve. What if he were detained at the border and questioned? He had rehearsed the statement: *I'm traveling to Paris to meet my father.* It sounded innocent enough. But everyone knew that instead of regular border guards, the border was now policed by the dreaded SS in their black uniforms with the swastikas on their armbands and the skull-and-crossbones emblems on their caps. That image alone terrified Karl. He wondered if he had it in him to be as resourceful as his father, who was working furiously to bring the family together, or as his mother, who had already saved them several times over. Yes, his mother had been more of a hero than he ever could have imagined. Could he follow in her courageous footsteps? He shook his head. He simply could not let his mind dwell on the danger. He had to hold on to the belief that he would be in Paris in several hours and happily reunited with his father.

A train attendant passed by on the platform and Marie stepped out to stop him. "Excuse me," she said. "My son has a ticket to Paris on the express train." As she spoke she reached into her handbag, withdrawing a sizeable amount of money. She rolled the bills into a tight wad and pushed them firmly into the attendant's hand. "You'll see to it that he is not disturbed and that he has a safe and comfortable journey, won't you?"

The steward looked down at the cash in his hand and then up into the steady gaze of the well-dressed woman in front of him. He glanced at Karl and then again at his own hand. Karl wondered if he suspected that they were Jewish or merely wealthy travelers. Finally, the attendant tipped his hat, bowed slightly, pocketed the money, and smiled at Marie. "Madame, if you would give me the young man's papers, I'll see to it that he isn't bothered the entire journey."

Marie reached into her bag once more and withdrew Karl's travel documents: his ticket, passport, and the all-important exit permit needed to get out of Czechoslovakia and safely into France. These would have to be presented at the border. She hesitated a moment, and then handed

KATHY KACER

them over to the waiting steward. He accepted the documents, tipped his hat once more, and signaled Karl to follow him.

There was only time for one more quick good-bye. "I'll give your love to Father," Karl said urgently as he embraced his mother once more. "And I will see you in a few days." Then, he picked up his suitcase and, with one last backward glance, he marched quickly after the attendant and jumped easily onto the train.

The attendant led Karl down the aisle of sleeping compartments and entered one at the end of the train car. As soon as Karl was inside the coach, the attendant pulled the curtain around the compartment. Before leaving, he turned to Karl. "I'll do my best to ensure that your trip is uneventful, sir." With that, the steward exited the car, and Karl was alone.

He took a deep breath and sank heavily onto the small bunk. He removed his jacket, laying it carefully at the foot of the bed, and took off his shoes. Then he lay back on the bed and closed his eyes, realizing suddenly how weary he was. Anxiety did that to you; it sapped you of energy and drained you of the wisdom you needed to stay sharp. And Karl needed his faculties for this journey.

He could barely wrap his head around the knowledge that he was leaving his home country, perhaps never to see it again. But he didn't want to think about that. Czechoslovakia had let his family down, had failed to protect them when they needed that protection most. Karl had tried to tell himself that he had little regret in leaving. But that wasn't entirely true. The sense of betrayal and the anger at being forced from his home threatened to overwhelm him. Instead, he squeezed his eyes shut tightly, trying to block the images of Rakovník, his house, and the familiar life of his childhood there. The attendant had said that he would do his best to make sure that Karl was not disturbed. Would his best be good enough, Karl wondered. With luck, he would wake to find himself in Paris. If not… who knew what his fate would be? The train pulled out of Prague station. Karl fell asleep to its rocking.

He awoke with a start. Where was he? What time was it? Karl stretched his cramped legs as cloudy images slowly began to coalesce. He felt the rocking motion beneath him, remembering that he was on a train en route to Paris. How long had he been sleeping?

A sliver of light slipped through the crack in the curtains at his feet, dancing playfully on his blankets. Karl sat up and cautiously pulled the curtain to one side. Swinging his legs over the side of the bunk, he stood up, balancing himself in the swaying train, and glanced out the window, trying to determine where he was. It was dawn and the sun was rising above a cloudless blue-gray sky. The train was traveling at a high speed and the countryside rushed by in a blur. In the distance, there were small houses and colorful fields picturesquely dotting the panorama. Here and there, Karl could make out small lines of traveling automobiles, trailing clouds of dust from the country roads. This landscape could easily be Czechoslovakia, Karl thought, but it was daylight, so surely he must have left his country behind hours ago.

Karl stretched his neck, eager to see a road sign, a marker – anything that might indicate where he was. A signpost suddenly appeared, speeding by the window too quickly for Karl to see. But shortly thereafter, another one rolled by announcing the name of the town in the distance. It was an unmistakably French name. With relief, Karl let out his breath and realized that he had been holding it for some time. The train had left Czechoslovakia. They were in France. If they had stopped at the border, he had not noticed it. He had slept through the night and no one had disturbed him. The bribe had worked.

There was a soft knock at his compartment door. It startled him in the wake of his momentary relief. Karl straightened his shirt and ran his fingers through his hair. "Come in," he said, as the steward entered his room carrying a tray with steaming coffee and a small croissant with jam.

He set the tray on a ledge and tipped his hat to Karl. "I trust you slept well, sir?" he asked.

Karl nodded. "Better than I thought I would."

The attendant smiled. "I promised that you wouldn't be disturbed.

I think you'll be needing these." He held out Karl's passport and other documents.

Karl accepted the papers. "Thank you...for your help."

"We'll be arriving in Paris shortly, sir." The attendant bowed once more, then turned and left.

An hour later, the train pulled into the Paris station and wheezed to a final stop. Karl grabbed his suitcase, checked to make sure he had his documents, and descended joyfully from the train into his father's waiting arms. Victor enclosed him in a big bear hug. "Thank God you're safe!" his father cried, unwilling to release his son.

Karl returned the embrace before stepping back to look at his father, startled at his appearance. Victor had aged dramatically in the four months since they had last seen one another. He was barely forty, yet he looked much older. Karl could see the signs of the stress and fear under which his father had been living in the deeply etched lines around his dull eyes, his graying and thinning hair, his stooped shoulders, and the slight tremor in his hands. Karl tried hard not to stare, but he was shaken by how worn his father looked.

If Victor noticed that Karl was taken aback by his appearance, he did not show it. He clasped his son's face in his hands. "I didn't know if I'd ever see you again." His voice caught in his throat. "Come," he said, pulling Karl by the arm. "I must call your mother immediately and tell her that the papers are good. She'll be anxious to hear that you've arrived safely."

A few days later, a jubilant Marie and Hana arrived in Paris to a joyful reunion with Karl and Victor. Their journey had not been without its drama, which Marie recounted when the family was settled safely into the small Hotel la Boétie where Victor was staying.

Two days after receiving the good news that Karl had arrived in Paris, Marie and Hana went to the Wilson train station in Prague to catch the overnight express train. Marie sought out and found the same steward who had attended to Karl on his journey. She spoke quietly to him while Hana looked on, and then handed over her travel documents and another substantial sum. The attendant happily accepted the cash and led mother and daughter to a private sleeping compartment on the train.

"I took care of the young man and I'll do my best to take care of the two of you," he said before tipping his hat, closing the curtains to their compartment, and withdrawing.

Marie felt confident that all would be well. "I knew that you had gotten through easily, Karl, so I couldn't imagine that I would have any trouble. Besides, who would want to bother a woman like me traveling with my daughter? I was looking forward to waking up in France." She and Hana began to settle into their small room and prepare for sleep when suddenly the attendant reappeared with Marie's documents in his hands.

He hesitated at the doorway of their compartment and looked terribly worried. Marie couldn't imagine what had happened. "Is there a problem?" she asked.

The man nodded, looked over at Hana and then back at Marie. "The passport is fine," he began. "Your daughter is listed here as your dependant." As Marie already knew, Hana did not require a passport. At only thirteen years of age, she could be listed on her mother's papers. Marie waited impatiently. "It's the Gestapo exit certificate," the attendant finally continued. "There's no mention of a daughter here. It could cause problems at the border...." His voice trailed off, leaving the rest to their imaginations.

Karl was stunned as he sat listening to his mother tell this story. This was just the sort of tight spot that he himself had dreaded might happen on his journey here. But true to form, Marie was undaunted by the predicament. She had faced innumerable obstacles in the past year and had surmounted them all. This one would not stop her.

Without blinking an eye, Marie reached into her handbag and pulled out a fountain pen. Then she reached for the Gestapo document and with the stunned attendant looking on, she wrote the words, "*und Tochter*" – and daughter – next to her own name on the papers. "And then I handed the document back to him and said, 'I trust that will do.'"

The attendant stared down at the papers. Marie's handwriting was in blue ink. The rest of the certificate was written in black. The blue letters stood out, unmistakably distinct from the rest of the document. It was like waving a flag above their heads and telling the enemy to come and get them! "I asked if there was another problem and the attendant didn't answer. I kept my voice even and firm and I didn't flinch. I wouldn't let him see that I was the slightest bit worried about this." Moments passed while Marie and Hana waited to see what the attendant would do. Finally the man, nodded, bowed slightly, and walked out of the compartment, leaving Marie and Hana alone.

"I have to admit, I didn't sleep much on the train," Marie concluded. "I was overjoyed to see the French countryside early this morning. And now, we are here!" She grabbed each member of her family in a fierce hug, her face exploding into the broadest smile Karl had seen in months. The family had been reunited. They had left so much behind in the country that had forced them out. But for the time being, none of that mattered. They were safe, they were free, and they were together.

A day after arriving in Paris, Marie and Victor received word that the Gestapo had come looking for Marie at the villa in Prague. Leila was taken into custody, threatened, and harshly interrogated about the whereabouts of the Jewish woman who had lived there. Leila had feigned ignorance and appealed to the Gestapo as an ethnic German from the recently acquired Sudetenland. She managed to convince the officials that she did not know what had become of Marie and she was released with only a verbal warning.

CHAPTER TEN

Toronto, February 23, 1990

THE GALLERY WAS FULL of people by the time Theo entered. It was the opening of a new exhibit – a collection of paintings by an emerging Canadian artist who, like Theo, had also originally come from Czechoslovakia. This young man's roots were much more humble than Theo's, his journey out from under the Communist thumb much more complicated. He was a skilled and multifaceted artist, crafting whimsical and mythical creatures that emerged on the canvas amidst thunderous storms and whirlpools of light. Theo had been drawn to his work and had been eager to coordinate this launch at the gallery. This was the part of his job that Theo enjoyed most, discovering the work of emerging artists and introducing them to a public eager to buy.

True, it was somewhat burdensome that this opening was taking place just a few weeks before his trip to Prague. Coordinating that excursion meant that there was already a lot on his plate. But his upcoming trip couldn't interfere with the work he had here in Toronto. Theo's eyes traveled the room. There was the artist in one corner, pacing with the proud but anxious look of an expectant father. Theo knew he would have to go talk to him, calm him down, and remind him about how good his paintings really were. But first he needed to work the crowd.

Fresh-faced young waiters wearing starched white shirts and pressed dark pants were serving wine from silver trays. Theo grabbed a glass and made his way through the gallery, stopping to welcome people he knew and introducing himself to the new faces. He was particularly interested in greeting those with an air of wealth – entrepreneurs and businessmen – the regulars who had come not only to look, but also to buy. He worked the crowd like a celebrity moving through his adoring fans. He shook hands warmly with men in dark suits, and kissed the cheeks of women in furs.

A group of people had gathered in front of a large canvas in which a fierce-looking helmeted head emerged from the top of a jeweled metallic shell. "I don't really understand it," an attractive woman was saying as she gazed at the painting. "It just looks menacing to me." She was younger than most of the other women in the room, and dressed in a tight skirt that exposed her endlessly long legs.

Theo moved to stand beside her. The scent of an expensive cologne drifted up toward him. "Allow me to explain," he said, leaning in to lightly touch her arm. He began to talk about the artist's upbringing in Czechoslovakia under a harsh Communist regime, briefly describing the politics of the country and the tyranny under which its population lived and worked. He maneuvered the woman directly in front of the canvas, pointing out the deep reds, peacock blues, and emerald greens that emerged from a dark and shadowy background. "Many of this artist's paintings reflect his personal journey from oppression to freedom, from suffering to joy. He is purging himself of fear – a catharsis of sorts – and moving toward renewal." While he spoke his arm moved to rest ever so slightly on the small of her back.

The woman smiled, leaning her body into his. "Thank you," she said. "How do you know so much about this?"

"Allow me to introduce myself. Theo Král. I'm the coordinator of the gallery. It's a pleasure to have you here. I'm always delighted to welcome a new face, particularly one as lovely as yours."

"I'll tell my father about the painting," she said, pointing to a balding gentleman on the other side of the gallery. "He's the one who comes to buy. I usually just come to look." She scanned Theo's face suggestively.

They spoke for a few minutes more and then Theo moved on, wondering briefly if she was available and whether or not he should pursue her. He had certainly had plenty of women over the years. Back in Czechoslovakia, his personal life had been one of the few areas where no one could interfere. For him women were not about politics or philosophy. They were simply about pleasure, like the art he acquired. He knew what to look for and what attracted him – and, when he saw one he liked, possessing her could become an all-encompassing enterprise.

He would come back to this one later, he promised himself. But for now, he needed to be host for the evening, to divide his time fairly among all of his guests, and to not let his fascination with this woman get the better of him. She had talked about the painting being menacing and she had been correct. There was something sinister and mysterious about these works that had also attracted Theo, touching a darker side of him, a side that only a few close to him knew about, and fewer still understood.

Theo had been drawn for years to an exploration of the occult – what he often referred to as the hidden and deeper truth about life that existed beneath the surface. He often wondered about the spirit that guided his life and the lives of all human beings. Was it a benign God that breathed life into the world and provided meaning, or did the spirit live in a world inhabited by demons? And how did these two forces exist in Theo himself? These were the questions that preoccupied his thinking. On the one hand, he was a dreamer, living life with an infectious, light-hearted carelessness, making friends with ease, maneuvering himself into the focal point of any situation, commanding attention with his charm and charisma. He made people happy. On the other hand, his zest for life teetered on the reckless. While he made friends easily, he lost them just as quickly. He used people for what he had to gain from them. It was as if he possessed an alter ego, a secondary though equally powerful personality. Theo was both charmer and conniver, entertainer and manipulator.

The woman smiled at him from across the room and Theo acknowledged her with a nod of his head and a slight bow. He knew he had
charmed this one and was already thinking about how he would convince
her to go back to his apartment later that evening. From the looks of
things, not too much persuasion would be needed.

His fascination with the hidden meaning of life had all begun years
earlier when a close friend had first introduced him to Hieronymus Bosch.
This fifteenth-century Dutch surrealist was known for his use of fantasy –
dreams and nightmares – to produce religious imagery in his oil paintings.
From Theo's perspective, Bosch demonstrated a moral and spiritual truth
in his work that was hundreds of years ahead of his time. Bosch's paintings
were sometimes erotic, often darkly gruesome, even occasionally amusing.
Some thought his paintings were created merely to arouse his audience.
Others believed his work was inspired by medieval heresies. It was perhaps
both sides of this artistic coin that fascinated Theo.

Years earlier, Theo had visited the Prado Museum in Madrid, specifi-
cally to see an exhibit of paintings by Bosch. The entrance to the museum
held one of Bosch's more grand and magnificent canvases, the three-panel
work known as *The Garden of Earthly Delights*. Each panel portrayed a
unique aspect of the origin of man. The panel on the left depicted Adam
and Eve in paradise with wondrous animals, calm reflecting ponds, and a
God-like figure in the forefront. The middle panel was a portrait of earthly
delights, with its nude figures, giant and mutating fruit, and life-sized sparrows and eagles. Hell was depicted in the panel on the right, where sinners
were represented in their descent into damnation. Theo had stepped as
close to the giant panels as he could, fascinated by the high level of detail,
the countless figures, and the great skill and craftsmanship of the artist.
The painting was intellectually and spiritually challenging. It was as if the
meaning of life, both the origin of humanity and the evil in the world, was
there in front of him, hidden from complete understanding. The painting
was marvelous and terrifying at the same time, and it had touched a place
in Theo that both inspired and confused him.

While gazing at this spectacular work of art, Theo noticed the terrible condition of the canvases, particularly the center panel. It was worn in many places, and the colors had faded and yellowed over time. There were nicks and cracks throughout. It appeared as if the entire image was wasting away, fading before Theo's eyes. He could not believe this degree of decay had occurred in a work of art as exceptional and irreplaceable as this one. Theo turned on his heel and made his way to the administrative offices of the museum. There he demanded to meet with the director. The startled assistant motioned Theo into a large office where he confronted the man in charge.

"That masterpiece has to be restored," Theo declared.

"Of course, you are right," the startled director replied. "But we have a limited budget here, and our Spanish painters like Goya and Diego Velázquez are more important to us."

Theo was undaunted. "What if I help you to secure the funds and organize the restoration?"

He immediately abandoned his work and plans, and for the next year, focused all of his energy and attention on the restoration of the Bosch painting. He begged money from friends and acquaintances, he smooth-talked funds out of European arts organizations, he demanded support from the city of Madrid. He even approached a major automobile company and convinced them to support the project. And, ultimately, he raised the tens of thousands of dollars necessary for a complete refurbishment of *The Garden of Earthly Delights*. There was nothing in it for him – not money, or even notoriety – just an intense desire to right an artistic wrong, and to save the work of the painter he admired so intensely.

"It looks like your opening is a success." The young woman had made her way across the gallery and now stood directly in front of Theo. He gazed around the room and at the crowd that was beginning to thin. The evening had gone well. Several paintings had sold and many of those in attendance had commented favorably on the gallery itself, promising to return for future exhibits. The featured artist of the evening looked dazed and relieved, and was slumped in a chair off to one side, surrounded by a few remaining admirers. Theo could now turn his attention to the woman in front of him.

"I have a few things left to do before I can leave," he said, reaching out to stroke her arm.

"My father's already gone," she replied. "I'll wait for you."

CHAPTER ELEVEN

Paris, Summer 1939

THE REISER FAMILY settled into an uneasy calm in Paris. As relieved as they were to have escaped Czechoslovakia, they knew they were not safe yet. They still needed their visas to Canada, and they had to book passage on a ship heading across the Atlantic. Both of these projects were proving to be complicated.

Despite George Harwood's promise that he would provide the family with the entry visas to Canada, Victor was having difficulty securing those papers. Visit after visit to the consulate proved futile and he would return home empty-handed. "It's just a matter of time," he assured his waiting family. "There are so many forms to fill out, so much information the Canadian government wants. But we'll have the papers soon. I'm sure of it." Victor sounded hopeful, but Karl wondered if his optimism was misplaced. What did they actually know about George Harwood, and what authority did he really have to assist them? Karl had watched his mother deal with enough dishonest people to question the intentions of anyone who promised to help, especially if that promise was secured with a bribe. Karl struggled with his impressions of Harwood. The man had agreed to save his family, but he was profiting from the family's desperation. Did that make him a hero or a criminal? Karl had learned that one had to be wary, trust few people, and anticipate the worst at every turn. That was the way to survive. And so, Karl and his family waited apprehensively as Victor made repeated visits to meet with officials at the consulate. Karl accompanied his father on one of those trips.

"What do they want to know this time?" he asked as he and his father climbed the stairs of the Canadian consulate one rainy day in early August. Karl had been in Paris for only two weeks, but already was feeling eager to move on. There was little for him and his sister to do here. Their days were spent listening to their parents discuss the arrangements to immigrate to Canada.

The rain and mist cast a gray pallor over Paris, further dampening his already melancholy mood. He thought fleetingly of Rakovník. He might have been swimming in the pond or bicycling through the countryside if he were home, instead of following his father on this seemingly endless mission to get out of Europe.

Victor sighed and stepped up the stairs. There was a limp there that Karl had never seen before, and a heaviness in his bearing that matched the depression that had settled over his personality.

"Haven't the officials already asked you every possible question?" Karl was persistent in the face of his father's silence.

"Who knows what they want, Karl," Victor replied, wearily. "I think the problem is just that there are so many people wanting to get into their country."

There were only two categories of people Canada was allowing in at that time: those who had agricultural knowledge and were willing to settle on a farm, and entrepreneurs who could invest a sizeable amount of money into a Canadian business, thus providing employment for local citizens. The Reisers were attempting to get into Canada under the stipulations of the farming category. "Even if we meet the conditions, there is little room for Jews in Canada's policies. So they are scrutinizing us even more closely," Victor added. Canadian government officials had become increasingly unreceptive to the prospect of admitting Jewish refugees from Europe. Notwithstanding the efforts of pro-refugee groups, the doors to Canada had all but closed by the summer of 1939, and the immigration policies under the leadership of Prime Minister William Lyon Mackenzie King and his cabinet were virtually impenetrable.

On this day, the meeting at the Canadian consulate would be a true test of Victor's knowledge and intuition. When Karl and his father were finally ushered into a meeting room, the official on the other side of the desk had some challenging questions for Victor.

Karl didn't even catch the name of the bland bureaucrat who barely acknowledged them as they took their seats. The man's desk was stacked with a mountain of files, folders, and other papers. He rifled through the heap and finally pulled a single sheet from underneath a pile of documents. "The Canadian government needs to understand how much you actually know about farming methods. This is just a short test that will help us determine your knowledge in the area of agriculture."

Karl glanced over at his father, wondering what Victor really knew about farming. Even though he had dealt with farmers in his transactions to secure grain crops, it was one thing to appreciate farming from a business perspective, and another to understand the detailed workings of the land. But Victor smiled evenly at the official and replied, "I'm happy to answer any questions you might have."

The officer continued to examine his documents without looking up. "Yes, yes," he mumbled. "Now then, how do you tell the age of a cow?"

"By the number of incisors in its mouth," Victor replied, instantly and confidently.

"And what methods would you use to increase soil moisture and reduce soil erosion?"

A half hour later, the questions had ended, and Victor stood to shake hands with the Canadian official. He had passed the test with no difficulty. "We will let you know about the entry documents shortly," the man said.

"We are eager to begin our lives in Canada working on a farm," Victor replied.

The official turned his attention back to the files that threatened to topple on his desk, and dismissed Victor and Karl with a wave of his hand.

"What now?" Karl asked, as he and his father walked quickly back to the hotel.

"Now we wait again," Victor replied.

Karl sighed and wondered once more if the waiting would ever end. He knew they were luckier than most. At least they were out of immediate harm's way. But this uncertainty was agonizing. And their ordeal was being made all the more tense by the grim news of the approaching war. Europe was mobilizing for battle. And while Poland appeared to be Hitler's intended target, France was highly vulnerable.

"There are rumors that Paris will be bombed," Marie said that evening as the family gathered to hear about Victor's test at the consulate.

Victor lifted tired eyes to meet his wife's concerned gaze and nodded. "The papers are full of warnings. The good relationship that once existed between France and Germany is gone, I'm afraid." It was well known that the governments of the two countries had for years agreed to ongoing consultation if international developments threatened either one of them. "Now, France has abandoned Germany in favor of a pact with Britain and Poland. And Germany will not look kindly on France's desertion. If Poland is attacked, France will have no other option but to go to her aid."

"Do you have any sense at all of when we might hear about the papers?" Marie asked.

Victor shook his head. "I believe that I have answered all of their questions. I'm certain we'll have the visas soon."

Marie took a deep breath. "I think we should get out of Paris now, before the bombs fall here." She had been pacing the hotel room for several days, glancing out the window, listening to news reports on the radio, devouring the papers. She was once more on high alert, tuned in to the pulse of the nation, and determining when she might need to mobilize her family. And now she sensed it was time to move. "We'll be safer in the country."

Victor did not disagree. He too had learned to trust his wife's instincts.

And so the family packed up once more and headed north of the city, this time to stay in a small rented château in the village of Vieux Moulin. Karl spent his days taking long walks along the Oise River and through the French countryside where cottages were separated by large squares of forest and meadow. Here amidst the trees and pastures, Karl felt lightness, something he had not experienced in a long time. The air moved more freely here, unencumbered by the compact architecture of Paris, the equally dense population, and the oppressive anticipation of war. Close by, in the city of Compiègne, the armistice had been signed in 1918, ending World War I. As the world stood on the brink of another war, the irony of this did not escape Karl.

Not only could he breathe more freely outside the big city, but he *felt* freer here in the country as well. Though there were no restrictions for Jews in France, no laws governing what they could and couldn't do, and no outright hostility, there was a sense that the French would make a distinction between "their" Jews and "immigrant" Jews. Local Jews would be protected if the conflict in the world escalated, while foreign Jews might be subject to deportation back to their home countries. Here in rural France, away from the political glare of the big city, the threat of deportation seemed less imminent, even though war was just on the horizon.

It was here in the countryside that Karl also dared to think about Canada, a country full of fields and meadows just like the ones surrounding him. That new land awaited his family if only they could reach it. Perhaps he would finish his education there, or work in a productive business, marry, and raise children. He had his whole life ahead of him, and the possibility of living it in a free country was overwhelming. It was after one such walk through the forest that Karl returned to the château to find his mother and sister packing their belongings once more.

"We're going back to Paris," Marie announced as Karl entered the house.

Hana looked up from her packing and smiled. "Father received word that the visas are ready to be picked up."

"We've done it, Karl," Marie added. "Now we can really start our new lives in Canada."

Karl could hardly believe what he was hearing. After all the months of uncertainty and waiting, could it really be that they had passed every hurdle and were going to be able to get out of Europe at last? They barely spoke to one another on the journey back to Paris. Despite the dire predictions, the city had not been bombed. However, like cities across Europe, it lay in anxious expectation of what would happen in the days and weeks to come. Each member of Karl's family was lost in private thoughts. *Would the papers really be ready*, Karl wondered, *or would the family be subjected to a new series of questions, forms, and tests?* Would they finally be able to leave for the safety of Canada, or would they find themselves imprisoned in a Europe destined for war?

When Karl and Victor entered the building of the Canadian consulate, they were ushered into the office of the same indifferent administrator. This time, he rose from behind his cluttered desk and extended his hand to Victor. "Here are all the documents required to enter Canada as permanent immigrants, Mr. Reiser," the man said. He handed the papers over to Victor. On top, Karl couldn't help but notice that Victor's passport had been altered slightly. Next to the line that asked for occupation, the consulate official had scratched out the word "businessman" and replaced it with the handwritten words "agricultural estate owner." "Good luck to you and your family," the official said.

Victor's eyes shone brightly and he stood a little straighter as he left the building clutching the visas to Canada. With the papers in hand, there was only one more thing left for Victor to do and that was to book passage on a ship sailing for Quebec City. With the world on the brink of war, Europe was filled with panicky North Americans scrambling to get home. There were long line-ups at the booking offices in Paris, where anxious would-be passengers pushed and shoved to get to the front. Fortunately for Karl and his family, George Harwood had come through for them again. While many others would be stranded in Europe, four tickets were waiting for the Reisers on the Canadian Pacific steamer *Empress of Britain*, which was due to sail from France on September 1.

This would be the last commercial voyage of this vessel before it was converted into a warship. A year later, it would be torpedoed and sunk by a German long-range bomber. The Reisers had no notion of the future fate of this liner as Victor happily paid for the tickets, and Karl and his family packed their bags one last time and boarded a train for the port city of Cherbourg.

The sun reflected off the gleaming white hull of the steamer as Karl stood on the deck, leaning over the railing and marveling at the crowd that had gathered on the pier to bid farewell to the travelers. More than one thousand passengers were on board, and these people would become his shipmates for the six-day journey across the ocean. People stood on either side of him, cheering and waving to friends, family, and even strangers on shore who waved in return. Pretty soon Karl found himself caught up in the fervor of the crowd and began to wave as well. His heart was pounding and his skin burned with feverish expectation. Ahead lay the vastness of the open sea and an unfamiliar country, a country that he was already beginning to call his new home. The horn blasted, the engine droned, and the anchor was cranked aboard as the *Empress of Britain* slipped its moorings and slowly moved out of the French harbor.

On that very day, German troops invaded Poland. Two days later, on September 3, Britain declared war on Germany for its unprovoked attack on Poland, and, a few hours later, France followed. At 11:15 a.m. that same day, Prime Minster Neville Chamberlain gave a speech to his nation and said, "It is evil things that we shall be fighting against – brute force, bad faith, injustice, oppression, and persecution – [but] against them I am certain that right will prevail."[5]

On September 7, 1939, with war descending like a shroud over the world, the SS *Empress of Britain* docked in Quebec City and Karl and his family disembarked in their new home.

PART II
LIFE IN CANADA

CHAPTER TWELVE

Toronto, June 1943

THE SMALL CLOCK next to his bed read twenty minutes to seven. Karl
checked himself again in the mirror and adjusted his tie. If he didn't hurry
up he'd be late to the meeting, and he didn't like arriving after everyone
else. The New World Club, which was organized by a Czech couple,
George and Edith Moller, met one evening a month at a small hall on
Charles Street. The Mollers had formed this club with the aim of bringing young Czech people together for social events. Several marriages had
resulted from introductions there. Karl had been attending for some time.

The club was a friendly reminder of home, the part of home that he
still thought about. There were many things about Czechoslovakia that
Karl did not miss. His former country had turned its back on him in so
many ways – disregarding his loyalty and casting his family out at the
start of the war. But he did miss his house and the lifestyle that he and
his family had once had. He glanced around his present living quarters,
a sparsely furnished bedroom in a small rooming house. Gone were the
expensive furnishings, artwork, and lavish existence. Karl shook his head
and shrugged off the moment of nostalgia. There was nothing here that

he lacked. In fact, he and his family had done quite well for themselves since their arrival four years earlier.

They had been dazed at first. Who could blame them? As relieved as each member of the family was to be out of war-torn Europe, Canada was unfamiliar territory, filled with strangers, unusual customs, and words that fell on their ears like dissonant musical chords. Notwithstanding Karl's English lessons, it was difficult to grasp the nuances and subtleties of this foreign language, not to mention the customs and practices of Canadians. In those early days, Karl spent hours wandering city streets, staring at passers-by and trying to absorb as much of Canadian life as he could. He tasted Canadian food, enjoying his first hamburger and Coca-Cola.

Their first stop after arriving in Quebec City had been Montreal. But they did not remain there for long. Victor had other plans for the family, and so they packed up once more and headed for Toronto. Their initial stay in the center of this big city was also brief, crammed into one small room at the St. Regis Hotel on Sherbourne Street, north of Carlton. A drop curtain that divided the room in two was the only means to secure some privacy. Victor made contact with other Czech acquaintances, and learned that many of his fellow refugees had settled on farms near the city of Hamilton, roughly sixty miles west of Toronto. He decided to do the same. Under the rules of his entry into Canada, Victor was required to develop a farming business. If he could do that within a Czech community, he reasoned, that would make the adjustment that much easier.

In Hamilton, the family was met by a friend from Czechoslovakia whose name was Arthur Brock. Arthur had arrived months earlier and already was a wealth of information about where to stay and what to do. Karl had a distinct and fond childhood memory of Arthur, who had owned a ceramics factory in Rakovník that also manufactured clay marbles. Arthur was a small, rotund, and good-natured man. Whenever he had visited Karl's family, he had come armed with marbles, gifts for Karl and Hana. Karl had had an enormous collection, all left behind in their wartime flight.

With Arthur's help, Victor made contact with a real estate agent who was known to cater to the refugee community, and began to look at various properties around the Hamilton area, eventually settling on a fifty-acre farm near the village of Carlisle.

Karl loved the farmhouse from the moment he first set foot over its threshold. It was a charming, two-story, red-brick building that had seemed instantly welcoming. Four large bedrooms on the second floor provided ample room for them. There was a big, inviting kitchen and an equally spacious parlor and dining room. The small barn in the back sheltered their livestock: four cows, two horses, and several pigs. A small coop to one side housed the chickens. This was a mixed-produce farm, producing wheat as well as dairy products.

Once they were settled in the house, Victor wrote to his former business associate in Holland, Mr. Kolish. In the weeks before fleeing Rakovník, Marie had sent him several cases of personal items – clothing, household objects, and delicate goods – to keep until the family was living somewhere safe. Victor requested that Mr. Kolish now send these cases to their new home in Carlisle. It was a joyful day when the boxes arrived at the Carlisle railroad station and Victor and Karl went to pick them up. Marie opened them and pulled out jackets, socks, dresses, and scarves, along with some pots, vases, and cooking utensils. There were even several small oil paintings that she had managed to pack in the crates – two works by the Czech painter Emil Orlik, and a painting by John Houston titled *Lady in Lace Dress*. Another was a canvas by Rudolf Puchold, Karl's former art teacher, depicting a scene from the courtyard of Rakovník's city hall. It was as if a piece of their Czech past had joined them here in Canada. But the joy the family felt at being reunited with some of their belongings from Rakovník was tempered by the realization that these objects could never make up for all that they had lost. There was both comfort and longing here in Carlisle.

But perhaps the most welcome thing of all was the warmth with which the community greeted the Reisers upon their arrival. In a country where the government had virtually sealed its borders to Jews escaping Europe, it was a surprise to discover how friendly the citizens were. The people of Carlisle had probably never laid eyes on refugees with European accents before. Still, they were warm and helpful in every possible way. Women would appear at the farmhouse door with baskets of baked goods and clothing for Marie. And men lent their expertise on farming techniques to Victor. Hana returned to high school in a nearby town and Karl even went so far as to join a youth group at the United Church across the road, participating in meetings, lectures, and dances.

As time passed, however, it became clear that Victor would be unable to coax a viable income from the farm. As Victor often joked, "The farm is too small to make a living, and too large to let us starve." In fact, it was the money that Marie had transferred out to the Crédit Lyonnais in Paris years earlier that had enabled them to purchase the land and that sustained them now. Victor knew little about how to grow wheat or maintain the dairy cows, and relied heavily on a hired hand who had come with the farm and was the only one who really knew how to take care of the land and the animals.

The English language, which had been difficult at times for Karl, had been a nearly insurmountable challenge for his father, who continued to stumble his way through awkward-sounding vocabulary and grammar. On top of that, he had never fully regained his health or strength after fleeing Czechoslovakia. Not only was Victor unfamiliar with farming routines, he was completely unaccustomed to physical labor. He always looked pale and on the verge of illness. His once strong body was stooped. His face was tense and troubled, and deep furrows like dry river beds were carved into his forehead. The limp that had appeared in France was worse. Victor walked with pain and it showed throughout his aging body.

In contrast, his mother had again proven herself to be amazingly adaptable. She had moved from a life of luxury to physically and morally sustaining the family here in Canada. The demands of this rural farming lifestyle had been as grueling for Marie as for the rest of the family. But she had met every challenge head on, cooking meals for everyone including the hired help, tending to the vegetable garden, cleaning the farmhouse. She even had the responsibility of rising in the middle of the night to keep the fire in the furnace going. She had done all this and more, selflessly and without complaint. Increasingly, her time had been taken up with caring for Karl's father.

Karl shook his head at all those memories as he finished getting ready for his meeting. He took one last look in the mirror, then switched off the lamp and left his small room. It was still light outside and the lingering warmth of the early summer evening seeped through his thin jacket and into his skin. He wound through the bustling streets of Toronto. Everywhere he turned there were reminders that the war was still on. Billboards glowed from atop high-rise buildings. One read, *You Serve by Saving: Buy War Savings Certificates.* Another poster advertising wristwatches proclaimed, *Canada's Finest Deserve the Best.* Two young boys stood on a street corner calling out to the passers-by to collect their metal, paper, and other waste to be recycled for the war effort. The *Globe and Mail* newspaper regularly reported on the heroism of Canada's soldiers overseas as well as the carnage of war and the suffering in its wake. The world had become fractured, and war had metastasized across Europe like a malignant cancer.

Who could ever have imagined that the conflict would turn into an event of global impact? Once the United States declared war on Germany after the 1941 bombing of Pearl Harbor, more than sixty countries were involved, and hundreds of thousands of soldiers were fighting overseas.

The war news in Czechoslovakia was always of particular concern and interest to Karl. Only a month earlier, he had read of the attack on SS leader Reinhard Heydrich outside the Prague castle. On May 27, as his automobile slowed to round a sharp turn on the streets of Prague, assassins shot at him, and threw a bomb at his car. He managed to crawl from the wreckage, but died days later from the wounds. In reprisal for the murder of Heydrich, Hitler had gone on a killing spree, looting Czech villages, and hunting down and slaughtering anyone suspected of being involved in the assassination.

The reports of the war in Europe were distressing for Karl and his family, particularly the grisly news that was trickling out about the treatment of Jews. Reports were spreading that Jews in Europe were being rounded up and relocated to forced labor camps. Many were never heard from again and the speculation was growing that "forced labor" was merely a euphemism for mass murder. By the spring of 1942, Hitler had already convened the Wannsee Conference to coordinate the Final Solution, his plan to exterminate the Jewish population of Europe. The Belzec extermination camp became operational in March 1942 and Jews from across Europe were already being deported to Auschwitz and Majdanek.

It was difficult to get information from those who were still in Europe. Letters arrived infrequently and one had to read between the lines to discern how much danger was present for those remaining in Europe. Despite these desperate circumstances, Canada had stepped up its policies prohibiting Jewish refugees from entering the country. No one was getting in despite the lobbying efforts of prominent Canadian Jewish groups. Karl marveled, as he often did, at how lucky his family had been to get out when they did. And he wondered if anyone would be safe in the face of Hitler's unrelenting campaign of hatred.

Karl walked up the steps of the small building on Charles Street and shook the thoughts of war from his head, wondering who would be at the New World Club meeting that night. Making new friends had never been Karl's strength. Even now, he tended to keep to himself. And while he had not personally experienced any outright acts of anti-Semitism here in Canada, he had learned to be cautious about being sociable. In 1943, there were still areas of Toronto that were prohibited to Jews, and the notice that a club membership was "restricted" meant that Jews need not apply. Indeed, despite the fact that the Reisers had arrived in Canada as landed immigrants, they were still obligated to report to the Royal Canadian Mounted Police once a month, a requirement that stemmed from the general misconception that, as refugees from a German-occupied country, they might be spies or Nazi sympathizers.

All this and more added to Karl's determination to establish his own independence and security without drawing attention. That's why he had moved to Toronto after living on the farm for only three months.

Education was the last thing on his mind. He had never excelled in school, had missed the opportunity to complete high school back home, and couldn't imagine going back to his studies after such a long hiatus. More than anything else, Karl wanted to work.

His first job in Toronto was at a machine shop owned by a Czech gentleman. After a year there, he had moved to de Havilland Aircraft. Now he was working on the Mosquito fighter, one of the most highly respected and best-known aircraft of the war. It was made almost entirely of plywood – hence its nickname, "the wooden wonder."

Karl's role at de Havilland was to design assembly fixtures, the connecting mechanisms that held sections of the aircraft together. He worked next to university graduates, pulling his intellectual weight with equal competence. His was a priority job and ensured that he would not be called up for army service. He could not face the thought of having to go back to Europe. His involvement in the war effort would be the designs he produced, and he threw himself into the work that was helping to defeat Hitler.

Karl entered the hall and looked around. A number of young men and women were already there, milling about the open floor. George and Edith Moller floated amongst the crowd, chatting up the young people and supervising the arrangement of desserts and coffee on a long table at one end of the room. The Mollers had hoped that young Czech immigrants and young Canadians would meet and mingle here, but few Canadians attended. Those in the room were also primarily Jewish, though that had never been the intention when the club was first formed.

"Karl! Over here." A voice from one corner of the room shook Karl out of his thoughts. He waved to the young man, Walter Picard, and moved over to shake hands with him. Karl had become friendly with this short, stout young man at these gatherings.

"How are you?" Walter asked.

Karl shrugged. "Aside from the lousy news coming from Europe, everything is fine. And you?"

Walter nodded in return. "And your father? I hear he's not been well."

At this, Karl's face fell. Victor had been battling kidney disease over the last few years, necessitating frequent hospital admissions. In addition to his ongoing physical deterioration, Victor had been growing increasingly depressed, emotionally slipping from the family's reach. And who could blame him? "He always thought that the fighting would be over in a matter of months," Karl said. "And we'd be back in Rakovník, picking up the pieces. He's beginning to realize that that will never be the case. It's been four years now and who knows how much longer this mess will go on."

"My family never imagined we'd be here this long," Walter said. "But Toronto is home for us now. I doubt we'll ever go back."

Karl paused at that. If the war were to end tomorrow, would he return to his home in Czechoslovakia? Not likely! Hitler had destroyed the illusion of a safe home in Europe. Canada was home now.

"It's not just the war, but it's the news of the treatment of Jews in Europe that's destroying my father's spirit," Karl said. "Every time the newspapers report that Jews are being imprisoned, or tortured, or killed in massive numbers, my father retreats further and further into his shell."

"And the reports are only getting worse, not better," Walter added.

The two young men stood in silence, eyeing the growing crowd. Despite the feeling of camaraderie in the room, Karl felt his spirits plummet. This was the way it always was, he realized. One couldn't engage in a conversation these days without a discussion of the news abroad, and a reminder of the deteriorating conditions for Jews.

"I'm moving my family here to Toronto," Karl continued. "The farm has become too much for my father, even with the hired help. And now my mother can't manage caring for him and everything else. I can help out with things much more once they're here."

The beautiful farmhouse had recently been sold, a crushing blow to all of them. Karl wondered if his father felt the failure of not having been able to manage the farm. It was hard to tell. The depression that had enveloped Victor hung like a cloud over every aspect of his being. The loss of the farm, the war, his health, the news of the treatment of Jews – it was hard to separate out which element affected Victor most. His depression became intensified every September around the anniversary of their arrival in Canada. He bore this date like a scarlet letter, a reminder that he had been ousted from the country he had thought would forever stand by him. It had never been his choice to leave Czechoslovakia, and while he was grateful for the freedom that Canada had provided, his adopted homeland was always a reminder of what he had lost, and not what he had achieved. He may have shifted continents, but he had never been able to leave his homeland behind.

The task of finding a new home for the family in Toronto had fallen to Karl, and he had taken it on with a sense of urgency, knowing that, with Victor's deteriorating health, Marie had wanted to see this move happen quickly. In midtown Toronto, there were a number of quiet, tree-lined streets, and charming residential neighborhoods with "For Rent" signs. Jews didn't appear to be restricted from purchasing homes, he noted with some relief. One house caught his eye and it proved to be the first and only home he looked at. He agreed to rent the house for his family for sixty dollars a month, and planned to reunite them there shortly. Hana would have to change schools, something that she might not be too happy about after having made some good friends at the school near Carlisle. But Hana was adaptable enough and would cope with the change. The important thing was that in Toronto Karl could look after his family, and not feel the pressure and guilt of living separately from them.

Karl glanced again around the hall, which was full now. He recognized many faces in the room, having seen them on a regular basis at these monthly meetings. One unfamiliar young woman, though, caused him to pause. She stood alone off to one side, eying the full room with a look of some indifference. She was very attractive with her stylish, short, curly hair and confident carriage. There was something about her that immediately interested Karl.

"Do you know who she is?" Karl nudged Walter and pointed toward the young woman.

Walter squinted in her direction and then shook his head. "No idea."

Karl made his way through the crowded room, pausing briefly here and there to greet acquaintances and exchange pleasantries. It took several minutes to reach the young woman. "Hello," he began, battling his shyness and extending his hand to shake hers.

The woman nodded, and a friendly but reserved smile crossed her face as she sized up the eager young man in front of her. She was small in stature and dwarfed by Karl's tall frame. He had to lean forward to hear her speak.

"I'm Phyllis Hoffman," she said quietly. "My parents are friends with the Mollers." She spoke impeccable English, not like the Czechs Karl was accustomed to meeting at these social gatherings.

"I'm Karl Reeser," he replied.

Phyllis cocked her head to one side. "Reeser? That doesn't sound like a Czech name."

"You're right," he replied. "It's not." Just months earlier, when they had finally become citizens, Karl had completed the paperwork to change the family name from Reiser to Reeser. After four years of having their name misspelled and mispronounced, Karl had had enough. No one in the family objected to the name change. If truth be told, Karl also wanted a family identity that was more anglicized. Their Judaism, which had plagued the family in Europe, was not going to be a factor in their assimilation into Canadian society. And so he left the name Reiser behind and with it any religious attachment. He was now Karl Reeser, a Canadian, and the name and identity felt right. Karl briefly explained this to Phyllis.

"And you?" he continued. "Were you born here?"

Phyllis shook her head. "I was born in Poland, but my family came here when I was two years old." She went on to explain that her father had finished his degree in chemical engineering in Czechoslovakia after Jews had been denied permission to go to university in Poland. "After he graduated, he couldn't get a job. No one would hire someone who was Jewish. So he decided to pack up his family and immigrate to Canada. He had two brothers who were already here." Phyllis paused and then added, "He never realized at the time that his decision to leave was the smartest thing he could have done." Phyllis was now in her first year at the University of Toronto, studying household economics.

Just then, someone called her name and she smiled a friendly good-bye and moved away. Karl didn't speak with her again that evening. But he thought about her the entire time, occasionally straining to catch a glimpse of her across the room and wondering if she was as aware of him as he was of her. She chatted amicably with people, laughing easily, seemingly oblivious to the young man who stood on the other side of the hall, following her every move. She intrigued Karl and, even after he had left the meeting that night, he couldn't stop thinking about her.

The next day, he appeared on his friend Walter's doorstep. "Please," he begged. "Make the call for me." Before leaving the meeting the night before, Karl had confessed his interest in Phyllis to the Mollers, who were only too happy to provide her telephone number.

Karl listened as Walter chatted with Phyllis on the telephone. Several minutes later, he handed the receiver to Karl and grinned. "Here," Walter said. "She said she was surprised to hear my voice. She thought it would be you."

Karl and Phyllis dated over the next few months. As their relationship blossomed, Karl knew that he had finally found his home in Toronto and he made plans to propose to Phyllis. Those plans were interrupted in April 1944, when Karl's father died. The many physical ailments that had plagued him over the years, compounded by his depression, finally caught up with him. Victor slipped into a coma at home and died peacefully with Karl, Marie, and Hana by his side. It was a heartbreaking day for the family who had watched this once strong and vibrant man deteriorate over the preceding years. His slow death had begun with the family's escape from Czechoslovakia, and it had been sealed by his inability to adapt to life in Canada.

Though still grieving his father's death, Karl finally proposed to Phyllis later that year. Her engagement ring had a beautifully cut diamond, one of two that Marie had sewn into her clothing when the family had left Prague. With her usual foresight, she had smuggled the jewels out just in case they might be needed one day.

F. 10 A.E.

R 4341

CERTIFICATE OF EXEMPTION

(Subject to cancellation)

Issued to persons who have been exempted from the provisions of the Defence of Canada Regulations relating to enemy aliens.

This is to certify that Mary REISER

at present residing at Carlisle, Ont.

(Post Office address)

born at Kladno, Bohemia, Czecho-Slovakia

a locality that was within the control of the German Reich on the 3rd of September, 1939,

Of 46 years of age; Weight 125 ;

Height 5'5'' ; of Medium complexion,

is by law entitle
person and to p
required by any
pliance with the
and to be immu
change his resider
certificate duly er
and may be rene
TIFICATE SHO
FYING THE RE

Dated at Hami..

day of JANUA

F. 10 A.E.

R 4319

CERTIFICATE OF EXEMPTION

(Subject to cancellation)

Issued to persons who have been exempted from the provisions of the Defence of Canada Regulations relating to enemy aliens.

This is to certify that Victor REISER

at present residing at Carlisle, Ont.

(Post Office address)

born at Rakovnik, Bohemia; Czecho-Slovakia

a locality that was within the control of the German Reich on the 3rd of September, 1939,

Of 51 years of age; Weight 160 ;

Height 585'' ; of Med. complexion,

is by law entitled and required to carry this certificate upon his person and to produce it for reasonable inspection as may be required by any peace or military officer. He is, subject to compliance with the requirements of the law, entitled to be at liberty and to be immune from interference provided that he shall not change his residence without notifying the Registrar and having this certificate duly endorsed. This certificate shall be good for one year and may be renewed thereafter. THE HOLDER OF THIS CERTIFICATE SHOULD NOT LEAVE CANADA WITHOUT NOTIFYING THE REGISTRAR.

Dated at Hamilton, Ont. , this 22nd

day of DECEMBER , 19 39

J. W. DesRoches Cst.

For Registrar General,
(J. W. DesRoches) Reg. No. 12945

Even as landed immigrants, the Reesers were still obligated to report to the Royal Canadian Mounted Police once a month, a requirement that stemmed from the general misconception that, as refugees from a German-occupied country, they might be spies or Nazi sympathizers.

The Canadian customs form indicating Victor's
acceptance of cases shipped from Mr. Kolish in Holland.

The family farmhouse in Carlisle.

CHAPTER THIRTEEN

Toronto, May 6, 1945

THE DULL SOUND OF BELLS in the distance and the muted strains of music and cheering voices drifted up from the streets of Toronto and floated through Karl's bedroom window. Somewhere in the house, a telephone was ringing. As in the early days of his childhood, he hunkered lower into his bed, reached for his covers, and pulled them up and over his head as he groaned and rolled over. It was Sunday, no work today, and the chance for some much-needed sleep.

In the preceding year, the tide of war had turned sharply and it seemed as if peace might finally be on the horizon. June 6, 1944, had been a significant and defining day. The newspapers had dubbed it D-Day when Allied forces landed on the coast of Normandy, France, in what had been called Operation Overlord, a major offensive against the Germans.

Believing that peace was at hand, Karl had realized that building airplanes for the war effort would not be a sustainable job. He looked around for a company that would thrive in the years following the end of the war, and had found a good position as a draftsman with Goodyear Tire. He enjoyed the new challenges and responsibilities of this job, which included the design of the conveyor systems transporting tires as they came out of the mold to the next stage of manufacturing.

Karl opened one eye, curious about the growing din in the distance. The chiming of church bells was a regular sound on Sundays. But why were there so many, and why were the bells clanging incessantly? Downstairs, the telephone rang again and he could hear his mother walking across the dining room and into the kitchen to answer it. The money from the sale of the farmhouse in Carlisle had enabled Karl's parents to purchase this home. Victor had lived here until his death, and now Marie, Karl, and Hana continued to inhabit the small two-story brick house. By now, Phyllis was a frequent visitor. The family had welcomed her into their fold warmly.

Karl sat up in bed as he heard the front door open and close, and then the telephone ring yet again. This time, he could hear his mother's voice rising in excitement. This much commotion so early in the morning on a Sunday was not necessarily a good thing. He waited a moment longer and then pushed aside his covers, reached for his housecoat, and bounded down the stairs. Marie and Hana were in the kitchen. Hana was sipping tea and watching her mother, who paced agitatedly in front of her. Marie looked up when Karl entered, and exclaimed, "It's over!" Karl glanced from his mother to Hana and back. "I don't understand…" he began.

"The telephone has been ringing all morning," Marie interrupted. "The war. It's over." Calls had been coming in from friends and neighbors. With the collapse of its defenses, the German forces had begun to surrender to the Allies. The war in Europe had ended. "The news is everywhere."

Karl quickly reached for the radio. The broadcaster's voice boomed out. "Victory flags are flying high, church bells are ringing, and people are celebrating in the streets. At long last, the Allies have secured victory in Europe." Karl didn't wait to hear any more. He grabbed the telephone and dialed Phyllis's number.

"It's so exciting," she cried. "I can hear the crowds outside my window. It's like New Year's Eve."

The sound he had been hearing in the distance must have been the din of cheering voices, Karl realized. Canadians were in the streets, celebrating the end of the war. "I'm getting dressed and I'll meet you downtown," he said. "We can't miss this."

It was only as he was buttoning his shirt that he paused to think about what had just happened. As imminent as the end of the war had been, this moment was still beyond comprehension. After six years, the war that had enveloped the world had come to an end. Memories flashed through his mind like the newsreel images he watched at the movie theater: the growing anti-Semitism in Rakovník, the flight from his home, the boat trip across the Atlantic, the years of waiting and wondering when it would all end. All of that was behind him and peace in the world loomed ahead. He imagined soldiers in fields across Europe, laying down their weapons triumphantly. He pictured families gratified to know that their sons and daughters would be coming home, and those who would never again see their loved ones. The news of Hitler's death had already reached North America days earlier. The reports suggested that he had committed suicide in his bunker underneath the Reich Chancellery in Berlin. Now, not only was this monster dead, but the evil regime that he had founded and led had fallen to its knees in defeat.

There was a soft knock at his bedroom door. Karl looked up as Hana poked her head inside and asked if she could come in. He nodded, moving aside some clothing so that she could sit on the bed.

"Do you believe this is really happening?" she asked. Hana, now close to twenty, had grown into a vibrant and energetic young woman. Since moving back to Toronto, she had been taking classes at Jarvis Collegiate Institute in the adult business department, working toward a diploma in secretarial studies.

Karl shook his head. "Hardly," he replied.

Hana paused a moment. "The first thing I thought about was Father, how he had longed for this day to come. He never got to see it." She looked up, her eyes moist.

Words caught in Karl's throat. It was true that his father had dreamed of the end of the war every day that he was in Canada. In the early days of their arrival, it had been one of the only things he had talked about

— when the war would end, when they might return to Rakovník, when they could reclaim some of their property. In the days leading up to his death, he had grown silent on the topic, perhaps resigning himself to a belief that he would never live to see the day when peace would arrive. Karl reached out to touch Hana on the arm and she smiled briefly in response. Then he shook the memory from his mind. He did not want the joy that he was feeling on this celebratory day dampened by his father's absence.

"I'm going out, Hana," he said. "You should, too. Go and call your friends. It's a day to rejoice."

Hana nodded, stood up, and left the room. Karl followed her down the stairs. In the time it had taken him to dress, the kitchen had filled with neighbors and friends. Marie was already busy serving up the cakes and biscuits that she always kept on hand in case there were guests. Among the visitors was Arthur Brock, the man who had helped them find their farm in Carlisle. Arthur's wife had died years earlier, and in the months following Victor's death, he had come around on a regular basis, offering support and friendship to the family. He had become a much-needed confidant to Marie. Karl watched as Arthur whispered something in her ear, and draped his arm affectionately through hers. She smiled and moved closer to him. Karl hoped they would marry. He himself already had one foot out the door with his pending marriage to Phyllis. He knew it wouldn't be long before Hana would follow suit. Though Arthur would never be Victor's intellectual equal, more than anything, Karl wanted his mother to be loved and taken care of. And Arthur was offering both.

Karl quickly maneuvered his way through the throng of visitors in his home, waved good-bye to his mother, and headed out into the streets. The buses were full of excited people chatting about the end of the war.

"The boys will be coming home soon," one man said.

"Life can only get better for all of us," another replied.

When Karl got off the bus, he was enveloped by a mob of cheering people. It was difficult to push his way through the masses. He strained to see above the crowd, searching for Phyllis. He finally spotted her standing on the steps of City Hall, waving and chatting amicably with passers-by.

They stood arm in arm in the middle of the festivities, reveling in the moment. There couldn't have been a more perfect day to celebrate. The sky was a deep and clear blue. The sun shone as brightly as the joyful faces of those who had come out to rejoice. Traffic had come to a virtual stand-still. The buildings on Dundas Street were already festooned with Union Jacks. The pavement was littered with confetti and more floated from the sky like unexpected snowflakes on an early spring day. The crowd pressed together until it was almost impossible to breathe. And the word that was on everyone's lips was "Peace!"

In the days that followed the newspapers carried detailed information about the end of the war. The headline in the *Toronto Daily Star* on May 7 proclaimed, "Unconditional surrender." The article that followed read:

Reims, France, May 7 – Germany surrendered unconditionally to the western Allies and Russia at 2:41 a.m. French time today. The surrender took place at a school house which is the headquarters of Gen. Eisenhower. The surrender which brought the war in Europe to a formal end after five years, eight months, and six days of bloodshed and destruction was signed for Germany by Col. Gen. Gustav Jodl....[6]

It would be three more months before the Pacific conflict with Japan would end with the dropping of atomic bombs on Hiroshima on August 6 and Nagasaki on August 9. The joy felt by everyone at the end of the war was dampened by the memory of fallen soldiers and civilian casualties in Europe. Tens of millions had lost their lives in the conflict.

As the reports of the losses were emerging, the news began to trickle in about the impact of the war on Jews. At first, the reports of the numbers of Jews killed under Nazi oppression were modest. But, as one concentration camp after another was liberated, the reported numbers of Jewish casualties grew to staggering proportions. And the conditions under which Jews had been killed were horrifying. Gas chambers, ovens, death camps, Zyklon B, all unheard of before the war, now became associated with the massacre of millions of innocent Jewish citizens across Europe. In North America, families were desperate for news of loved ones, friends, and neighbors.

No one was exempt. Luck was being measured not by whose families had escaped death, but by how few family members you had lost.

"Sometimes I think it's a good thing your father isn't here to hear this news," said Marie one night as the family sat around the radio. This was now becoming a daily ritual, first scouting the newspapers for the most recent reports of Jewish victims, and then listening intently to the radio to try to understand how so many could have died with no one coming to their aid.

"How could the government not have known what was happening?" asked Karl angrily. "The armies of Canada, the United States, and Great Britain knew everything that Hitler had been planning as far as his armies were concerned. I can't believe they didn't know that Jews were being slaughtered by the millions."

The photographs and movie news reels haunted them all, skeletal figures staring in dazed confusion at the camera with ghostly eyes that seemed to say "Thank you for rescuing me," while at the same time questioning "Why did you take so long?"

It was inconceivable to Karl, as it was to so many, that the death camps could have existed under the noses of Allied military intelligence and planning. And it left Karl and others enraged and helpless at the same time. All they could do was wait and hope that someone they knew, a relative, friend, colleague, or neighbor, might have survived the carnage. And, slowly, letters began to arrive along with other bits of news.

Phyllis's Aunt Renia, her mother's youngest sister, had survived. One of Karl's cousins, Vicky, was also alive. It was Vicky's sister Irene who had married Mr. Schmahl, the man who had brought Victor the four paintings. But the Schmahls had not survived. In fact, there were few in Karl's and Phyllis's families who had made it. It was as if the Nazis had taken a machete to their family trees, hacking off limbs and branches and discarding them.

There was one bit of happy news. Karl discovered that his beloved nanny, Leila Adrian, was still alive. She had left the country right after the war had ended, when Czechoslovakia had expelled all remaining Germans in what the country believed was retribution for years of Nazi occupation. Despite the fact that Leila had cut her ties to the former Sudetenland years earlier, her identity as an ethnic German marked her and millions of others as traitors to the country. Leila was now living in a village near Frankfurt. The letter that Marie received from her was a bright spot in an otherwise bleak picture.

In the days following, Karl's family learned about more and more of their friends and acquaintances who had also perished. The Zelenkas were all gone, caught in the Nazi net when they stayed back to care for an ailing son. The day that Hana learned that her good friend Rita Popper had perished was just as hard. In fact, no one from George Popper's immediate family had survived, with the exception of George himself, who had managed to get to the United States, aided by an uncle who had sponsored him to go to university. Hana recalled Rita's lovely smile and sweet innocence. "I can't believe anyone would want to harm her," Hana said. "Why?"

But that was a question no one was equipped to answer. *And why were we so lucky?* Karl wondered again and again. *We never really saw the future, never imagined the scope of what was to come. How is it that we made the right decision to get out when we did? How did my mother have so much foresight? If only there had been more like her.*

On June 28, 1946, Karl and Phyllis were married. The man who performed the ceremony was Rabbi David Monson, known affectionately as the "people's rabbi." The exchange of vows took place in his basement recreation room where he had constructed a permanent *chupa* – or wedding canopy – for these occasions. Only a handful of people were present: Karl's mother and Arthur Brock, Hana, a couple of uncles and an aunt, and Phyllis's parents and a few close relatives of hers. Neither Karl nor Phyllis wanted a lavish wedding. In truth, this Jewish ceremony was not even part of their belief system. But civil ceremonies were unheard of at the time, so this was the only possibility. Following the service, the family and a few other friends gathered at the King Edward Hotel for a small luncheon, and then Karl and Phyllis left for Niagara Falls and Lake Placid on their honeymoon.

The couple settled into a small apartment in the west end of Toronto, close to Phyllis's parents and Karl's work at Goodyear. With his mother's marriage to Arthur a few months later in early 1947, Karl felt as if his life was indeed settling into a normal and fulfilling existence. He was content. He had found a loving partner in Phyllis. Hana was grown and becoming more and more independent. Karl had a good job and even dreamed of one day starting a family of his own. It therefore took him by surprise when Marie announced shortly after her marriage that she and Arthur were moving back to Prague.

"What do you think you'll find there?" Karl asked after listening to Marie explain that she had been thinking about this return nonstop since the end of the war was announced. "Go for a holiday. Go and see if our home is still there. But don't give up everything we've established and worked for here for something that may not even exist anymore."

"I think about our house so often," Marie continued. "And everything we had before the war. Since discovering that Mr. Schmahl was amongst those who perished, I've wondered more and more about the paintings that he gave us."

Karl listened but did not respond. It was virtually impossible for him to think about the Czechoslovakia he remembered from before the war.

"The paintings were all beautiful, but I especially loved the one of the children washing up. I haven't had any letters from Alois Jirák," she added, naming the colleague who had taken possession of the paintings along with the power of attorney for their estate. "I wonder if he even managed to get through the war safely, let alone take care of our things. It would be a miracle if any of it is still there," Marie said. "I know they were just things, irrelevant compared to the loss of lives, but I can't help but wonder about everything we left behind."

Marie's eyes revealed her unshakeable determination, a look that Karl had seen many times. "The Nazis took everything and forced us out," she said calmly and deliberately. "We had to run, like mice from a sinking ship. Well, now the war is over and it's time to return, to take back our country and our home."

"This is home," countered Karl, shaking his head emphatically. "That's only an illusion."

But Marie's mind was made up. "I have to find out what's left," she said firmly. "I have to try to get it back. If necessary I'll spend the rest of my life fighting to regain our property."

At that, Karl fell silent, knowing that once his mother had resolved to do something, there was no stopping her. He knew that if anyone was capable of reclaiming their property and belongings, his mother certainly was.

Karl and Phyllis, 1947.

CHAPTER FOURTEEN

Toronto, March 10, 1990

WHEN THE POST OFFICE called a couple of weeks later to say that there was a package waiting for him from Prague, Theo was perplexed. He was not expecting another shipment of art. The most recent lot had arrived with all of the paintings intact – the "legal" ones that he had cleared through the National Gallery in Prague.

Theo had been organizing regular buying expeditions to the city of his birth for years, ever since he had realized that he could acquire fine art there at a price that was a fraction of its worth, and sell it here in Toronto for many times its value. The first five paintings he had bought in the early 1980s had sold easily, and Theo had profited well from those sales. The next time he had traveled to Prague, he had returned with ten paintings. On the next trip, he had bought twenty, and then thirty. Not in his wildest imagination had he ever dreamed that this business would do so well. He had made a good profit for the gallery and for himself over the years, acquiring the kind of wealth that allowed him to enjoy a lifestyle similar to the one in which had had been raised, though, in truth, he cared little about the money. He would have somehow managed to maintain his lifestyle whether he had the means or not. More surprisingly, the business he had developed was entirely legitimate. The paintings he selected were all approved by the infamous National Gallery of Czechoslovakia, one of many arms of the Communist government. It could have easily denied permission for the export of valuable paintings, or taxed them so heavily as to make their attainment too costly to be worth the effort. So how was it that Theo had come to be a regular here at the post office, routinely picking up bundles of paintings that he had bought in Prague and legally cleared for delivery to Toronto?

The answer was that he knew what to look for when he shopped – eighteenth- and nineteenth-century European oil paintings. Recently he had begun to include some twentieth-century impressionist oils. Most of the paintings he bought were done by Czech artists. František Jakub was a favorite. Jakub's pastoral scenes of peasants, plump nude women, and cherubic infants were in high demand in Canada. Paintings by artists such as Alfons Mucha, František Ženíšek, and Václav Brožík were also desirable. Occasionally, he managed to acquire works by German and Austrian painters. Theo chose mostly landscapes, interior scenes, and still life paintings. No portraits – he had learned that Canadian art collectors didn't like them – and no religious scenes. There was no market in Canada for those either. Most importantly, he knew that all of the paintings he selected would easily pass the scrutiny of the National Gallery and its panel of commissioners who granted permission for export. The Gallery considered these paintings to be too bourgeois and of little value. Theo chuckled at that. *What did they really know of art*, he wondered. It helped that most of the panelists on the jury were women. Theo had learned how to please and even manipulate them to turn a blind eye to some of the paintings he slipped into the bundle. It was remarkable how far an engaging smile, a kiss on the cheek, and a bottle of fine cognac could go.

But over the years, while on his buying sprees, Theo had occasionally come across pieces that he knew with certainty would not pass the inspection, no matter how charming he might be. And yet, he longed to have these works. He knew that if he could somehow get them out of the country and sell them in Canada, he would hit the jackpot. And that's when he began to smuggle paintings out, using sources and acquaintances that, for the right price, were eager to help him with this illegal activity. Once they had crossed the border from Czechoslovakia into Germany, it was simple to bring these additional paintings overseas into Canada. Getting them *into* Germany was the hard part. It was a complicated procedure and anything but safe. If he were discovered trying to smuggle valuable artwork out of Czechoslovakia without the Gallery's approval, the secret police would be on him in seconds. He would be arrested, thrown in jail, possibly tortured, and perhaps never heard from again. His Canadian citizenship and passport would not protect him if he were suspected of being involved in some clandestine scheme to smuggle goods out of the country. Karl Reeser's request to retrieve his family paintings would require one of these complicated maneuvers. Was it worth the risk? Theo knew that the answer to that question was a definite yes.

"I didn't expect to be back here so soon," Theo said as he entered the postal building and approached the desk. The clerk, a young man with a bright red face and awkward bearing, recognized him immediately and bent to confer with him.

"I'm the one who called you, Mr. Král," the man said. "I'll get your package if you'll just wait a minute. There's a bit of a problem with it." He frowned and shrugged before leaving the main room to search in the back.

Two mysteries, thought Theo, as he waited for the clerk to return. Who was sending him a package? And what was this problem? His mail from Prague was either about the artwork that he was in charge of shipping or the occasional letter from family or friends. Neither posed any problems, unless the Czech government was somehow involved in this. At that thought, Theo paused and his mind flashed back to when he had first arrived in Toronto.

It had been a shock to his family when Theo decided to leave for Canada in 1978. It wasn't that he hated the oppressive regime. Quite the contrary. He knew the system well and had learned to move quite freely within it. He went where he wanted and spoke his mind. After graduating from film school, he had secured a good job working in the Czech film industry. This had also been a political position. Theo's job had been to function as a "commissar." He organized film festivals and screened movies for the government, ensuring that those chosen for the public adhered to the strict rules of propaganda and politics. His was a senior position, supervising a large contingent of people in the film industry. It was expected that he would also observe all behaviors of those below him, and report any activities of interest or concern to the Central Committee. While others would have readily acted as spies for the government, at this, Theo drew the line, refusing to satisfy the Communists and become an informer. It was important to him that he not intentionally hurt anyone, even within this position of power. And he walked that line well. If he had wanted, he could have risen within the party to a position of authority, probably within the Department of Propaganda. With his charm and organizational skills, he would have done well for the system.

So why leave what was, for all intents and purposes, a good life? The truth was that Theo had seen the writing on the wall long before the regime began to falter. He envisioned the future of Czechoslovakia with the kind of foresight that he was known for, and he knew there was no future here for him. Besides, Theo was increasingly unhappy in this homogeneous society defined by identical three-story walk-ups and fearful citizens. He no longer wanted to live by someone else's rules. It was time to live entirely by his own.

No one understood his reasoning, least of all his parents. They cornered him and went at him with every argument they could muster.

"You are leaving all these comforts – your home, your position, your security," his father said. "Are you really willing to abandon all of this?"

"You are leaving *us*!" his mother added, more gently. "When will we see you? It's not so easy to travel outside of Prague." Travel visas were next to impossible to obtain. The government did not trust that those who left the country would ever return.

"Do you understand the seriousness of what you are doing? You'll

KATHY KACER

probably be denounced and stripped of your citizenship," his father concluded grimly.

Theo shrugged. "I'm still going."

Earlier in his life, he had become involved in a Christian peace organization. It's not that he subscribed to any kind of religion. But the group had afforded him the opportunity to travel to various countries to participate in local symposia. A conference was being held in Toronto and, using his affiliation with this group as a rationale, he applied for and received the exit permit needed to travel to Canada, knowing full well he would not return.

Theo had to admit that those first few months in Toronto were difficult. He was homesick and spent evenings playing old Czech songs on the record player and poring over photographs of castles and châteaus from the Czech countryside. For the first time in his life, he felt truly alone. He had no Canadian friends, missed the old connections, and hated the isolation, something he had never experienced before.

But still he would not return to Prague. He ignored the letters that began to arrive from friends and family members begging him to come back. The Communists even went so far as to release his parents for a visit to Toronto to persuade him to return. But he remained firm. He was not going back. He was determined to weather those early days in Toronto and concluded that this was his destiny. The responsibility for establishing a new life lay with him now. *Lazy people do better in a socialist system where you're not allowed to think for yourself,* he concluded. That was not the life that Theo craved. He had his sights set on greater adventures. Eventually, he was expelled from the Communist party. He had been a golden boy within the system and his defection was viewed as a slap in the face.

The postal clerk returned and placed a small box on the desk between them. It was square, possibly holding a book or two, thought Theo. But more important than its contents was the condition in which this parcel had arrived. The paper was ripped and hung in strips, as if it had been torn apart and then hastily repackaged. The string had been retied, and tape had been applied haphazardly to hold the shreds of paper together. The clerk's face, red before, now seemed almost to explode with color as he gestured apologetically at the pile of paper and string. "It arrived like this from Prague, Mr. Král," he said. "I don't know what happened to it. Looks like it got kicked around a bit."

Theo knew instantly what had happened, though for a moment he couldn't speak. Anger rose in his throat like bile. This was no accidental damage. The package had clearly been torn apart and then rewrapped. It looked as if someone had been searching for something here, and Theo was certain that the ones doing the inspecting were the Czech secret police. The young clerk was speaking again, though Theo barely heard him through the fog of fury that he felt at this assault on his property. "You'll have to sign here, Mr. Král. Just so we know you accepted the parcel as is. If there's any damage to the stuff inside, you can fill out this form as well…."

The young man was still talking but Theo was already on the move. He signed blindly, grabbed the package and stumbled out of the building and toward his car. Once inside, he spent a minute calming himself before peeling aside what was left of the packaging so that he could view the contents.

It was indeed a book, a gift from his parents, as the enclosed card read. This book was a detailed exploration of the history and meaning of Tarot cards, a topic near and dear to Theo's heart. This volume was unavailable in Canada and his parents had been promising they would send it for some time. But if the paper that enclosed the box had been torn apart, it did not even begin to compare with the damage to the book itself. The front cover was ripped at the edges and had been peeled back in layers as if to reveal something hidden within the cover or concealed in the spine. Pages were missing along with the back cover. And, as Theo held the ruined book in his hands, he knew exactly what it was that the secret police had been looking for. It was common knowledge that they regularly searched for microchips containing information about their government and possibly concealed in books, gifts…or even paintings.

There was nothing subtle about this defacement of his property, and no attempt on the part of State Security to hide its search. Their message here was loud and clear: *We are watching you and we are suspicious of your activities*. And there was nothing Theo could do about it, no complaint that he could lodge, and no form from the post office that could help him. And all this practically on the eve of his departure for Prague. He would be extra vigilant, he assured himself, as he tossed the book on the passenger seat and revved the engine of his car. He would not be deterred. If anything, this arrogant gesture on the part of the Communist police goons only strengthened his resolve to retrieve Karl Reeser's paintings. His trip was only days away.

CHAPTER FIFTEEN

Prague 1947–8

SHORTLY AFTER Marie and Arthur's departure to Prague, Karl and Phyllis gave up their apartment in the west end of the city and moved into the family house on Rosedale Heights Drive. There they waited for news from Marie. It was difficult to get information. Through sporadic letters and even more infrequent telegrams, Karl was able to learn the full details of what unfolded in Prague only many months later.

When Marie and Arthur returned to Czechoslovakia, they took up residence in a spacious flat in Prague and began to take stock of what had happened to the country following Nazi Germany's surrender. Like many European countries, Czechoslovakia was in the process of rebuilding, and in April 1945, the Third Republic of Czechoslovakia came into being. This was a coalition government consisting of three parties: the Communist Party of Czechoslovakia – Komunistická strana Československa (KSČ) – the Czechoslovak Social Democratic Party, and the Czechoslovak National Socialist Party. At the time there was great support for the KSČ, which had strong ties to the Soviet Union, the country that had liberated Czechoslovakia in the final days of the war and was now directing much of its future. The KSČ was determined to become the country's primary political force.

In the spring election of 1946, Edvard Beneš, who had resigned in the aftermath of the Munich Agreement, returned to Prague and was formally confirmed to his second term as president of the republic. However, the election results gave the KSČ a majority of the vote. More importantly, the Communists were able to gain control of all key ministries, with power over the police, the armed forces, education, social welfare, agriculture, and the civil service. The Communist leader, Klement Gottwald, became prime minister. He was viewed as a moderate who would respect the Czech tradition of democracy; this was reinforced when he proclaimed his desire to lead the country to a thorough "democratic national revolution."[7]

It was into this new and promising political climate that Marie and Arthur arrived. Those early days in Prague were good. The country seemed to be thriving in the promise of prosperity for all. It almost felt to Marie as if life had returned to what it once was. There was a free press in place, freedom of religion, equal rights for women, an independent judiciary, jobs, and the right to education and recreation. Wealth was being restored, and art and music were thriving.

In the early days, Arthur was happily reunited with his son, who had managed to survive the war in one of the concentration camps of Poland. Karl could only imagine Arthur's joy at this happy discovery. Almost immediately, Marie started looking for news of the fate of the Jewish community in Rakovník. The first discovery was devastating. Not one other Jewish family in their hometown had come through the war intact. Apart from the Reisers, only George Popper had survived. Everyone else had remained in town when Marie had packed up the family and fled to Prague, and all had been arrested by the Gestapo shortly thereafter, eventually perishing in Hitler's death camps. The grief cut deeply as Marie remembered her friends, her neighbors, the dinner parties with the Poppers — everything was gone. It was unthinkable. The Rakovník that she had known no longer existed.

The only thing that remained was the house on Husovo Náměstí, the central square, and Marie focused on it as though getting it back would restore one small piece of the world she had once known. She discovered that the family home had indeed been confiscated by the Gestapo shortly after they had fled. When Marie inquired as to the property's current status, she learned that the house was now in the possession of the Czech government and had been converted into the local headquarters for the Communist party. Despite her best efforts and those of the attorney she had retained, there was nothing she could do to reclaim the house. Everything that Victor had worked for, everything that they had built together, their entire estate had vanished, swallowed up first by the Nazis and now by the Communists.

But Marie would not stop there. Seized by the realization that she would never be able to reclaim the family home, she believed that there was perhaps one part of the family property that had escaped Nazi confiscation. And that was the four paintings that she had left in the possession of Alois Jirák. Marie clung to the hope that the paintings had been moved to Jirák's son-in-law's home in the country for safekeeping, and had remained safe there, out of the Nazis' hands. To Marie, the paintings seemed to represent, more than anything else, the freedom that the family had once enjoyed. They were all that remained of the family's legacy.

Marie tracked down Alois Jirák. Mr. Jirák, she discovered, had made it through the war with his family, living in his estate outside of Rakovník. Like many Czech citizens, he had managed to do his work and remain under the radar of the Nazi machinery.

Marie's reunion with him was not a friendly one. All of the respect that he had shown to Victor when they had done business together was gone, replaced with a cold reserve and disdain for Marie and her circumstances. After a short and awkward greeting, Marie got down to business.

"I'm not here to talk about our estate," she began. "The property is gone – in the hands of the government now. And I realize there is nothing I can do about that."

Mr. Jirák nodded, his eyes narrowed, and he stared at Marie without responding.

"I'm grateful that you handled our power of attorney back then," she continued. "You helped my husband and me to hold on to the funds that enabled us to get out of the country safely. Not everyone would have helped in that way."

Mr. Jirák continued to stare.

"But before we left Prague, I entrusted you with four paintings that hung in our home in Rakovník."

At that, Mr. Jirák raised his eyebrows slightly. "Paintings?" he asked.

Marie nodded. "Yes, four of them. Surely you remember. At the time, you said that you were going to take them to your son-in-law's estate in the country. You said they'd be safer there in case the Nazis came looking. I'm assuming you still have them and I'd like to take them back now."

Mr. Jirák turned his head and gazed away. A long moment passed and neither spoke. Marie held her breath in anticipation of what Mr. Jirák would say. Finally, he turned back to face her.

"Yes, I remember now," he said. "Four of them, you say?"

Marie nodded.

"Right. Well, I'm afraid they're gone. The Gestapo came to search Václav's house – my son-in-law, Václav Pekárek. Everyone was being searched, you know. You think only the Jews were in danger? Well, that's not the case. We all were. The Nazis wanted everything they could get their hands on." Mr. Jirák paused. When he said the word *Jew*, Marie sensed his contempt and she felt her anger rising. She fought to control herself.

"At any rate," Mr. Jirák continued. "They searched the home several times, went through all of our things, and, on one such search, they confiscated the paintings – took them off the wall and carried them out the door. Who knows what became of them. I did my best, you know," he added. "As you yourself said, there were not many like me who were willing to help you and others in your situation. Be grateful you got away with your lives. Not everyone was as lucky as you were."

Mr. Jirák continued talking, but by now Marie had stopped listening. The paintings gone? She couldn't imagine it and, what's more, she didn't believe it. Maybe it was the fact that Mr. Jirák would not meet her eyes, or that he claimed too emphatically not to have the paintings. That intuition, so predominant in Marie, kicked in once more and convinced her that Mr. Jirák was lying. The rest of the property may have been taken, and for that there was no recourse. But in her heart Marie believed that the paintings were safe, and she became even more determined to get them back.

Almost immediately after leaving Alois Jirák, Marie proceeded to the law office of Václav Jukl, where she described the events of her family's departure from Czechoslovakia, Alois Jirák's role, and her strong suspicion that he was now in possession of her property. With her usual determination, Marie made the decision to begin legal action against Alois Jirák.

Several letters were exchanged between Marie's lawyer and the attorney that Jirák retained upon learning that Marie was planning to sue him. It did not take long for Mr. Jirák to confess a new version of his story. In this account, he claimed that the paintings had remained safe in his home during the war. He reiterated that the Gestapo had searched the house, and had questioned him several times as to the origin of the paintings. He reminded Marie of the consequences that might have resulted had they discovered that he was hiding Jewish property. Jirák stated that he had sold the paintings a couple of years after the war ended. He claimed that it was his belief that the power of attorney granted by Victor and Marie entitled him to dispose of the paintings in any way he wished, since he had had no way of knowing whether or not the Reiser family had even survived. Marie's arrival back in Prague had come as a complete shock to him, which had prompted his first lie. The paintings, however, were still gone, he continued to claim, and there was nothing more that anyone could do to retrieve them.

Once again, Marie was not convinced. Several more letters passed between the two attorneys. Marie's lawyer continued to press for the return of the paintings, while Mr. Jirák hung on to his story that the paintings were gone and Marie should abandon her mission.

Meanwhile, back in Toronto, Karl wondered and worried about his mother. By the summer of 1947, the political situation in Czechoslovakia was again becoming precarious. All of the assurances of a moderate transition to power for the Communists, one that would respect the Czech tradition of democracy, were rapidly disappearing. The Communist-dominated police, under the control of the Ministry of the Interior, began to increase its intrusiveness in the lives of Czech citizens. The KSČ, with Soviet support, was beginning to accelerate its drive to total power. Toronto newspapers were filled with ominous predictions that Czechoslovakia would be caught up in the whirlwind of conflict that was spinning and escalating between the Soviet Union and the United States.

"'Moscow's strategy will be to spark revolutions throughout Europe. And Czechoslovakia will be the first step.'" Karl was scanning the papers and reading sections aloud to Phyllis as the two of them discussed for the umpteenth time the declining circumstances abroad. "Look here. This reporter compares the stand-off between the Soviet Union and the U.S. to a contest between neighbors who are trying to see who can live the longest. The rules of the contest provide that the survivor gets the property of the one who dies first, so it's more than mere academic interest at stake. It is a real 'we or they' proposition."[8] He looked up incredulously. "I can't believe the world is in this position again. There are some who are even talking of a Third World War."

"Your mother hasn't written much lately," Phyllis replied uneasily. "But even the letters that we've had from her say so little about what is going on there politically."

"Mother would never want to worry us. Don't you know that's her style? She'd rather write about what she can buy with whatever declining currency she has than talk about any danger to her or to Arthur." In her sporadic letters to Karl, she had written that she was trying to do as much shopping in Prague as possible. Remarkably, the money that she had left in the country years earlier was still there, in bank accounts that had remained untouched, in the same financial institutions where Karl had lined up daily to withdraw small amounts of cash. Now Marie was trying to use up as much of it as possible, though she admitted in her correspondence that there was little to buy.

Karl pointed again at the newspapers. "Look, they're saying that Czechoslovakia is a key location in Europe." He sat back in his chair, shaking his head. "No wonder Hitler was anxious to control the country years ago. And Stalin is the same. He won't let it be. And he won't stop there. Even if the West ignores what's happening to Czechoslovakia, anyone who thinks appeasement will work on the Communists doesn't know what they're talking about."

There was a tense silence in the room. "There's nothing you can do," Phyllis finally said. "You know your mother will decide things for herself."

"All I know is that I wish she'd leave Czechoslovakia behind and get back here safely." He looked up suddenly. "My father must have felt like this when he was in Paris and we were stuck back in Prague before the war." No wonder his father had suffered so much in the absence of his family. Karl now experienced a feeling of complete helplessness. In the face of the rising animosity between the United States and the Soviet Union, he was terrified that if the situation deteriorated, his mother might actually be trapped in Czechoslovakia again, this time under Communist rule.

Karl wanted his mother home for personal reasons, too. By late 1947, he and Phyllis were expecting their first child, and he hoped his mother might be there for the birth of her first grandchild.

Back in Czechoslovakia, the lawyers remained at an impasse. Then, in late 1947, there was a new turn of events. Mr. Jirák finally confessed that he was in fact in possession of the four paintings. Despite his continued insistence that the Gestapo had searched his son-in-law's house on several occasions, Jirák admitted that he had managed to keep the artwork hidden away. The paintings were safe. A letter from his lawyer stated that Mr. Jirák was willing to return three of the four paintings: the children in the bathhouse, the dancer, and the forest inferno. The fourth one, the one called *Die Hausfrau*, would remain in the possession of his son-in-law as payment for having taken such risks to hide the paintings in the first place. It was only fair, the letter stated, that Mr. Jirák and his family be compensated for all they had done for the family during the war. One painting would settle this dispute once and for all.

Jirák's offer was not what Marie wanted to hear. At first jubilant over the discovery that the paintings were indeed safe, she was angry to think that Jirák would hold one back from her. She could acknowledge that he had risked his family's life to hide their belongings, and for that, she was extremely grateful. Indeed, she would have given him a substantial reward for having kept the paintings safe, anything except one of them in payment. It was her decision to determine the fate of the paintings, she reasoned, not his.

More and more, the paintings were taking on a particular symbolic importance for Marie. There were four paintings; there had been four members of the Reeser family. Keeping the family together in their pre-war flight from Europe had been Marie's primary objective. Keeping the four paintings together was now taking on the same significance. "They are all that is left of our home and belongings, and I will not abandon any of them. I would no more leave a painting behind than I would have left a member of my family behind during the war," Marie declared. "I will not separate the paintings."

The response letter from Marie's lawyer was emphatic. In it, he stated that Mr. Jirák's responsibility had been to protect the paintings as per Marie and Victor's instructions. Jirák had no jurisdiction to sell them or keep them, no matter how much time had elapsed since the end of the war. Marie wished to settle the matter quickly, but under no circumstances would she relinquish one of the paintings. With this stalemate firmly established, there appeared to be no alternative but to move to a court hearing. The fate of the paintings would have to be settled in a courtroom before a judge.

In December 1947, Hana traveled to Prague to be with her mother. Taking a break from the stress of the pending court hearing, the family decided to go on a skiing vacation to Špindlerův Mlýn. This scenic resort in the Krkonoše Mountains was one of the most popular sites in northern

Czechoslovakia, famous not only for its skiing, but also for its hiking and biking trails. Cottages, chalets, and hotels dotted the valleys in the shadow of several giant mountain ranges. The air was crisp, and the green tops of the pine trees looked beautiful as they emerged from under cascades of snow. Here, it appeared as if nothing had changed from before the war. The trip was a reminder of days gone by when the family had taken many such vacations.

Hana was a strong and accomplished skier. It was while she was there with her mother and Arthur that Hana was introduced to Paul Traub, a man ten years her senior. Paul was a quiet, intelligent, and deeply thoughtful man who had studied to become a physician before the war began. His relatively young life and career, like that of so many others, had been tragically interrupted by the war and his arrest and subsequent deportation to the Auschwitz concentration camp. He had survived while most of his family members had not, and, in the wake of the war, he too had decided to return to his homeland. Paul and Hana decided to ski together, but while descending a particularly difficult mountain, Paul fell and broke his shoulder. This ended his skiing holiday, but it was the beginning of a growing affection between himself and Hana. They knew they were meant to be together.

When the family returned to Prague, there appeared to be a growing political tension in the air. The news was filled with the dissension between the United States and her allies in the west and the Union of Soviet Socialist Republics in the east. Czech military forces were being trained to handle the Soviet equipment and weapons that were regularly arriving in the country in large quantities. It felt as if Czechoslovakia was arming for war. Unbeknownst to anyone, Klement Gottwald and his KSČ party were beginning a covert plan for a Communist seizure of power. They would not wait for the elections due to take place in the spring, and allow the possibility of defeat.

It was during this time that a strange turn of events occurred with respect to Marie's attempts to reclaim the paintings. In a letter from her attorney to Jirák, she appeared to abandon her mission. The correspondence indicated that, while she did not relinquish her right to ownership of the paintings, she did wish to withdraw legal action. In addition, she agreed to cover the legal costs that Jirák had incurred in the intervening months. From Jirák's perspective, this was a complete victory and a vindication that he had done the right thing all along.

When Karl heard that his mother was abandoning the lawsuit, he was somewhat relieved. "At least this means that she will get out of there before the political situation worsens," he reasoned. Marie must have anticipated that a Communist takeover was imminent. Knowing that she would have to leave or be caught in this new oppressive net, Karl assumed that his mother had come to the conclusion that there would be no point in proceeding further with the lawsuit.

"But the paintings," questioned Phyllis. "After all she's tried to do to get them back, why would she stop now?"

It was a good question, and Karl had no answer. "She still maintains that all four paintings belong to her and to our family," he said. "Knowing my mother, she may even be thinking that once this new political unrest has passed, she'll go back to Czechoslovakia and pick up the fight where she left off. I'm sure this isn't the end of the road."

In February 1948, the Communist party under Klement Gottwald assumed full control over the government of Czechoslovakia. The country became a satellite state of the Soviet Union. This event would become significant beyond the impact on Czechoslovakia alone, as it paved the way for the drawing of the Iron Curtain, and the full-fledged Cold War between the East and West for the next four decades.

Karl's heart nearly came to a standstill when he picked up the newspaper in Toronto in late February and read the headlines. "Lesson for appeasers seen as Bolshevists grab Czechoslovakia." The article that followed read:

So democratic little Czechoslovakia has gone the way of all countries upon which bolshevism has managed to obtain a firm grip.

Czechoslovakia's absorption is one of Moscow's greatest successes. As the *London News Chronicle* pointed out a few hours before the coup was achieved, if the Communists gained complete control in Czechoslovakia it would be their most important victory in Europe, because out of all their conquests the Czechs would be the first with an instinctive belief in western democratic freedom. Well, bolshevism reigns in freedom-loving Prague – at least for the time being.[9]

Marie knew that she would have to get out of Czechoslovakia quickly. The borders were about to close. The memories of fleeing Prague once before rushed back into her consciousness. It was mind-boggling that her country was again forcing her to flee. She had returned believing that she and Arthur could build a stable home in the country she loved. And for a short while it had appeared as if that might be true. But now her heart ached, first for the homeland she was losing for the second time, but perhaps even more so for the loss of her precious paintings. They would remain behind, sealed within the same borders that were forcing her out for a second time. Marie, Arthur, and Hana quickly packed a few suitcases and boarded a plane for Toronto. Paul Traub, the man Hana intended to marry, was not allowed to leave with her. He was refused an exit visa by the new Minister of the Interior on the basis that, as a physician, he was needed by the country. In response, he claimed that his arm, which he had broken while skiing with Hana, made it impossible for him to practice any longer. Eventually, after paying a substantial bribe, Paul managed to get the necessary exit visa. He left the country quickly, taking no belongings, and was met in New York by a relieved Hana.

Karl was thankful to have his family back on Canadian soil. Upon his mother's arrival in Toronto, Karl questioned her about the paintings and the lawsuit. Marie's response was clear and firm. "You can forget about them," she said. She and Karl never spoke of the paintings again.

4.března   8.

Dr.Pi/Cho   Vážení páni manželé
                             Inž.Václav a Božena Pekárkovi,

                             P e t r o v i c e .

                  Vážený pane inženýre!
                  Dnešního dne po Vašem odchodu volal mě
nový právní zástupce pí Reiserové a sdělil, že převzal
zastoupení po dru Feiglovi, že si spisy prostudoval a že
pí Reiserové doporučil zpětvzetí žaloby s tím, že se
nevzdá nároku na vydání obrazů, ale útraty s tím vzniklé
podle soudního rozsudku, že uhradí.
                  Paní Reiserová dle jeho sdělení s tím
projevila souhlas a v důsledku toho odpadá také stání
dne 17.t.m.. To tedy znamená Vaše úplné vítězství pokud
jde o žalobu, kterou pí Reiserová na Vás před časem poda-
la.
                  Těší mne, že Vám mohu oznámiti tento
výsledek a zatím znamenám

                             s projevem dokonalé úcty

A letter from Marie's lawyer advising that she has agreed to withdraw legal action for the return of the paintings, while not relinquishing her claim to them.

JUDr. VÁCLAV JUKL
advokát
PRAHA II, NA STRUZE 3
Telef. 26267

V Praze dne 27. V. 1949.

Vážený Pán,
pan Ing. V. Pekárek,
Václavy čp.43
p. Petrovice u Rakovníka.

Věc: pozůstalost po V. Reisrovi / vydání obrazů /:

Vážený pane inženýre.

Potvrzuji tímto příjem Vašeho ctěného dopisu ze dne 22.t.m. jehož obsah jsem vzal na vědomí. Ujišťuji Vás, že mám opravdovou snahu věc likvidovati k úplné spokojenosti všech súčastněných. Moje mandantka jest ochotna přijmouti jakékoliv rozumné řešení avšak nemůže přistoupiti na darování jednoho obrazu. Doufám však, že s panem prof. Jirákem věc uspořádám tak, aby všichni súčastnění se necítili poškozeni.

Děkuji Vám za Váš ctěný dopis a znamenám
v dokonalé úctě
oddaný:

Written by Václav Jukl, Marie's attorney in Czechoslovakia, this letter states that Marie is prepared to accept any reasonable solution to the matter of the four paintings, except relinquishing one of them.

A statement from Alois Jirák to his laywer, which lists three of the paintings and describes that the fourth one was promised to his son-in-law, Václav Pekárek, "who risked his life and property to safeguard the paintings from occupation forces."

PART III

A CHANCE AT RESTITUTION

CHAPTER SIXTEEN

Toronto, March 15, 1989

THE MAIL HAD ARRIVED earlier than usual that day. Karl paused on his way to the kitchen, newspaper in hand, glancing down at what appeared to be bills, the usual useless fliers, and a bank statement or two. There was an advertisement for a membership to a tennis club that looked interesting. Now sixty-eight, Karl had maintained a youthful vigor. While he had long ago given up skiing and cycling, he walked and hiked regularly, and was still an avid and skilled tennis player.

As he flipped through the remaining envelopes, one caught his eye. It looked like an invitation of some kind, but the return address and postage were Czech. *Who would invite me to Czechoslovakia*, he wondered. *And what kind of event would be taking place there at this time?* In the early spring of 1989, Czechoslovakia was still an oppressive place under a Soviet regime that ruled with tight, unyielding laws. State Security, the infamous secret police, was everywhere, watching its citizens and arresting dissidents. It was common practice for them to wiretap telephones, watch apartments, open and read mail, and search homes without warning. Individuals were frequently arrested for what became known as "subversion of the republic." Citizens, at all levels of society, were "encouraged" to watch their neighbors and report any suspicious activity, or risk falling under suspicion themselves. Informers were strategically placed within businesses, schools, and community groups. The people of Czechoslovakia lived in constant fear.

There had been a brief period of liberalization, known as the Prague Spring, which began in January 1968 under the leadership of Alexander Dubček. Under his rule the country saw a loosening of regulations inhibiting free speech, travel, and the press. Many Czechs rallied behind these progressive changes, and called for even more rapid advancement toward democracy. But this alarmed the Soviet Union, and, fearing that these reforms would lead to a weakening of the Communist Bloc during the Cold War, the Warsaw Pact nations, including the Soviet Union, East Germany, Poland, Hungary, and Bulgaria, invaded Czechoslovakia on August 21, 1968. Approximately ninety civilians were shot and killed, and close to 3,500 fled the country, many finding refuge in Canada which, in contrast to its policies during the Second World War, this time opened its doors to escaping Czechs. Gustáv Husák replaced Dubček as president of Czechoslovakia and reversed almost all of his reforms. The party was purged of its liberal members, and intellectual elites were dismissed from public office and professional jobs. Control was gradually restored, and hard-line Communists were reinstated as leaders. Twenty years after the Prague Spring, Czechoslovakia was still a repressed country. With its closed borders and restricted opportunities, there were few if any celebratory events or occasions that might have prompted someone to send an invitation to Karl.

He turned the envelope over in his hands and then carefully broke the seal, removing a stiff cardboard note with formal black lettering. Its contents startled Karl. The card requested his presence at the fiftieth anniversary reunion of his former high school in Rakovník. And, as he stared soberly at the invitation, memories stirred.

March 15, 1989 – it was fifty years to the day that Germany had invaded Czechoslovakia, setting off the string of events that would plunge the country and eventually the world into the chasm of war. And it was fifty years to the day that Karl and his family had fled Rakovník to the temporary safety of Prague, and, ultimately, Canada. Karl had only visited his former homeland once in the years since his family had been forced to flee. But the truth was, he had never had any desire to return. Any sentimental attachment to Czechoslovakia that he might have retained in the early days of adjusting to life in Toronto was gone. It was as if that part of his life had ended and a new chapter – one that represented freedom and security – had been born to take its place. Despite the slight remnant of an accent that still identified him as European, Karl felt and *was* more Canadian than Czech. His entire adult life had been formed in Canada. He had found a home and a career here, had married, and had raised two children with Phyllis. Linda taught marketing in the business schools of two universities. Ted had his own successful business distributing restaurant equipment. Both had married and had had children of their own, a source of additional pride and joy for Karl and Phyllis.

Karl stared again at the invitation, wondering how the organizers had even tracked him down after all these years. Then he shook his head and smiled wryly as another thought flashed through his mind. He had not even graduated from his high school! That place was one more reminder of the virulent anti-Semitism that had plagued his country even before the war. Karl tossed the invitation aside, marveling at how the letter had instantly propelled him back to a place and time he had worked hard to forget. Memories had that power, he realized. The slightest event or object could catch you off guard and hold your mind hostage to the past.

He took another deep breath, wondering where Phyllis was. He needed a cup of tea, and wanted to talk to her about the invitation. The dog whined softly at the door, anxious to go for a walk. "Later, Quinta," Karl said firmly. At Karl's command, the brown Welsh terrier sniffed and reluctantly turned away.

Karl was just about to head for the kitchen when one more envelope caught his eye. This one had been at the bottom of the pile and might have been overlooked completely had it not been for its familiar onionskin wrapping. It was an airmail envelope, Karl realized, and also from Czechoslovakia. Two letters from his former homeland in one day! It was more than he had received in years. But it was the salutation on this envelope that made Karl catch his breath.

Mrs. Marie Reiserová or anybody from the family.*

More memories! Marie had died five years earlier. Her heart had begun to fail her in her advancing years. One mild heart attack followed another, and gradually she began to fade. This was followed by a series of ministrokes until, in her ninety-first year, Marie ended up hospitalized for what would prove to be the last time. Karl visited her every day, sitting by his mother's bedside and often helping to feed her. Her declining health and the countless physical examinations by the doctors at the hospital frustrated her terribly. Karl talked about his children and grandchildren, and these conversations always put a smile on Marie's face. Though she now had difficulty speaking, her mind was as sharp and clear as ever. It was here in the hospital that she also reminisced about Czechoslovakia.

"You know, in spite of losing so much, I can honestly say that my life has been happy," she said one afternoon, propped up in her hospital bed. Karl was astounded that, in spite of her frailty, she maintained this strong and positive attitude. "There were only a few things I missed of what we had to leave behind," she continued. "Our possessions were only objects, nothing compared to the fact that all four of us were able to get out alive. But, I've always been sorry I had nothing to leave you and Hana. There should have been a family legacy." She paused and turned her head to stare out the window while Karl looked on. It was the closest she had come to talking about the four paintings and her ill-fated attempt to retrieve them since returning from Prague in 1948.

In 1984, Marie passed away. She had outlived Karl's father by forty

---

* Czech surnames identify individuals as male or female. Here, the feminine form of Reiser is achieved by adding the suffix "ová."

years, and had outlived Arthur Brock by more than thirty years. Her second husband had died of leukemia in 1951. Karl was grateful for the long, productive life Marie had lived, though his heart still stung from the void that her absence had created.

He tore open the envelope and quickly scanned the letter inside. It was written in English – that alone was unusual – and by a man who identified himself as Jan Pekárek. It took a moment for Karl to register who that was. And then, slowly, the realization began to sink in. Jan Pekárek was the grandson of Alois Jirák, with whom Marie had fought for ownership of the paintings. As Karl recalled, Jan had even attended school with his sister, Hana, back in Rakovník. Karl went back and reread the letter, more slowly this time, trying to process its contents.

Dear Mrs. Reiserová!
By examining the inheritance which has been left by my parents I have found some paintings. From the correspondence which we have found, we have learned that these paintings belonged to Mr. Victor Reiser. These paintings were kept back by my grandfather during the German occupation and have stayed in his house until now.

I suppose that these paintings are very valuable, and since they still are your ownership, I would like to hand them to you or to your descendant.

Let me know, therefore, in what way it would be possible to hand them to you. I advise you, however, upon the fact that first of all these paintings should be examined by our authorities for the purpose to obtain the permission for their exportation. As soon as I receive some instructions from you I can start an action in this sense. I suppose, however, that the best way would be a personal contact with your descendant or with a person to whom you trust. This dealing must take place in Prague as we cannot normally travel abroad.

From the above mentioned letters I also notice that some misunderstandings had occurred between our families. I shall be only too happy to have this matter settled in a calm way and to restore a friendly atmosphere between our two families....

With kind regards,
Yours sincerely,
Jan Pekárek

"What's wrong? You look as if you've seen a ghost!"

Karl looked up. He had been so absorbed in reading the letter that he had not heard Phyllis approach. At sixty-seven his wife was still attractive and as spirited as ever. But now her face only registered concern.

"Karl, what's the matter?" she repeated, reaching out to touch her husband's arm. "You've gone quite pale."

Karl was dazed. "You won't believe this," he began breathlessly, and then proceeded to read the letter aloud to Phyllis. When he finished, he looked up to meet his wife's startled gaze. "I believe Mother secretly hoped that one day she and the paintings might be reunited. She never lived to see that day." He paused and rubbed his eyes.

"What are you thinking?" Phyllis asked.

Karl shook his head. "I'm not sure," he replied. What *was* he thinking? On the one hand, it appeared that Karl might have a chance to achieve what Marie had had to give up – a chance for the family to be reunited with their possessions. Karl knew that his mother had gone to her grave wishing and praying for their return. It appeared that here was an opportunity to fulfill that dream. But how? "There's nothing here in this letter to tell me how I might be able to retrieve the paintings," he continued. "I can't just ask this Pekárek fellow to ship them to me!"

Indeed, there was little chance that anything of value could be sent in or out. Without understanding the exact details, Karl knew that goods of worth that entered or exited Czechoslovakia were meticulously examined and heavily taxed or even confiscated. "Even traveling there to pursue this could pose a problem," Karl continued. A visa was required to enter the country, and those were only provided if the reason for the visit was legitimate enough to satisfy the government. On what pretext would Karl be able to go?

"You know the biggest irony in all of this?" Karl asked, shaking his head. "A moment ago I was thinking about how it would be fine with me if I never set foot in Czechoslovakia again. And now this comes along!"

Karl rifled through the discarded mail and retrieved the letter from his old high school. Could that invitation now be of help? He read it through again. The reunion was to take place in May – two months from now. There was ample opportunity between now and then to write to Jan Pekárek and begin to explore the options available. He looked at the reunion invitation again and then glanced up at Phyllis.

"You know," he said, "this might be the answer. Look at this invitation that also came today." He held it up for Phyllis to see. "Perhaps I should attend."

Phyllis read it through quickly. "Why would you ever want to go to this?" She was well aware of Karl's bitter disappointment and contempt for his old school.

"I don't! But don't you see? The reunion gives me a legitimate reason to be in the country, and a valid basis on which to apply for a visa. Once I'm there, I can at least sit down and talk with this Jan Pekárek and find out about the paintings firsthand." Karl knew that it was impossible to even think of doing anything about the paintings from outside the country. "I think I should respond to this man's letter and tell him that I'm planning to be in the country in May." Karl was speaking as much to himself as to his wife.

Phyllis looked worried. "But even if you go and see him, that still isn't an answer as to how you'll be able to get the paintings out."

"No, it isn't. But between now and then I can start to explore the options available." He reached up to rub his eyes again. He needed that tea more than ever, and Quinta was chomping at the bit to go for a walk.

"It's a step, and it's all I can do right now." He looked at his wife with new resolve. "Yes, that's it! I'm going to reply to the invitation and say that I will plan to be there for the reunion. Then I'll write to Mr. Pekárek and tell him that I would like to visit Prague in May. In the meantime I'll see what I can find out about getting goods out of Czechoslovakia."

"Karl, what about our trip?" Years earlier, Phyllis had created a company called Phyllis Reeser Tours. She developed and led photographic excursions to countries around the world. This passion for photography had been ignited in her after Karl had resumed his interest in taking pictures while on a trip to Switzerland. The two of them were actively involved in the local Toronto Camera Club. Over the years, Phyllis's proficiency in photography had increased, and even surpassed Karl's, leading her to start her business. Karl usually accompanied her on these photo tours. Her next excursion was coming up in May, an expedition that would take her and a group of amateur photographers through Turkey. Karl had been looking forward to this trip, a chance to explore a country he had never seen before.

He was silent for a moment, "This could all work well. It will mean that I will have to cut my tour of Turkey short. But I could go with you for the first part, and then arrange to fly to Prague from there."

The coincidence of Phyllis's trip, the high school reunion, and the revelation about the paintings, now seemed more remarkable than ever. Though Karl had little idea of what he was getting himself into, he felt drawn to this journey with an urgency he could barely contain. There was a voice from the past calling to him. Perhaps it was Marie's, guiding him back to their belongings. She had called the paintings their family's legacy. Maybe it was time to finish what Marie had begun. It was time for family restitution.

CHAPTER SEVENTEEN

Toronto, March 13, 1990

IT WAS DARK in Theo's apartment and he turned on a lamp, casting a spotlight on the dining room table and on the deck of Tarot cards that lay in the center. Before sitting down, Theo switched on the stereo, moving the dial past the droning voices of news broadcasters until he reached a station where soft music was not broken by commentary. John Lennon was singing and the lyrics of "Revolution" drifted from the radio. How ironic and wonderful, Theo thought, that Lennon's voice should fill his apartment at the same time as he was about to do his Tarot card reading.

Theo had a deep admiration for John Lennon. It was both the artist and activist in Lennon that Theo identified with. A man who constantly questioned the government and authority was a champion as far as he was concerned. Lennon had lived his life daringly and publicly and had stood up to the establishment in much the same way that Theo believed he had stood up for his own independence from the Communist regime. "It's the dreamer in both of us," he often remarked to friends who questioned his obsession with the former Beatle. And while Lennon's notions were sometimes naive, Theo argued that if enough dreamers would come together, perhaps they really could change the world. It was an inspiring mantra to hold on to as he was about to embark on a journey to reclaim a family's property.

He took a deep breath and sat down at the table, picking up the worn pack of cards and shuffling them with deliberate and purposeful movements. His interest in Tarot cards had emerged from his journey of exploring mysticism and the occult, a practice that had occupied his life and thinking for years now. While he had never had readings performed on him, some years earlier he had learned to do the readings himself, believing that he could gain insight into current and future situations, and tap into the spiritual force that guided him in his life. He often referred to Tarot cards as "little mirrors into the soul." And that's what this experience was for him, an opportunity to gaze inward and seek a greater understanding of his thoughts, desires, and wishes at this time. It wasn't as if this reading would give specific instructions about particular circumstances of his mission, but the cards would provide one more spiritual glimpse into this upcoming journey, a look into the past, present, and future – one more avenue into the wisdom he would need to go to Czechoslovakia, retrieve Karl Reeser's paintings, and get out safely.

He placed the shuffled deck in front of him and cut it into two piles, moving his hand over each of them to feel the energy that vibrated upward and into his palm. The telephone rang in the next room, but Theo ignored it. He selected one of the piles and began to lay the cards out in a specific pattern. On this evening, he was using a particular placement or spread of cards designed to peer into the nature of a creative project or undertaking, to illuminate and evaluate its many components. Lennon's voice drifted into the background as Theo began to turn the cards over in sequence, contemplating and interpreting each revelation before moving on to the next. Several cards caught his attention.

The card at the top represented emotion, or the feelings aroused by a project. This card suggested one who was filled with vitality and passion for life. There was boundless creativity here and a lust for a change of both pace and place. The card suggested travel or escape.

Theo reflected on his upcoming trip. Everything finally seemed to be in place. His business dealings had been attended to, luggage packed, and contacts made. The gallery would be fine for the next week or so without him. There were no new openings scheduled, no client relationships to nurture, and no other business opportunities on the horizon. His passport and visa were up to date and ready to go. The last things to go in his briefcase had been the photographs of the four paintings. Theo had stared at them before dropping them into a side pocket. "Hang on," he had said quietly, as if he were speaking directly to four people and not four inanimate objects. "I'm coming to get you." The card he was staring at reflected a person who was daring in action, cocky in attitude, and utterly without fear.

The card on the left was a symbol of thought or the analytical process of organizing a project. This card suggested some lack of concern at the possibility of gaining all or losing all. There was extravagance represented here, along with intoxication with life – a place where ultimate knowledge and oblivion are unified.

Karl Reeser had come by weeks earlier to give Theo his advance payment. Karl's gratitude to him for agreeing to the project was poignant, so much so that it put the monetary remuneration in second place behind Theo's genuine desire to help this man. "These paintings became the focus of my mother's attempts to regain our property when everything else was unattainable," Karl had said as he pressed the envelope of cash into Theo's hands. "She did everything she could to achieve that goal and she was unsuccessful. Please don't fail us now." Karl's eyes had been pleading. Theo was certainly feeling unconcerned about the money, as the card suggested. And extravagance was a part of his being, whether he had the means or not. Still, he couldn't deny that it always helped to have that extra cash on hand.

The card on the bottom was a symbol of the imagination. This was an indication of the creative force of an undertaking, and represented someone who was known as a con artist; one who could ignite a dangerous situation and send the most stable venture spinning wildly out of control.

At this, Theo paused. What spiritual guides would he have to be attuned to in order to complete this expedition safely? He had already acknowledged the dangers that were inherent in his trip, given his intention to illegally smuggle goods across the border. There were forces here that might impair his ability, and while he would try to steer clear of obvious dangers, one could never fully anticipate what might happen. There was only one thing of which he was certain. He knew that if anything were to go wrong with his plans, if he even smelled the faintest whiff of trouble, he would back away from this mission as quickly and as quietly as possible. Nothing was worth risking his life for, he assured himself. Not even a nice gentleman with a compelling family story. On that, Theo was clear.

On and on he went, turning the cards over, reflecting on their meaning, and then moving on to the next. By the time he had finished the reading, he felt at peace with the process and with his upcoming trip. There would be some excitement brewing ahead, as evidenced by some of the cards. But the reading had suggested that this was a journey that was important for him, and one for which he was prepared. Skill, creativity, intuition, and passion: those were the qualities that would see him through.

Lennon's voice was still singing from the radio. *The station must be playing a retrospective of his work*, Theo thought. Knowing that John Lennon also had an interest in mysticism – dreams and nightmares – had further endeared him to Theo, along with the fact that Lennon had also expressed an affinity for Hieronymus Bosch. Lennon had once said, "I dream in color and it's always very surreal. My dream world is complete Hieronymus Bosch and Dali. I love it. I look forward to it every night."[10] When Theo had first read that quote in a book of Lennon sayings, he had been dumbfounded. He saw this as another association that drew the two of them together. Lennon would be with him on this journey, an additional spiritual guide.

As Theo prepared for bed on the eve of his departure to Prague, he felt confident that his mission would be successful. He was Theo Král – the king – in this case, the king of smugglers. And while others might see that proclamation as tremendously arrogant, for Theo it was simply the truth.

CHAPTER EIGHTEEN

Zurich–Prague, May 22, 1989

KARL ADJUSTED his airline seat into a reclining position and closed his eyes, trying to take advantage of the only solitude he might have for some time. He was on a Swissair flight from Istanbul to Zurich, a two-hour journey. He would spend one day in Zurich and then board a plane for Prague. But it was difficult to relax. His mind beckoned him back and forth in time, a siren call to the events of the preceding weeks, and those that lay ahead.

He had been fully engaged in the tour of Turkey, immersing himself in history and photography as he always loved doing, and enjoying this fascinating country. He had explored archeological sites, museums, mosques, and scenic countryside in a jam-packed tour from Ankara to Istanbul. But as captivating as Phyllis's itinerary had been, Karl had often felt his mind turning to the pending trip to Prague and his meeting with the grandson of Alois Jirák. At the thought of Jan Pekárek, Karl felt a fresh stirring of anxiety and uncertainty. Pekárek had never responded to Karl's reply letter in which he had indicated that he was coming for this visit.

So many things could have gone wrong already, Karl thought. Perhaps his letter had never arrived in Prague. It was entirely possible that it had been opened and confiscated by the secret police who regularly tampered with the mail. In that case, who knew what might have already happened to Mr. Pekárek? He might have been interrogated or arrested for trying to conceal valuable goods from the government. In another scenario, Karl imagined that perhaps Pekárek had received the letter but was too anxious to go any further. One letter confessing to the fate of the paintings might have been enough and now, in response to Karl's eager reply, perhaps Mr. Pekárek wanted to withdraw his offer to finally reunite Karl with his family's property, and regretted that he had even initiated the process.

But, more than anything else, Karl feared that by now the paintings had already found their way into the hands of the Communists. If Pekárek had indeed begun to inquire as to how to get the paintings out of the country, then the authorities may well have become suspicious. It was unlikely that anyone would put forward such a request if they didn't have property of value to inquire about. Could he come this close to fulfilling Marie's dream only to have it dissolve into thin air once more?

On top of that, Karl was feeling skeptical of Jan Pekárek's offer to return the paintings. What motive would he have for contacting Karl after so many years? Was he after a reward? Karl wanted to believe that Pekárek's intentions were genuine. But with Alois Jirák's history, Karl worried that his grandson might be similarly deceptive. It was entirely possible that Karl was traveling all this way, possibly risking his own safety, only to discover that Jan Pekárek had some kind of an ulterior motive.

If that were not enough to consume his thoughts, Karl was also wondering what Prague would be like upon his arrival. The Prague of his memory reflected its rich history dating back more than a thousand years: buildings with gilded archways, concert halls where world-famous musicians had once performed, baroque statues, and tree-lined parks. That memory was interrupted with a vision of how Prague had been transformed by goose-stepping Nazi soldiers marching along banner-lined streets in a terrifying display of propaganda and pageantry. Karl had visited Czechoslovakia once briefly, when Phyllis had arranged a photo tour there in 1985. Despite the beauty that was still in evidence throughout the country, there were also noticeable signs of the oppression the country was enduring under Communist rule. Buildings were neglected and in disrepair. Goods of any kind were in short supply. The people looked solemn and disconsolate.

Phyllis had been encouraging and supportive when Karl had said good-bye to her in Istanbul earlier that morning. "You're doing something wonderful for your family," she had reminded him. "Your mother would be so proud," she added, watching Karl pack his things at their hotel. At the same time, she couldn't help but voice some concerns. "I'm worried about you being in Prague and doing something illegal." At that, her eyes penetrated Karl's, searching for reassurance, answers, anything to allay her fears. Karl returned her stare calmly.

"I won't do anything foolish," he had replied, though he wasn't even certain what he *would* be doing. There was absolutely no blueprint for this trip, just a series of ideas and possibilities. He couldn't confess this uncertainty to his wife. She was worried enough already. "And I will try to call you as often as I can, just to let you know I'm all right," he had added reassuringly. He knew he wouldn't be able to discuss much with Phyllis over the telephone. Everyone knew that phones in Prague were wiretapped, and anyone and everyone could be watched.

Phyllis tried to smile. "If it were up to me, I would never have tried to go after the paintings. I would have abandoned this plan from the start. But you were always the brave one – and persistent! You can't let things go. I guess you have more of your mother in you than you think."

Those words echoed in Karl's ears as his plane touched down in Zurich and he disembarked and headed for his hotel. A fax from his son, Ted, was waiting for him when he checked in. The reply letter from Jan Pekárek had arrived in Toronto after Karl and Phyllis had already left for Turkey. That was good news. It meant that Pekárek was still engaged in the process of trying to return the paintings. However, the letter did not contain the news that Karl had hoped to receive. In it, Mr. Pekárek acknowledged that he had begun to inquire about the procedures necessary to receive permission to export the paintings. He explained that it would have to be determined that Karl was the legal heir of Victor and Marie Reiser. Karl would have to produce death certificates for his parents along with birth certificates for himself and his sister. Documents were also required to prove that Victor and Marie were Czech citizens at the time of their death. That, in and of itself, could be enough to bring Karl's efforts to retrieve the paintings to a grinding halt.

As soon as the legal ownership of the paintings was determined, a "judicial adjuster" would have to be appointed by the government to assess the value of the paintings. They would then impose a tax – a percentage of their assessed value – that Karl would have to pay. The National Gallery would then have to grant permission for the paintings to be exported. Finally, export permits would have to be issued by the customs department. The entire process was onerous and did not at all guarantee that, at the end of the day, Karl would receive authorization to have the paintings leave the country, even if he did meet the requirements and pay the tariff. Recognizing that the situation was complicated, Jan Pekárek stated that he had contacted a solicitor who was an expert on the "affairs of the property of foreigners." This person had confirmed all of the stated requirements and had expressed his willingness to meet with Karl during his stay in Prague. He also warned that the process of settling the matter would be a long one – not something that was going to be completed in the short time that Karl was in Czechoslovakia.

As Karl read the fax, his heart began to sink. The conditions were overwhelming and daunting – simply impossible! Even if he were able to produce the required documentation, he knew that once this matter was in the hands of the Czech authorities there was little chance that they would actually release the paintings, particularly if the National Gallery assessed their value to be substantial. And Karl knew that the paintings were indeed valuable. He read the fax again, realizing that the prospect of reclaiming the paintings was slipping away. Given that Jan Pekárek had already begun a process of investigating the procedures necessary to export the artwork, Karl was more convinced than ever that the Czech authorities had already taken possession of them. It was even more disheartening that this news was reaching Karl on the eve of his departure from Zurich to Prague. Had he traveled all this way only to discover that his goal was unattainable?

As soon as he settled into his room, Karl picked up the telephone and called Ted in Toronto. Karl's voice was tired and resigned as he voiced his concerns and apprehensions to his son. "I'm troubled by the whole matter," Karl said. "There are at least a dozen obstacles facing me right now, and each one of them is complicated."

"I agree," said Ted. "But I've already contacted someone I know at the Department of External Affairs in Ottawa, a man named Lynch. He's with the legal advisory division there." Ted was typically practical and matter-of-fact, traits that Karl needed at this time. Doubts and misgivings would not service this project.

"I don't trust the lawyer that Pekárek has contacted in Prague, notwithstanding his supposed expertise in foreign property affairs," said Karl. For that matter, he did not trust anyone in Prague. Most people there had ties to the government, or, if they didn't actively support the Communists, then they were likely under suspicion from them. Either way, this contact was unreliable. Both Ted and Karl agreed that the only way in which this plan had any possibility of succeeding was to seek legal advice from someone with the Canadian government.

"Mr. Lynch has suggested someone in his department who is an expert in dealing with estate matters in Eastern Europe," Ted continued. "He's willing to forward Pekárek's letter to the Canadian embassy in Prague and see if the ambassador there can advise you in some way. After all, the embassy is there to look after the welfare of Canadians. Perhaps they would be willing to assist you in retrieving the paintings – without all the Communist nonsense and red tape."

As Ted and Karl continued strategizing, Karl experienced a resurgence of hope. It was good to talk to his son, and energizing to brainstorm some ideas to move the plan forward. At the end of their conversation, Karl decided that he would personally contact the embassy and seek the counsel of the ambassador. "I'm going to try to make an appointment with him for when I'm there," Karl said. "I need to meet with someone face-to-face and see if there is anyone who can really help me with this."

"Your grandson is over eleven pounds," Ted said as he and his father concluded their conversation. "That's more than double his birth weight!"

Karl laughed. "Send him and Elizabeth my love," he said, referring to Ted's wife. "I'll keep you posted on my progress here."

As soon as he hung up, Karl dialed information to get the telephone number of the embassy in Prague. He was soon connected with the office of Chargé d'affaires Robert G. McRae. Keeping details to a minimum, Karl explained that he would be in Prague for a few days, and was requesting an appointment. A meeting was scheduled for May twenty-fourth at two o'clock.

Karl's plane touched down in Prague and he collected his belongings and joined the line moving through passport control. It was long, and many ahead of him were being stopped and interrogated by the police. Karl checked and rechecked his papers; he could not afford for anything to go wrong at this point. When it was his turn, he handed over his documents and politely answered the questions about where he was from, and the purpose of his visit, silently giving thanks once more that the organizers of his high school reunion had inadvertently but conveniently planned the event for this time – a perfect reason to be entering the country. The border official scrutinized his passport and visa, and then scrupulously rummaged through his suitcase. Finally, he stamped Karl's documents and waved him through the line.

During the taxi ride to his hotel Karl observed the city. Prague had suffered considerably less damage during the war than most other European cities in the region. But things had changed. The splendor of this city now lay hidden under a cloud of neglect. When the Communists had descended, Prague had plunged into disrepair. The once stately buildings that had been its landmarks, majestically towering over the streets and waterways, were now gray and aged, almost sagging under the layers of soot and dirt that had settled on them over the years. In place of fine architectural apartment buildings, the Communists had built tall, box-like concrete structures to house the people of the city, each one identical and uniformly drab. The citizens of Prague looked as worn down and dull as their surroundings. They walked quickly on overcrowded sidewalks, robotic, heads down, minding their own business. Broken-down motorbikes crawled along the congested streets, and were chased by dilapidated Škoda and Lada automobiles that spewed black exhaust from engines sputtering like rapid gunfire at every turn. There were no military officers, not uniformed ones at any rate, but Karl knew that the members of State Security were everywhere, spying on the movements of their citizens and their visitors. Karl's frame of reference for the past fifty years had been the freedom of Toronto, and it was unsettling at first to think that he might be watched.

But there was something else that Karl knew about the situation in Prague. He was aware that the political system that had ruled so decisively for the last thirty years might actually be in decline. In recent years, the Soviet Union, long considered the primary enemy and rival of the West, was being regarded as less and less of a threat. The Soviet economy was floundering, and with it, its hold on its surrounding Communist-dominated countries. Shortly before Karl had left on this trip, there had been an article in the Toronto newspapers stating that Canada was calling for the release of Václav Havel, the renowned Czech playwright and dissident, who many were touting as the possible next president of a new democratic Czechoslovakia. Havel had been imprisoned for the last nine months for his part in demonstrations in Prague protesting the ongoing Soviet occupation. More and more protests of this kind were occurring on city streets across the country. And while the Soviets had quickly clamped down on these demonstrations, there was a sense that it was only a matter of time before the Communists would be forced to back down, or withdraw, and Czechoslovakia might once again claim its freedom from oppression.

It was against this backdrop of political entrenchment coupled with potential transformation that Karl arrived in Prague and proceeded to the InterContinental Hotel. He was surprised and impressed that the hotel had maintained its rather luxurious state. The first order of business after checking in was to call Jan Pekárek.

"It's good to hear from you," Pekárek said. "We must meet." There were few details exchanged over the telephone. Pekárek's voice was guarded and cautious. Karl could sense his anxiety and felt it as well. Both of them knew that someone could be listening in. "Please come to my place," continued Pekárek. "We will talk."

Karl took down the details, hung up the receiver, and headed outside to catch a cab. The warmth of the springtime air soaked through his light jacket and he squinted at the morning sun. He could hear the sound of the Vltava River flowing rapidly beneath the Charles Bridge, its waves lapping up against the break-wall. The scent of magnolia blossoms wafted through the air. Karl breathed in deeply and climbed into a cab. Despite the pleasant spring morning, he realized that he still bore the emotional scars of having fled this city for his life years earlier. Each corner was a reminder of those days in 1939: that street where Nazi soldiers patrolled; that bridge where Hitler had surveyed his troops; that park, once forbidden to Jews; that building that had flown the swastika. His breath quickened as his cab wove its way through the labyrinth of winding cobblestone streets, many too narrow for two cars to pass, before finally coming to a stop in front of a modest four-story apartment building.

He disembarked, glancing up. Jan Pekárek lived on the top floor and there was no elevator. After climbing the dark staircase, he reached the fourth floor and rang the doorbell. Pekárek opened the door and greeted Karl warmly.

"Please come in," Pekárek said. "It's good to meet you." He stepped aside, and Karl entered a shabby but tidy apartment. He faced Pekárek and sized him up. The man was of medium build, rather pleasant looking, with thick, round, dark-rimmed glasses. He wore a tired old sweater and worn trousers. When he smiled, he showed his yellowed and crooked teeth, evidence of the country's lack of adequate dental care.

Karl quickly learned that Pekárek was a medical doctor – an immunologist and a scientist of considerable reputation. He had written hundreds of research papers, which had been delivered in countries around the world, though sadly not by him. "This government would rather send a loyal comrade and Communist director abroad to represent the country, not a scientist like me. Foreign travel is a political reward here. My papers are the means to provide that to others." Pekárek chain-smoked unfiltered cigarettes as the two of them sat talking. The ashtray in front of him overflowed with cigarette butts, and the smell of stale smoke hung in the air. Pekárek had been an enthusiastic Communist at one time. "But that was a long time ago," he continued. "I've seen how this government has suppressed individual rights and abused civil liberties."

His political journey had been a complicated one. During the Second World War, he had actively opposed the German fascists and had become an ardent Communist, even going so far as to join a group of partisan soldiers whose goal was to smuggle supplies to a group of saboteurs who were operating in the forests around Rakovník. He continued to be a vocal and passionate Communist after the war, supporting the country's overthrow of President Beneš in 1948. Years later, he began to recognize the decline of cultural, social, and educational resources under Communist rule. And as he witnessed firsthand the restrictions on freedoms, he became disillusioned with his country's political system and was now an outspoken critic.

"Mr. Pekárek, by speaking out, are you not afraid of arrest, or, at the very least, of losing your position at your research institute?" Karl asked. Pekárek was employed at one of the state-run laboratories in Prague. How did he have the courage to oppose the system so overtly and vocally, and particularly as he had a wife and young daughter? In this regime, even those who were related to, or associated with, dissidents could be blacklisted. The risk to his family was enormous.

Pekárek shrugged, and then answered matter-of-factly, "It seems that my position as a preeminent scientist has had some advantages. I'm quite simply irreplaceable. But please," he continued. "I insist that you call me Jan. There is too much history between our families for such formalities." It was a perfect opportunity to move the conversation to a discussion of the events of the war. "How did your family ever manage to get out of Czechoslovakia?" Jan asked. "I understand that it wasn't possible for most Jewish people to leave once the war had started."

"You're right. It was virtually impossible," Karl replied. "We left days before the official start of the war, and only because my father had connections out of the country, and my mother managed to pull together the necessary papers within the country." He quickly filled Jan in on the details of their flight to freedom. "We were lucky," he added. "Most of our friends and family members never made it out. They perished in Hitler's gas chambers."

The two men sat in silence. Karl wondered how much Jan really knew of the events of the war and the suffering of Jewish citizens in Czechoslovakia and elsewhere. He was Hana's age, and would have been a young teenager then, living in a rural town, raised in a milieu of latent anti-Semitism and then overt persecution of Jews. Those events would have been the norm for Jan. Furthermore, after the war, he had lived within the confines of Communism, and his life had been impacted more by those circumstances than by the events of the Holocaust. Besides, even today, most Jews living in Czechoslovakia still kept their Jewish identify a secret.

"Tell me how your sister is?" Jan broke into Karl's thoughts.

"She's well, thank you. She's married and has three children and several grandchildren. She and her husband live in Toronto, not far from my wife and myself."

"And your mother – I was sorry to hear of her passing. I didn't know her, but I can tell from the documentation regarding the paintings that she must have been a strong woman."

Here was the opening that Karl was waiting for, a chance to talk about the paintings. "Yes, my mother was indeed passionate," he said as he leaned forward. "You mentioned in your letter that you had found some documentation. My mother spoke very little about this after she returned to Toronto in 1948, except to say that she had not been able to recover the paintings." He knew he was skirting some of the facts. After all, in Karl's mind it was due to the greed of this man's grandfather that Marie had failed to reclaim her property. But Jan had expressed his willingness to return the paintings, and Karl was being careful not to offend him.

Jan stood and walked over to a large wooden desk in the corner of his apartment. He rummaged through a stack of file folders, retrieved some papers, and returned to sit next to Karl. "These are the letters I found amongst my grandfather's belongings after he and my father had died."

Karl took the papers and quickly read through them. There they were: the letter affirming that the four paintings belonged to Victor and Marie, along with letters from Marie to Alois Jirák's attorney demanding the return of the artwork, and Jirák's refusal to do so. It was all there in front of him, the evidence of the unpleasant exchange that must have taken place between the two parties. He looked up at Jan, unable to speak.

"Take them and get some copies made," Jan said. "I would like the originals back." He seemed unperturbed by the documentation that implicated his grandfather in this way. "It was so helpful to see this material in writing. That's what led me to your family after my grandfather died."

Karl nodded, folded the papers, and put them inside his jacket. "I gather from your letters that it will be difficult if not impossible to get the paintings out of the country." Karl was still fighting to calm his beating heart. He felt the need to steer the conversation away from their family feud, and to discuss the current status of the paintings.

"Yes, I've made inquiries, and the regulations are impossible to say the least." Jan proceeded to outline the conditions that he had previously listed in his letter to Karl.

Karl hung his head. "My mother dreamed of bringing the paintings to Canada. I just can't accept that there isn't a way to fulfill her wish." Once again, it felt as if he had come to a dead end as far as his family's treasures were concerned.

"Would you like to see them?" Jan asked. Karl looked up puzzled. "The paintings," Jan repeated, "would you like to see them?"

"Of course I would," Karl replied. He had not even dared to ask this question. Surely by now the paintings were in the hands of the authorities who had come to collect them following Jan's inquiries. But perhaps Jan still had access to them. "Can you arrange for me to look at them?" asked Karl. "Where are they?"

Jan smiled. "Come with me," he said. "I'll show them to you."

The second letter that Jan Pekárek wrote to Karl outlining the procedures he would need to follow in order to export the paintings from Prague.

CHAPTER NINETEEN

Prague, May 22, 1989

JAN ROSE FROM THE COUCH and motioned for Karl to follow him. Karl stood and reached for his jacket, wondering where they were going. But to his surprise, Jan turned and headed down the hallway to a bedroom at the back of the apartment. Startled and puzzled, Karl followed behind. The small back room was sparsely furnished with one large four-poster bed piled high with a feather comforter and quilted bedcover. A small chest of drawers sat in one corner, and a rectangular wool rug lay over the worn hardwood floor. Jan went first to the window and quickly drew the curtains. Soft light penetrated through the thin blinds. The room became dimly lit, though not dark. Glancing back at Karl, Jan moved over to the bed and began to strip back the bedcovers, comforter, and several blankets. Finally, he pulled away a large sheet and there lay the paintings, neatly stacked one on top of the other and separated by more blankets and sheets. Each one was carefully wrapped in paper and tied with string. Jan unwrapped the top painting and stood back.

"I made those inquiries to the Czech authorities anonymously," he said, turning to smile at Karl. "No one knows about the paintings."

Karl was dumbfounded. Not in his wildest imagination had he thought that the paintings might actually be here in Jan's home, and buried in a bed! He stumbled toward the bed and ran his hand lovingly over the top painting. It was the Geoffroy – the children in the bathhouse – the one that may well have been his mother's favorite. It was in perfect condition, preserved here in this bed cocoon as if it had been hanging in a gallery. It appeared that all of the paintings were still on their stretchers, though the gold frames were gone. Karl did not know what had become of them and it didn't really matter. What mattered was that the paintings were here, all four of them, all together and safe.

"Please help me to stand them up," Karl asked hoarsely. He still felt light-headed. Together, he and Jan unwrapped the remaining paintings, lifted them, and propped them up, each one placed against one of the four walls of the small room, nearly dwarfing the two men who stood in front of them. Even in the dim light, Karl could make out the exquisite details of each painting. The young children in the Geoffroy looked playfully and innocently at their teachers. The forest flames from the Swoboda filled the canvas with their radiance. The Spanish dancer's face in the Paoletti stared back at Karl with expectation and longing. And the housewife in the Vogel looked demure and thoughtful. Though as a youngster Karl had barely paid attention to these works of art, they now felt as familiar to him as members of his own family.

"The paintings were kept in my father's home, and we only found them after he and my mother had died." Jan was talking and Karl pulled himself away from the paintings. "My grandfather said that the Gestapo searched the home on several occasions – even interrogated my father about the paintings."

Karl wondered about this. He couldn't imagine how it would have been possible to conceal four such large paintings, particularly if the Gestapo was intent on finding and confiscating them. But he didn't question Jan.

"After I read the documents that had been left behind, and realized that there was a dispute about the ownership of the paintings, I felt uneasy about it," Jan continued. "That's why I contacted you. I'm convinced that the paintings are yours."

Karl was gratified to hear Jan proclaim that he and his family were the rightful owners of the paintings; it was absolute exoneration for the legal dispute that had taken place between his mother and Jan's grandfather. And yet, this moment was met with deep regret that his mother had not lived to hear this pronouncement. This vindication was wedded to another sorrow as well. Karl knew that Czechoslovakia would never surrender these paintings to him. The restitution of Jewish property was unheard of here in a country that had fenced itself in behind a myriad of complicated laws that enabled it to justify what the Nazis had done. In fact there were three injustices here: Jewish property had been taken during the Nazi regime, not returned to the rightful owners after the war, and stolen again by the Communists. But that thought only strengthened Karl's resolve to get the paintings out of Czechoslovakia. Right then and there, he vowed that one way or another he would transport these family heirlooms to Canada.

With a deep sigh, Karl stepped back from the artwork. Then he and Jan lifted the four paintings and laid them gently back onto the bed. Karl rewrapped and tied each one in its paper and string, once again laying sheets between the canvases to protect them. With one last glance, Karl replaced the down comforter and tucked the quilted bedcover back in place, as if he were tucking his children in for a long night. He hated to leave them, but there was much to do and his mind was racing with the speed of a locomotive.

"I'll drive you back to your hotel if you'd like," Jan offered. Karl gratefully accepted. Before leaving the apartment, Jan went to his desk, opened a drawer, and withdrew two rusted windshield wipers. "Everything is in short supply here in this country as I'm sure you've noticed," he said in response to the quizzical look on Karl's face. "Even these old windshield wipers are valuable. People are likely to steal them if I don't remove them from my car every night!" They left the apartment, walked down the long staircase, and emerged on the street. Jan's jalopy was as dilapidated and decayed as the wipers. It squealed and sputtered its way through the narrow streets, finally and miraculously coming to a safe stop in front of the InterContinental Hotel.

The two men had said little to one another during the car ride. When they reached the hotel, Karl finally turned to face Jan. "I have to figure out how I'm going to get the paintings to Canada," he began. "I'd like to try to do something while I'm here in the country." The less he said to Jan about sidestepping government regulations, the better. Besides, at this point, he had no concrete plan, only the determination to do something in the few days he had available. "I will call you on May twenty-fourth, after I've returned from the high school reunion." He wished with all his might that he didn't have to attend the gathering. It felt like a bigger nuisance than ever, and a hindrance to proceeding with the important work of getting the paintings out of Prague. But he had no choice. The reunion was the reason he had been granted entry into the country, and following through on that plan was essential to keeping his alibi intact. "Thank you," he added, somewhat awkwardly.

Jan nodded. "I leave the plans in your hands, and I look forward to hearing from you."

As soon as he entered the hotel lobby, Karl headed for the front desk. He had the documents that Jan had given him specifying the ownership of the paintings and documenting the legal dispute between Jan's family and his own. He needed to photocopy these papers before his meeting at the Canadian embassy. All his hopes rested on the possibility that someone there would be able to help him. At the front desk, he was directed to a small business center in the corner of the lobby.

"Excuse me," he said, stepping up to speak to an attractive young woman behind the reception counter. He reached into his jacket pocket and removed the letters that Jan had given him. "I'm wondering if you might photocopy these papers and letters for me."

The woman glanced down at the papers and then up at Karl. She eyed him suspiciously and Karl felt the hairs rise on the back of his neck. There was important evidence contained in those letters, information that documented the paintings, their presumed value, and the dispute that had taken place between his family and Jan's. Could she be one of the informers that were placed in every business and company to report on the activities of locals and even guests? Karl had unwittingly, and perhaps foolishly, provided personal information to this complete stranger. In that moment, he wished he could reach across the counter, withdraw the papers, and disappear from the lobby. But it was too late.

"A moment, sir." She turned her back and moved into a small office behind the desk. Karl could hear the copy machine being turned on and the cover raised. The buzzing of the machine was loud and with every click, Karl realized that the woman was making two copies of each of his documents. Even here in this four-star American hotel, the secret police were close at hand. One photocopy of the papers would be for Karl. But where would the second copy be sent? He didn't know, but every fiber of his being told him that he needed to get his plans in place for the transport of the paintings and do it soon, before the authorities became suspicious and moved in on him.

"Here you are, sir." The woman returned and placed the documents in Karl's hands. He thumbed through them. The originals were all there along with only one duplicate of each, just as Karl had suspected. A second wave of fear gripped him. He cleared his throat, thanked the woman behind the desk and proceeded up to his room, being careful to double-lock and bolt the door behind him.

Karl slept little that night. He tossed and turned, wondering and worrying about everything. Would he be able to come up with a plan to safely export the paintings back to Canada? Would someone at the Canadian embassy be prepared to help him? Would Czech authorities stop him before any of this could come to pass? He had just handed the evidence of his family's history over to a hotel staff person and probable Communist disciple, who had collected the evidence that the authorities would need to come after him and Jan. Perhaps he had already blown his chance to recover the paintings.

Along with this jumble of thoughts and uncertainties, Karl also reflected back on his meeting with Jan Pekárek. It was hard for Karl to determine how he really felt about the grandson of Alois Jirák. Certainly he was grateful that Jan had contacted him and was prepared to return the paintings. But Karl couldn't deny that he was also deeply suspicious of him. After all, were it not for Jan's family, Marie would have reclaimed the paintings years earlier. She would have fulfilled her dream of being reunited with her treasured belongings, the paintings would have already found their true home in Toronto, and Karl would not be here risking his safety! And while Jan was doing the right thing by returning their family possessions after his grandfather had vigorously tried to prevent it, Karl didn't believe that this made Jan a hero. It merely made him an honest human being. In the end it didn't feel to Karl as if Jan was doing anything *generous* by making this offer of restitution. It felt as if he was simply putting something to rest, and in doing so, he was cleansing his own hands of the misdeeds of his family members.

Was he being harsh in judging Jan in this way? Perhaps so. But emotions that he didn't fully understand and couldn't control were battling inside of Karl. He had seen what the loss of their family property had done to Marie. He felt a deep loyalty to his mother and was angered by her inability to retrieve the paintings before her death. In the absence of Alois Jirák, the only place Karl could put that anger was on the shoulders of Jan Pekárek. Perhaps that wasn't fair, but it was what he felt. He saluted Jan for coming forward to right this family wrong, but rightly or wrongly, that was as far as it went.

Karl groaned aloud and checked the clock next to his bed once more. Dawn was fast approaching. Tomorrow was the school reunion, the next day was the meeting at the Canadian embassy, and then he was due to meet with Jan once more. He wished he could close his mind to the memories, not to mention the worries. He wished he could turn his brain off but that simply wasn't possible. As the early morning rays of daylight seeped into his room, Karl finally gave in to his insomnia. He rose and began to prepare for the day ahead.

CHAPTER TWENTY

Prague, May 24, 1989

TWO DAYS LATER, Karl found himself seated in a small café across the street from the office of the Canadian embassy. Due to Canada's opposition to the Communist takeover of Czechoslovakia in 1948, the embassy had not been established here until April 1965. Before that, there had only been a diplomatic mission to Canada present here in the country, under the direction of a resident chargé d'affaires. The embassy building was quite lovely from the outside – a stately villa, surrounded by a high black wrought-iron gate. Trees lined the boulevard in front of the building, which sat in a quiet residential area. Close by and down a sloped bank, the familiar Vltava River flowed aimlessly toward the Charles Bridge. The red and white Canadian flag stood guard in front of the building and fluttered slightly in the early afternoon breeze that lifted and unfurled it from its flagpole.

Karl glanced at his watch. He was early for his two o'clock appointment with Robert G. McRae, but that was deliberate. He needed to compose himself and formulate his thoughts for this all-important meeting. He touched the breast pocket of his jacket, checking again to make sure his passport and visa were there. He had other papers as well, those that documented the family's former property in Rakovník, as well as the evidence he had collected verifying that the family had had to abandon their home in advance of Hitler's armies. Finally, there were the copies of letters that Jan Pekárek had given to him. Who knew what papers would be helpful for this meeting with McRae? But better to be prepared, thought Karl. And better to know what he was going to ask the embassy for! At that, he paused. What was he asking for? He knew that he would never report the paintings to the Czech authorities. Of that he was certain. Discovering them in Jan's apartment had settled that matter in his mind. Relinquishing them to a government inspection would likely mean he would never see them again. So what alternative was there? And how could the Canadian authorities assist him? Surely as a Canadian citizen he was entitled to some protection under Canadian law. But did that protection extend to property – especially property that had been held here in this country for so many years? And would the Canadian government be willing to defy the edicts of a ruling government?

Karl ordered a second cup of coffee. He ran his hand through his hair and rubbed his tired eyes. He had not slept much in the last two nights.

The high school reunion had passed in a blur. He had been picked up at his hotel early in the morning by his old school friend, Miloš Nigrin, one of the few boys from his childhood with whom he had stayed in touch. Miloš had not aged well in the fifty years since they had seen one another. Once a handsome young man, he now had that same gray pallor that branded most Czech citizens these days, a pastiness that came from years of cigarette smoking combined with inadequate health care. Though still tall and slender, it startled Karl to see a friend whom he remembered so well from childhood now reduced to this withered man.

Miloš led Karl to his car, an old Simca automobile that looked as brittle as Miloš did. Once inside, the first thing the two men did was to exchange currency. Karl handed over American dollars for Miloš's Czech crowns.

"I'm planning a trip to Vienna next year, if the Communists let me out of here. These American dollars will come in handy," said Miloš.

As for Karl, he would not have to contend with the unreasonably high exchange rate imposed by the government in the banks. The trade was of benefit to both of them. "It's good to see you, Miloš," said Karl warmly. "Tell me how you've been – how is your family?"

Miloš quickly pocketed the money, glancing first in the rearview mirror and then out the window before replying. "I'm finally retired," he said. He lit a cigarette and dragged on it deeply. He was a chemical engineer and had worked in a state-run company for many years. "I must say, I was a bit surprised when you wrote to say you were coming for the reunion. Don't get me wrong – I'm delighted that you're here. But as I recall, you were never too fond of this school of ours." Miloš smiled and coughed loudly into his sleeve.

Karl nodded. He had never forgotten that Miloš had been an ally back in the days when they attended school together, one of the few schoolmates who had not participated in the taunting and bullying that Karl had been subjected to because of his religion. "It was time to come for a visit," he replied, deliberately vague. "I was curious about what was happening here in this country. It feels as if Czechoslovakia may be on the verge of a new awakening, politically speaking." It was important to steer the conversation away from the real reason for his visit. He couldn't be honest about his motive for being in the country, not even with his old high school chum.

Miloš shrugged. "I'm not so excited about politics anymore. I survived the war *and* the Communist takeover. My life will change little, no matter who is in power."

Karl reacted strongly. "But the secret police. Surely if things change, you and others will be able to relax and stop looking over your shoulders."

"The secret police? Yes, there's always the possibility that a colleague or neighbor might turn you in. And for what? Looking at someone the wrong way. Maybe even exchanging crowns for American dollars." He patted his pocket and glanced once more in the rearview mirror. "I've seen others disappear for less. But the truth is, I've stopped worrying so much about them. What would they want with an old man like me?"

How ironic, thought Karl. *Those same words were once uttered by many Jewish families in advance of Hitler's campaign!*

The drive to Rakovník took Karl west out of Prague, through some of the most picturesque countryside of Czechoslovakia. Industrial buildings gave way to fields of sunflowers that dotted the side of the road, thrusting their blooms upward into a clear blue sky. Thick green forests lay beyond the meadows, rising into undulating hills. Karl had picnicked many times in pastures and woodlands just like these. He had skied on those distant mountains, and bicycled on those hilly trails. Out here in the countryside, there was less of a feeling of oppression. Karl rolled down his window and breathed in the fresh morning air. He was reminded once more of the splendor of his former homeland, a beauty all the more bittersweet given the passage of time and the world events that had ensued.

Soon the terrain flattened out as the hills gave way to towns and villages, and the road became even more familiar as the car approached the town of Rakovník. Karl's breath quickened. There was the High Gate, the city's landmark. Somewhere over there was the old cemetery where his grandfather had been buried. Karl wondered if it still existed, or whether, like so many Jewish graveyards, it had been destroyed by the Nazis or neglected after Jews had been forced to leave their hometowns. Miloš navigated through the narrow streets, finally emerging onto Husovo Náměstí, the central square. He came to a stop in front of the Hotel Družba.

Karl descended from the car and glanced across the street. The hotel that was hosting the reunion happened to be located directly across from Karl's former home. Curtains fluttered through an open window on the third floor that had once been Karl's bedroom. The red-tiled roof reflected the mid-morning sun. Karl closed his eyes and could almost see the salon on the second floor where the four paintings had once hung. The exterior white stucco of the building had grayed over time, but, mostly, the house of his childhood looked as it once had, still quite grand and stately. There was, however, one major difference. The house was now the district headquarters for the Communist Party. A huge banner hung above the street level windows, proclaiming: *Proletáři všech zemí, spojte se! – Workers of the world, unite!* The sign of the hammer and sickle punctuated the end of that edict. Around the corner and next to the front door, a second sign said, *Okresní Úřad Rakovník* – District Office of Rakovník. With a shudder, Karl turned away and entered the hotel.

The reunion passed by in a jumble of faces he didn't remember and names he barely heard in the noise. His schoolmates, now all elderly, were polite and pleasant enough. He tried to be similarly courteous in turn. He reminisced about the years spent in high school, and he and his schoolmates walked over to the cemetery to see the grave of Mr. Puchold, the art teacher who had been particularly well-liked and respected by the students, including Karl. He also discovered that Mr. Ulrich, the dreaded geography teacher who had been openly anti-Semitic, had been killed in a Czech prison after the war for being a Nazi sympathizer.

After several hours with his former schoolmates, Karl could feel himself becoming restless. He was anxious to get back to Prague and resume his efforts to recover the paintings. And, deep down, he was experiencing a sense of irritation with these men, and with the shallow nature of this reunion. Karl had reappeared in the lives of his schoolmates after fifty years and yet his presence was met with only superficial interest. He had expected that they would be more curious about him and his life; particularly how he had escaped in 1939 and how he and his family had survived. But conversations were awkward and felt forced. No one expressed sympathy that he had left school so abruptly without completing his *matura*. No one asked about his father, who had been a prominent businessman in this community. No one mentioned his home, which was now a Communist command center. The fact that his family had been forced to flee, and that his home and belongings were gone, appeared to be a non-event for these men. In fact, from Karl's perspective, his former schoolmates seemed largely indifferent to the fate of the Jews during the war, and indifferent to Karl and his circumstances. The only thing they were curious about was the fact that Karl still had his real teeth!

But he realized that he had been naive to have expected more. These former acquaintances had never been his true friends. They would likely have turned him over to the Nazis years ago. Perhaps they were even amongst those who had entered his home after the Gestapo left, and ransacked it for his family's remaining property. He wondered if he would discover a lamp, rug, or even a painting that had once belonged to his family if he were to walk into their homes today.

He knew that he was being harsh to castigate his old schoolmates in this way. Surely, at the very least, they must have felt some remorse or shame at what had happened to Jews in the war. Perhaps they were avoiding the topic for that very reason. But, in the end, Karl knew he had been right to dread this reunion, and he reminded himself again that this gathering had only ever been a means to an end.

Karl glanced at his watch and realized it was almost time for his appointment with the chargé d'affaires. He paid for his coffee and was just about to rise when a commotion broke out across the street. A black Tatra automobile came to a screeching stop in front of the embassy gates. Two men, dressed in dark suits and carrying briefcases, walked out of the embassy building, climbed into the car, and sped off, tires squealing. It was a puzzling moment, but Karl had no time to dwell on it. He left the café, rang the bell next to the iron gates, and climbed the stairs to the embassy.

"I have an appointment with Mr. McRae," he announced to the receptionist behind the glass partition. "My name is Karl Reeser."

The woman was instantly sympathetic. "Oh dear," she began. "I'm terribly sorry, Mr. Reeser, but Mr. McRae has been called away for a pressing and unexpected meeting at the Hradčany Castle. He's just left with Ambassador Mawhinney."

That must have been the car that had departed with such urgency, Karl realized with a sinking heart. Seeing the look in Karl's eyes, the receptionist quickly continued, "Mr. McRae would be happy to see you tomorrow, or, if you wish, you could meet with the vice consul right now."

What to do, wondered Karl. He had so little time here in the country and had serious misgivings about delaying his meeting for another day. He needed to see someone immediately if he had any hope of putting plans together for the discreet export of the paintings. But it was McRae who had been sent a copy of Pekárek's letter explaining that he had the paintings and wanted to return them. It was McRae who had spoken with Karl from Zurich and had agreed to this appointment. What would this new man know of his situation? Karl stood in the vestibule of the embassy building, shifting from one foot to the other, and looking distressed and hesitant. Once again the receptionist spoke up.

"I assure you, the vice consul is familiar with the reason you are here," she said, reassuringly. "He and Mr. McRae have discussed your situation. The vice consul's name is Richard VandenBosch. I think it would be worth your while to meet with him."

Karl knew he had to act quickly. He nodded to the receptionist and followed her down a long corridor.

Richard VandenBosch was a tall, energetic man in his early thirties with an engaging smile and charming demeanor. He jumped from his chair as soon as Karl entered his office, and came around his large wooden desk to greet him. "Hello, Mr. Reeser," he exclaimed warmly, pumping Karl's hand. "So sorry for the mix-up with the meetings. Robert expressed his regrets that he couldn't be here to talk to you. It couldn't be helped. But I'm pleased to fill in for him. Come, sit down."

Karl felt instantly at ease in the presence of this likeable young man. He seated himself in a comfortable armchair next to Richard VandenBosch and waited expectantly.

The two exchanged pleasantries: Karl's early impressions of Prague, the hotel in which he was staying, his high school reunion. Then VandenBosch got down to business. "My wife and I have a great interest in art, and I'm most curious to hear the story of your paintings." He stared attentively at Karl through large, dark-rimmed glasses.

"I know you must be a busy man," Karl began. He sensed that he should be brief or he would lose the opportunity to present his case. And yet, Karl believed that he would have to take Richard VandenBosch back to March 15, 1939, and Hitler's invasion of Prague in order to do his story justice. To Karl's surprise, the vice consul was relaxed and in no hurry. He seemed to want to engage in a long conversation.

"I'm somewhat of a history buff," he interjected. "Especially personal history. So please take your time and start at the beginning. How did your family escape from this country back in thirty-nine?"

Karl let out a deep breath and settled into the armchair as he unfolded the details of his family's history. Each time that Karl tried to abbreviate parts of his story, or gloss over details, Richard interrupted him, insisting that he go back and fill in the missing information. He was particularly fascinated with the story of how Marie had bribed the Gestapo officer in order to obtain their exit visas when they were first trying to leave Prague. "You mean she actually walked into one of the Gestapo headquarters in another city, *by herself*, and offered money to an official?" he asked, shaking his head in disbelief. "What incredible guts she must have had." The meeting that Karl imagined would last no more than ten minutes stretched to over two hours.

"My parents were from the Netherlands," Richard said as Karl was wrapping up his story. "My father was the first in his family to go to Canada in the 1940s. And while he had it relatively easy during the war, he also had to leave everything behind when he left his homeland."

Richard VandenBosch tilted back in his chair and stared intently at Karl. He had been stationed here in Prague for almost two years, after a string of postings in cities around the world starting in 1978. This was a career that he had fallen into quite by accident. As a child growing up in Ottawa, he had never been a particularly strong student, and had been on the verge of being kicked out of school many times. At the age of seventeen, he left school to join the RCMP as a civilian, doing shift work in their office while attending night school to complete his studies. It was while he was working with the RCMP that a friend offered him a position in external affairs. Since he already had police clearance, a requirement of his job, he thought he might give this new opportunity a try. He was interviewed and hired.

As a consular officer in Prague, VandenBosch was responsible for looking after the visa and immigration concerns of Canadians who were visiting or working in Czechoslovakia. The issues that he dealt with were varied and often extremely compelling. Most recently he had helped a Canadian who had been hit by a car while in the country. Helping solve the predicaments and crises facing fellow Canadians was something that gave Richard VandenBosch a great sense of satisfaction. Karl's story moved him instantly and deeply. He was in awe of Marie, who had so boldly protected her family in the face of great odds. He was impressed with Karl, who was determined to fulfill his mother's dream of restitution. And he was captivated by the story of these family treasures that had resurfaced after so many years.

For his part, Karl felt an immediate kinship with this inquisitive, interested young man. He didn't know why he should trust him so completely. But he sensed that this man was honest. How ironic, Karl thought, that he had hesitated in agreeing to a meeting with VandenBosch. This was proving to be a lucky outcome. It was a relief for Karl to be able to tell his story, and gratifying to find someone so keenly interested and stirred by it. In spite of the previous nights of sleeplessness, Karl had never felt more awake as his mind struggled to find a solution to his predicament, and a way for this man to help him.

And then an idea came to him. Karl composed himself, faced Richard VandenBosch, and looked him straight in the eyes. "It seems to me that it will be useless for me to apply to have the paintings legally exported from this country. There is no question in my mind that they would be seized by the Czech authorities, and then they would be as good as lost to me."

Richard nodded thoughtfully in agreement. He too knew that if the authorities got hold of the paintings, Karl would be in a battle with the government to extort money from him. There would be no victory in this for Karl, no happy ending, and no return of family property.

"I need to make sure that the Czechs do not get their hands on the paintings," continued Karl. "I would like the Canadian embassy to take possession of them." It was the only alternative. If he could get the artwork into a Canadian shelter, he reasoned, the Czech government would then no longer have access to them. "The embassy could provide a kind of asylum or sanctuary for the paintings until I figure out what I'm going to do." Karl leaned forward in his chair, suddenly quite animated. "I need to do all of this in the next few days," he added. "I'm due to fly back to Canada on May thirtieth, and I don't want to leave this country without securing a safe place for the paintings. I don't know when I can return, and I don't know how I'm actually going to get the paintings out of the country. But for now, and with your help, I'd like to deliver them here to the embassy. I want you to hide them and protect them until I can find a way to get them out of here."

The bold request hung in the air between the two men. And then Richard VandenBosch responded, and with the words that Karl had hoped to hear. "I have no problem with that," he said.

The meeting concluded shortly after that. Richard agreed to personally accompany Karl to Jan Pekárek's flat where they would take possession of the paintings and transport them to the embassy. VandenBosch would provide the automobile and the two of them, along with Pekárek, would do the lifting and carrying. Richard told Karl to call him two days later. "I need to check out some details with my colleagues," he said.

Karl agreed, noting that he also needed to confirm the arrangements with Jan Pekárek. "This man thinks that I'm working with the Czech authorities to export the paintings from the country. I don't want to compromise his personal safety in any way with this change of plans."

Richard nodded. "We're going to have to try to get the paintings here to the embassy on Saturday," he added. "You may have noticed the renovations that are currently underway here." Karl had seen the scaffolding outside the building and the workers in the hallway. "Most of the construction workers do not have security clearance." In other words, surmised Karl, these people might be spies working on behalf of State Security. It was an effective and simple way for the government to keep watch on the embassy's business – simply plant party people, in the guise of construction workers, within the building. "We don't want anyone noticing that you and I are transporting goods into the building," continued Richard.

"On Saturday, the embassy is empty except for a Canadian Forces security officer. And he can be trusted. We can safely move the paintings then."

The meeting was over. Karl stood and shook hands with Richard VandenBosch, once again giving silent thanks for having had the good fortune to meet with this man. The future of the paintings now rested with him and with the Canadian embassy. One more step in this complex operation had fallen into place.

Karl's former family home in Rakovník – now the district headquarters of the Communist Party.

CHAPTER TWENTY-ONE

Prague, May 1989

SHORTLY AFTER Karl left his office, Richard VandenBosch headed down the hallway to meet with Robert McRae. He knocked softly on his door and entered, sinking heavily into an armchair across from his desk.

"How was the appointment with Mr. Reeser?" McRae asked. He had just returned from his meeting at the Hradčany Castle and was still extracting notes and binders from his briefcase. As soon as VandenBosch sat down, McRae put aside his papers, perched himself on the edge of his desk, and waited expectantly.

"Incredible!" Richard replied. "I need to talk to you about this." McRae was not only Richard VandenBosch's superior, but had become a valued friend over the years. They had met while posted together in Yugoslavia. It was McRae who had recommended him for the position here. Richard respected and often sought out McRae's advice. "This man's story – his life – is quite remarkable," he continued. Just as Karl had done for him, he unfolded the history of the paintings. "Mr. Reeser wants the embassy to take possession of the paintings while he figures out a way to get them out of the country," he went on. "If he goes through the 'legal' channels, you and I both know that they will be confiscated. Housing them here will give him time to figure out a better plan."

McRae nodded thoughtfully. "And what did you tell him?"

"I said we'd have no problem with that."

McRae nodded again but did not reply. The calm and acumen he possessed came from years of having worked in diplomatic service. Robert McRae had seen and heard it all.

"As far as I'm concerned, the paintings are the property of a Canadian citizen," Richard continued. "The letter we have from this Jan Pekárek proves that. That makes the artwork Canadian as well. I don't care how long it's been here in this country." He leaned forward in his chair to face McRae. "Look, there's no way we should let the Communists get their hands on this stuff. Our job is to help Canadians in need, and this guy is desperate for our help."

It was no secret that Richard VandenBosch had little fondness for the government of the day. He had witnessed firsthand the repressive activities of the police and had seen the impact they had on the people of this country. Over the nearly two years that he had been here, his emotions had turned from sadness for the country, to irritation, and then to outright anger. He was tired of the crude campaign of harassment carried out under the guise of conducting government business. He sometimes wondered what the authorities thought they might uncover with this constant scrutiny, but he also knew that it was the very act of surveillance that kept the citizens cowering and on guard.

He had also had personal experiences of being watched and spied upon, notwithstanding his diplomatic immunity, which was meant to protect him from interference or intimidation by a host government. Most days, he could look out the window of his office and see the barely concealed undercover agents, training their long-lens cameras on the embassy building. He had answered telephone calls in the middle of the night where no one would reply on the other end, and he knew that his phone had been bugged.

There had even been a time, the previous summer, when he and a group of diplomatic families had all gone out for a weekend picnic. Twelve cars with diplomatic license plates headed out of the city toward a spot in the countryside. Richard had his wife, Anne, and his two young sons, Alexander and James, in the car with him. They eagerly anticipated spending a relaxed afternoon in the fresh air and away from their small, dank apartment where there was always a taste of burning coal in the back of their throats.

The families had found the perfect spot in a small valley where green fields dotted with daisies butted up against gently rolling hills. They had parked their cars, spread blankets on the grass, and pulled out baskets of sandwiches, sweet cakes, and beer for the adults. The children had begun kicking a soccer ball around the open field. But in the distance, on a sloping hill and clearly visible to all, a line of black cars was also parked. A half a dozen or more plain-clothed agents were standing in front of their automobiles, binoculars and long-range cameras aimed directly at the embassy families below. Big Brother was always watching.

Now that there was a sense of change in the political landscape of Czechoslovakia, the demands on the Canadian embassy to assist people had increased dramatically. Recently, people had been escaping from East Germany and were coming through Prague to get to the embassy in West Germany. Cars were being abandoned in the city as people tried to flee. Tents had sprung up in the gardens of public buildings, housing families who were desperate to get papers to go overseas. No one really knew what would happen to the citizens of Czechoslovakia if the Iron Curtain collapsed. And no one could predict what would become of personal property.

"I don't like people getting ripped off," he continued, springing from the armchair in McRae's office and beginning to pace back and forth. He hadn't even seen the paintings, but was already drawn in by Karl's vivid description of them. "They'll be sold, and some corrupt Communist is going to pocket the cash. Or they'll end up on some party official's wall, someone who will never know or care about them, or the blood, sweat, and tears it took to get this family out of the country during the war."

VandenBosch had listened to many stories over the years. But this one, Karl's story, had something more. It was the fact that his family had miraculously escaped unscathed in 1939, when so many other Jewish families had met a devastating fate. It was the injustice of having entrusted valuables to someone, only to have that person betray that trust. And it was the miracle of discovering their goods still safe here in Prague, and yet still unattainable.

He finished pacing and faced McRae. "This family defied the odds by getting out of here before the war," he said. "Now it's time to reunite them with what is rightfully theirs." He sank back down into the armchair and waited for McRae's response. But he was not worried. He and the chargé d'affaires were like-minded civil servants. They shared the same concern for the welfare of Canadians in need, and both were equally determined to right the wrongs committed against fellow nationals.

"I'm with you on this one," McRae replied. "Let's see what we can do."

The two officials sat down to formulate plans. Richard would accompany Karl to retrieve the paintings and the two of them would transport them in a diplomatic vehicle to the embassy. The diplomatic car would provide immunity, ensuring that they would not be stopped or searched during the transfer. McRae agreed that this all had to happen on Saturday, two days later, when the workers doing renovations in the building were off. "If we're going to do this, then let's do it with as few eyes on us as possible."

Richard nodded. "I'm just waiting for Mr. Reeser to confirm things from his end, and then we're all set," he concluded.

"As I said, I support this one hundred percent," said McRae. "But we should probably discuss what might happen if the Communists do get wind of this plan."

VandenBosch shrugged. Of course he had considered this possibility already, and knew there could be consequences for the embassy if it colluded in a scheme that defied the protocols of its host country. At the very least, this could be embarrassing for the embassy. At worst, it could have international implications.

"If they find out, I suppose I could be thrown out of the country for contributing to the theft of what they consider to be their property," Richard said. "That certainly wouldn't look good on me or our country. But I'd fight any suggestion that we're breaking the law," he added. "As far as I'm concerned the paintings are Canadian, and we are perfectly within our rights to help Mr. Reeser get them out." He would not be intimidated by the possibility of this plan being discovered. And even if the Communists found out what the embassy was doing, at the end of the day, he knew that he was protected by the rules of the Geneva Convention, providing him immunity from prosecution. His personal safety would not be compromised.

"I know you're a passionate man. But just promise me you won't be a cowboy, okay?" McRae stood to signal the end of the meeting. VandenBosch smiled. It was in his nature to fight for the underdog, and this case would be no exception. "I need to brief the ambassador on all of this, just to be on the safe side," added McRae. "But I think he'll agree with everything we've decided. Let me know when Mr. Reeser confirms things. By the way, I'm looking forward to seeing those paintings myself."

When Karl left Richard VandenBosch's office, he headed straight back to his hotel and immediately placed a telephone call to Jan Pekárek. Keeping the discussion brief, he arranged to meet Jan and his wife for dinner the next evening. It would be easier and safer to have a discussion about the plans in a public place, rather than over the telephone. Next, he placed a call to Phyllis. Again, it was difficult to have the full conversation he yearned to have with his wife.

"How is everything?" she asked. Karl could hear the veiled anxiety behind her simple question.

"Things are going well," he replied, deliberately trying to keep his voice light and even. "Moving forward, in fact." There was so little he felt comfortable saying. Throughout the call, he waited and listened for the click to indicate that the line was being tapped. But he did want to reassure Phyllis that he was safe.

"I can't wait for you to be home," Phyllis said.

"Only a few more days. Don't worry," he added. "Prague seems to be looking better than ever right now." He chuckled to himself, wondering if Phyllis would guess what he meant by that oblique statement. "I'll tell you all about it when I'm home. Love to you and the children."

When he got off the telephone, there was a call waiting for him from Richard VandenBosch. Anxiously, Karl returned the call.

"We're all set here," the jubilant voice of Richard VandenBosch boomed over the telephone, immediately allaying the fears that had crept into Karl's mind. This call signaled to him that all of the authority figures at the embassy were on board with the plan. "Can you meet me here Saturday morning, as we discussed?" he asked.

Karl took a deep breath. "I'm having dinner with my friend, tomorrow evening." He was deliberately vague about naming Jan on the telephone. "If you don't hear from me, then you can assume that I will be there first thing Saturday morning."

"I'm looking forward to seeing you then," Richard replied and the two men said their good-byes.

The next evening, Karl caught a cab to the Hotel Paris where he was to meet Jan Pekárek for dinner. He entered the formal lobby and was once again overwhelmed with nostalgia for this once fine establishment. His father had been a regular guest of this hotel on his business trips to Prague. And while he and his mother and Hana had lived in Prague after escaping Rakovník, this hotel was also the place where Marie had made her telephone calls to Victor in France. She had parked herself in a private telephone booth in this lobby, anxiously awaiting his calls, filling him in on the details of her attempts to secure their travel documents, and trying, unsuccessfully at times, to sound strong and dispel his fears for the safety of his family. At each step Karl felt that he was following in the path of his mother.

Despite the shortages and the general shabbiness of the city, the Hotel Paris restaurant was still quite elegant and bustling with activity. A familiar

Czech folk song played softly through overhead speakers. Karl was led to a quiet table in a corner of the room. He was early for the dinner meeting, and, while awaiting the arrival of Jan and his wife, he composed himself, concentrating on the details that he needed to have in place for Saturday. Even though things were far from resolved as far as getting the paintings out of the country, Karl already felt lighter knowing that he would be able to move them to the embassy.

Karl rose from his seat as Jan entered the restaurant, right on time. He waved, and Jan and his wife moved toward the table. Karl was introduced to Jan's wife. She smiled, accepting Karl's outstretched hand, as he invited them both to sit. He was anxious to talk about the paintings, but decided they should first order and enjoy their dinner. The meal was classic Czech fare, not unlike the meals Karl remembered from his childhood – beef with dumplings and thick brown gravy, and sweet and sour pickled cucumbers on the side. They washed all of this down with several glasses of local beer. The conversation with Jan was light. They discussed Karl's life in Toronto and Jan's work at the lab. His wife, a pleasant-looking woman, was largely silent, drifting into the background of their discussion and seeming somewhat subjugated by her husband's obvious intellect. It was only after the three of them had received their coffee and dessert that Karl and Jan finally put their heads together to talk about the plans for the paintings.

"I've made arrangements to move the paintings from your home to the Canadian embassy," began Karl, glancing around. The waiters had moved back from their table to a respectable distance. Still, he lowered his voice. Briefly, Karl reviewed his meeting with Richard VandenBosch and told Jan of the embassy agreement to temporarily accept custody of the paintings.

"So you've decided not to go through conventional channels," Jan interrupted at one point.

Karl nodded. "I won't do anything that jeopardizes your safety," he added. "You have my word on that."

Jan looked thoughtful. "It's probably a wise decision to *bypass* the government," he said after a short pause. After that, he asked few questions.

It was not necessary to know too much, simply the part that he would have to play in all of this. His wife was silent, glancing periodically at her husband and listening closely to what was being said. "I'd like to come for the paintings tomorrow, Saturday morning," Karl concluded.

Jan, who had been nodding at everything Karl had said, frowned unexpectedly and lowered his gaze. Karl was instantly ill at ease. Had Jan changed his mind? Would he refuse to relinquish the paintings? Everything hinged on this part of the plan. Karl stared at Jan, waiting for him to speak. But Jan was not backing out.

"There's a man in our apartment building – an administrator," Jan began anxiously. "Every building has one." At that moment, a waiter moved toward the table to refill coffee cups, abruptly silencing the conversation. Only when the waiter had finished pouring and moved away did Jan lean forward and resume speaking. "We must be careful when this administrator is there. He watches everything, everyone. That's his job, and if anything out of the ordinary were to happen, he'd be the first to report it."

Another tense moment passed.

"He's a party appointee. He's meant to let the Communists know about the business of each and every tenant, particularly those activities that are suspicious or out of the ordinary." Jan leaned even closer and lowered his voice to a whisper. "We could never chance moving something as large and obvious as the paintings with him in the building. He would report us in a moment."

Karl exhaled deeply and closed his eyes.

"This man goes out to work during the week. That's when no one is around to watch the tenants, and we'd be freer to move about," Jan continued. "But on evenings and weekends, this fellow is home. We simply could not be seen moving anything on a Saturday. I think it would be better to move the paintings on a weekday. Would that be possible?"

Karl's heart sank. The one day that the paintings could safely be moved into the embassy was the one day that they were at risk of being discovered in Jan's home. "No!" he replied. "A weekday is impossible. The embassy is undergoing renovations, and workers are crawling all over that

building like ants. They're all watchdogs according to my contact there."
He thumped his fist on the table, at once irritated and frustrated with the
circumstances. "How do you live under this toxic microscope?"

The question, unanswerable, hung in the air and Jan shrugged his
shoulders and looked away. In that moment, his wife reached out unexpectedly to touch his arm. She whispered something to him. He nodded,
and then turned back to Karl. "There is one slight chance," Jan said.
"This fellow, the informer, has a cottage in the country. He often spends
his weekends there, unless his wife is working in town. She occasionally
moonlights as a cloakroom attendant in one of the museums. You'll have
to call me early tomorrow morning. I won't know his plans until then.
With luck, the weather will be good, and he and his wife will decide to
leave for the weekend."

Karl nodded. It was all he could do for now. He wished that he could
leave this dinner meeting with the moving plans firmly in place. But that
was not to be. Karl and his dinner guests finished their coffee, said their
good-byes, and left the restaurant.

He spent another restless night at his hotel; his sleep was constantly
interrupted with thoughts of the paintings. At one point, the telephone
rang shrilly, the sound cutting through the silent shadows in Karl's room.
He groped for the receiver, but when he put it to his ear, no one was there.
It must have been a wrong number, he reasoned, as he replaced the telephone
and lay back down on his pillow. But was it as simple as that? Or was he
now the target of some investigation by police agents?

Would he be able to safely move the paintings to the embassy? He
imagined himself being stopped outside Jan's apartment door, the paintings in hand, secret police surrounding him. The paintings would be
confiscated, but what of him? Would he be arrested? Expelled from the
country? *The paranoia in Czechoslovakia choked you,* Karl thought, *worse
than the pollution in the air, or the smoke that hung in the restaurants and
bars.* He turned over in bed and tried to close his eyes to the fear.

Early the next morning, Karl picked up the telephone. Holding his
breath, he dialed Jan's number.

"We're in luck," Jan said as he answered the phone. The coast was clear. The informer had gone to his cottage for the weekend. The plan was on.

Richard VandenBosch on the Charles Bridge, while stationed in Prague, 1989.

CHAPTER TWENTY-TWO

Prague, May 27, 1989

THE WEATHER REPORT in Prague that morning called for warm temperatures and sunny skies – truly a bright new day, Karl thought, feeling on the verge of a new beginning. *Don't be overconfident*, he quickly cautioned himself as he rose. There was still much to do before he and the paintings would be safe.

Over a quick breakfast, Karl had the opportunity to glance through the local newspaper, *Rudé Právo*, or the *Red Right*. There on the front page was the smiling face of President Gustáv Husák. It was not surprising to see him in fashionable dress, meeting with visiting dignitaries and talking about the country's deep interest in cooperating with its citizens and the desire for expanding freedom and democracy. This rhetoric was typical of the kind of manipulation that took place here on a daily basis. But while Husák and others were trying to put a new face on the totalitarian regime, life here was still empty and restricted. More than ever, Karl could not wait to finish up his business here and get back to Toronto.

He arrived at the Canadian embassy by mid-morning. The receptionist smiled him through the entrance and escorted him down the hallway to Richard VandenBosch's office. Their footsteps echoed down the long, empty hall in a synchronous drumbeat, the only sounds on this quiet weekend morning, Karl noted with satisfaction. There were few staff to be seen and, more importantly, no non-embassy construction workers in the building.

Karl and Richard shook hands and exchanged warm greetings. "I'm so grateful to you and the embassy…" Karl began, but was instantly stopped by Richard's raised hand.

"No need to thank me. Let me get my car keys and let's go get your paintings."

The words were music to Karl's ears. The two men walked quickly out of the building and across the gated courtyard where embassy automobiles were parked. There were several vans, a black official-looking Tatra that was probably used to transport the ambassador, and several smaller vehicles. VandenBosch bypassed the larger cars and headed straight to one corner of the lot where a small blue Honda Civic was parked. He proceeded to unlock the driver's door. Karl stopped dead in his tracks. The good news was that the car had diplomatic license plates. It would not be stopped driving through the city. The bad news was that there was barely enough room in this car for the two men. There was no way that the four paintings were going to fit.

"Perhaps I didn't explain about the size of the paintings," Karl started as he turned to face Richard. The young diplomat waited, quizzical. "They're big," Karl stammered. "I mean to say, they're huge, bigger than this back seat, bigger than this car!" Unless they planned to strap the paintings to the roof, the vehicle was completely inadequate. He gestured helplessly, stretching his arms out and over his head to demonstrate the expanse of the paintings.

Richard stood rooted to the spot for another minute. Finally, he scratched his head and let out a long, low whistle. "I guess perching four priceless oil paintings on the roof of my car isn't going to work, is it?" Karl snorted, then laughed out loud and shook his head. A moment later Richard joined in.

"Wait here," he said, still laughing. He reentered the embassy building, emerging minutes later with a security officer who led the two men to a Volvo van. This vehicle had the same protective diplomatic license plates, but was much more suitable for their cargo. Richard smiled and winked at Karl. "I believe this one will work better."

The two men drove in silence to Jan's apartment. The streets were pulsing with activity. Richard expertly wove the van in and around the traffic mayhem, dodging other cars, motor scooters, and pedestrians who brazenly stepped out across the boulevards. Karl watched it all through the van window, his heart racing as rapidly as the traffic around him. No one out there knew or cared about what he and Richard VandenBosch were about to do, he realized. But Karl felt as though he were part of some kind of conspiracy plot, driving to the scene of the heist!

They parked directly in front of Jan's apartment building and climbed the stairs to his flat. Jan opened the door after the first knock and welcomed them in. Karl quickly introduced Richard and then followed Jan down the hall to the back bedroom. Richard gasped when the blankets and bed sheets were pulled back. Even though the paintings were still wrapped in paper and tied with string, he could easily appreciate their size. "I see what you meant about the car," he said, shaking his head. Karl nodded and motioned Jan and Richard to position themselves at the corners of the bed to begin lifting the paintings.

Without much discussion, the three men raised the top painting and carried it down the long staircase and into the parked van. Then back up the four flights of stairs to get the second painting. The men moved quickly, so Karl had little time to dwell on the knot that rested in the pit of his stomach. He was wary, glancing around and over his shoulder all the time. It was one thing to know that the informer in Jan's building was away for the weekend. They were safe from that scrutiny. But Karl did not want to meet up with any other residents of the apartment building, either. He had no desire for anyone to snoop around or ask any questions.

An old man opened his apartment door as they passed. The resident's expression was unreadable as he gazed passively at the three men carrying an oversized wrapped package. He looked as though he had watched events in his country for decades and had learned how not to react. Jan nodded to him and muttered a greeting. The man returned the nod and retreated into his flat.

Karl's hands felt slippery and he quickened his step. No time to dwell on the old man. No time for fear to take over. Just get the paintings down the stairs and into the van. Every minute in the open was a moment of potential detection. No one else seemed to be around. The hallways and staircases were deserted, and the street in front of Jan's building was equally quiet. The only pedestrians were a couple of elderly women who walked by carrying baskets of groceries. They barely lifted their chafed and wrinkled faces to acknowledge three men carefully placing oversized wrapped packages inside a parked van.

The paintings were heavy, and by the time they had finished descending the staircase for the fourth time, Karl was panting. It was close to noon and the humid air was stifling. Sweat glistened on his forehead and he reached into his pocket for a handkerchief to wipe across his brow. Jan and Richard were out of breath as well. Before closing the van door, Karl placed several more sheets and blankets from Jan's bed around the stacked paintings to provide additional protection for the drive back to the embassy. Finally, he slammed the door shut and turned to face Jan.

"Well, that's it, then," he began, glancing once more down the deserted street in front of Jan's apartment building.

Jan reached out to shake Karl's hand. "Good luck, Karl. I hope you are able to get your paintings to Canada quickly and with no difficulty."

"I'm so relieved that this worked out today," Karl said.

Jan nodded. "I am too."

There was so much more on his mind that he couldn't bring himself to say. He still grappled with what he thought about Jan Pekárek and his motives. But, in the end, gratitude won out. He pumped Jan's hand and muttered, "Thank you for contacting me."

Jan nodded again and began to step back onto the sidewalk. But Karl stopped him. He reached into his jacket pocket and pulled out some papers. "Your documents," Karl said, handing them over to Jan. "I know you wanted these back."

Jan accepted them gratefully and handed Karl a single sheet of paper. "A receipt," he said. "Or at least an acknowledgment that you now have all four paintings and our business is done."

Karl quickly scanned the document. Written in Czech, it read as follows:

Receipt

The below undersigned certifies that on the 27th of May 1989, Engineer* Karl Reiser received from Dr. Jan Pekárek, residing in Bechynova ulice 5, four paintings which the family Pekárek hid during the occupation for the family Reiser from 1945 until today.

The paintings are as follows:
1. Geoffroy: École maternelle
2. Antonio Ermolao-Paoletti: Woman at the Ball
3. Rudolf Swoboda: Forest Fire

The fourth painting, Die Hausfrau by Hugo Vogel, was supposedly promised by the late Victor Reiser as a reward for hiding the paintings during the Nazi occupation, and became the subject of a legal dispute between our families.

The document was not signed. It was curious to Karl that Jan had chosen to include a reference to the legal clash between the families as to the ownership of the Vogel, and that he had claimed this fourth painting in writing as having been promised to his family. Karl did not comment on that. He thanked Jan for the receipt, shook hands once more, and then climbed into the van next to Richard VandenBosch.

---

* This is often used as a title of respect.

"Next stop, the Canadian embassy," Richard said, as he quickly edged the van into traffic.

Once again, Karl was quiet during the drive. And again, he could feel his heart pounding inside his chest. But this time, it was exploding with excitement, knowing that the paintings were with him and would soon be safe inside the embassy building. He thought again of his father, who had never lived to see the end of the war, and of his mother, who had never lived to see the paintings returned. He felt so close to fulfilling his family's mission that he could barely breathe.

Richard parked the van behind the iron gates of the embassy courtyard, and the two men began to carry the paintings into the building. Only once they were safely inside the hallway next to Richard's office did Karl begin to remove the string and wrapping paper. Then, they lined them up, leaning them against the walls. Finally, they stood back to view the paintings.

Richard was taken aback by how impressive they were. "These are wonderful!" he exclaimed. "Each one is special in its own right. Look at the detail on the dancer's dress," he said as he admired the Paoletti, "and the expression on this lady's face." He pointed at the housewife. He turned to the last two. "You can almost feel the heat of those flames. And the faces of these children – quite simply remarkable."

For his part, Karl was utterly speechless. Aside from those few moments inside Jan's darkened apartment when he had first laid eyes on the paintings after fifty years, he had not had a chance to stand back and fully admire them as he did now. And he knew that VandenBosch was right. They were remarkable, from their size, to their vibrant colors – amazingly well preserved – down to their detailed and intricate brushstrokes. They had meant little to him in Rakovník. Today was another story. Today they meant everything. And from the shadow of the dark hallway in the embassy building arose the presence of Marie and Victor. Standing in front of the paintings was a moment of victory for his entire family, and Karl wanted to savor it. *You didn't get everything*, he thought silently of the war and Hitler's reign of terror. *You didn't tear us apart as you tore apart so many others.* This property, his family property, had eluded the Nazis first, and the Communists, at least for now, as well. It was a triumph.

Karl was so absorbed in staring at the paintings that he didn't realize Richard had left him. When he finally came out of his daze, he saw Richard walking toward him down the long hallway, accompanied by another gentleman. He carried a sheet of paper in his hand.

"This is Mr. Lalonde," Richard began. "He's a fellow Canadian, and a security officer here in the embassy." Karl shook hands with the smiling young man. "I've asked him to witness this receipt acknowledging that we now have the paintings and that you will endeavor to find a way to get them out of the embassy and into Canada."

Karl scanned the document. The receipt also released the embassy from any responsibility for the welfare of the paintings. Karl noted this, resolving once more to do everything in his power to get the paintings out of Czechoslovakia as soon as possible.

"I'm not planning on going anywhere in the near future," Richard added. "But in case plans change, you should have this as evidence of your ownership of the paintings. Once the paper is signed and I've made a copy, I'll drive you back to your hotel."

Karl nodded, still absorbed in his memories. He signed the form which was then cosigned by Richard and witnessed by Lalonde. Before leaving, he snapped photographs of the paintings and then, with one more backward glance, he left the embassy.

Outside the InterContinental Hotel the two men turned to face one another. "I know I've got a lot of work to do before the paintings are out of the country," Karl began, haltingly. "But it already feels as if they are free."

Richard nodded. "This is a great moment for me as well," he replied. "To know that I am a small part of the recovery of this art gives me a great sense of satisfaction."

"I know I've said this before, but this would not have been possible without you." Richard silenced him with a wave of his hand. Karl took a deep breath. "I will be in touch. As soon as I have any information regarding the transport of the paintings, I will let you know."

"We'll keep them safe until then," Richard replied. "You can be sure of that."

The two men shook hands warmly. Karl looked deep into the vice consul's eyes, trusting what he saw – the honesty and integrity. He felt an intense solidarity with this man who, only days earlier, had been a complete stranger. It was hard to express the full extent of the appreciation he already had for everything Richard VandenBosch had done. Karl climbed out of the car. He watched it disappear from sight, and then turned to enter the hotel. People stared as the bellman held open the door. In his arms, Karl still carried the crumpled sheets and blankets that he had taken from Jan Pekárek's bed to cushion the paintings. He planned to return them to Jan later that day. It was an enormous bundle, making it difficult to get through the door, and turning a few heads. Karl lowered his eyes, suddenly self-conscious, and focused on getting to the elevator as quickly as possible.

When he entered his hotel room, he picked up the telephone to call Phyllis in Canada. "My work is done here," he said. "My flight leaves on Monday, so I will be home in a couple of days."

This time, the relief in her voice was palpable. "I can't wait to see you," she said. "Is everything okay?"

"It's more than okay," Karl replied. "It's perfect!"

It was only after Karl had locked the door to his suite and sunk down onto his bed that the full impact of the events of the previous few days began to sink in. "The paintings are safe!" He repeated this mantra over and over. And, while they were still technically inside Communist Czechoslovakia, they were on Canadian soil. And even though he had no idea at that time how he was going to get the paintings out of this country and into Canada, he knew that he had surmounted one enormous hurdle. Along with the exhilaration of having reclaimed the paintings, Karl also realized how exhausted he was. He had not allowed himself a moment to let down his guard, and the strain of having plotted and planned for the delivery of the paintings had left him drained, emotionally and physically. He lay his head down on the bed, thinking he would rest for a few minutes, and was instantly asleep.

As he lay there, dreaming about the day he would be able to enjoy the paintings from within his own home in Toronto, there was a sudden sharp rap at the door of his hotel room. Karl bolted awake. How long had he been sleeping? A few minutes? Several hours? A second sharp knock and Karl felt his mouth go dry and his heart begin to pound uncontrollably. His immediate thought was that he and the paintings had been discovered. All the pleasure and relief of the day left him. How arrogant on his part to relax, he thought, when he was still on Communist soil and still in some danger of being discovered.

When the knocking began for the third time, Karl stood up and cautiously approached the door. Blood pulsed in his veins, sending flashes of heat up to his face. He opened it a crack and peered into the hallway only to see a housekeeper standing there staring back at him. "I've come to check the minibar," she said. Karl let out the breath that he had been holding and chuckled out loud as he stood aside to let her enter, admonishing himself for his paranoia. He was safe and the paintings were safe. Still, there was much to do before he could rest completely.

As soon as the housekeeper left, Karl went back down to the lobby. This last disturbing event had decided something for him. He did not want to remain in the country for one minute more than he had to. Every glance, every knock at the door, every person he passed merely heightened the anxiety he was feeling. And in his current state of apprehension, it was better to get out as quickly as he could. His flight home was scheduled to depart on Monday afternoon. He was flying on Swissair, which only flew out of Prague on weekdays. Karl had chosen this flight over Czechoslovak Airlines, which flew from Prague on weekends, because he had balked at the thought of flying on a Communist airline. But now, he didn't care how he flew. His only desire was to leave Prague as soon as possible.

There was a desk for the Czechoslovak Airlines in the lobby of the hotel, and a helpful attendant quickly rearranged Karl's flight so that he could leave the next day. Satisfied and relieved, he returned to his room, though not before stopping at the concierge desk to pick up another copy of the newspaper, *Rudé Právo*. In his room, he settled back on his bed, promising himself he would spend a few minutes reading the paper before packing his belongings for the flight home.

The newspaper carried the usual array of fanatical Communist worker resolutions and pronouncements. Karl quickly scanned the articles, paying little attention to what was reported. One item of local news, however, caught his eye. A Czechoslovak Airline plane, en route from Prague to the spa town of Karlovy Vary, had been hijacked by an armed man several days earlier. In the scuffle on board, the hijacker had discharged his gun, piercing the hull of the plane. Had it not been for the skill of the pilot, the plane would have crashed. In the end, it landed safely and the man was arrested. The pilot was being hailed as a hero. Though this incident had ended well, it left Karl shaken and in doubt once more. He didn't know what was worse, taking his chances by staying in Prague for a couple of extra days, or risking his life on a Czech plane! Neither alternative was appealing. But surely this incident was an omen, he thought. He went back down to the lobby where he transferred his airline ticket back to the Swissair flight leaving on Monday. Under the circumstances, perhaps it was better after all to travel safely back to Canada on an airline he trusted.

That afternoon, he delivered the sheets and blankets back to Jan Pekárek's apartment. Then, armed with his camera, he spent the final two days in Prague wandering through the old part of the city. He crossed the Charles Bridge, stopping to rub the golden toe of the statue of St. John of Nepomuk. Legend had it that this action would bring luck, and Karl closed his eyes and wished with all his might to get himself and his paintings safely out of the country. He passed a large statue of Christ encircled with Hebrew letters. The text on the crucifix had been added in 1696, placed there as punishment for a Prague Jew who had been accused of debasing the Cross. The golden letters had always been a matter of controversy for Prague's Jewish community. Karl's walking journey took him past the Church of St. Mikuláš,* where Mozart was said to have played the organ.

---

* Church of St. Nicholas

The St. Vitus cathedral, inside the grounds of Prague Castle, were so massive that, up close, it was hard to get a clear perspective of them. The walls rose up as a sheer edifice, overwhelming and magnificent, blackened by years of wear and disrepair, scattered with gold carvings, menacing gargoyles, and imposing statues that seemed to defy their years. Karl also passed by the famous Astronomical Clock mounted on the Old Town City Hall. The dial of the clock represented the position of the sun and moon in the sky. The clock chimed on the hour, at which time the "Walk of the Apostles" – a parade of figures moving above and across the face of the clock – took place. Four figures flanked either side of the clock, and were also set in motion hourly. The figures symbolized four sins. One figure, looking in the mirror, represented vanity; a skeleton represented death; a turbaned Turk represented threats to Christianity; and the fourth statue, a Jew holding a bag of gold, represented greed or usury. Tourists happily snapped pictures of the colorful clock and its parade of figures, seemingly unaware of the meaning behind the sculptures. Karl joined them.

This old section of the city was under restoration, and despite the seeming lack of interest in refurbishing public buildings, there were signs that the once splendid architecture of Prague was being uncovered and renewed. This was the Prague that Karl remembered from his youth, and it did his heart good to see scaffolding against the marble and brick facades, and view the workers as they cleaned and repaired previously neglected segments of the city's fine architecture. Tourists filled the streets, along with dozens of prostitutes openly soliciting customers. As Karl strolled through the winding cobblestone lanes, he pushed all thoughts of the paintings from his mind. He would have plenty to do and think about once he returned to Toronto. For now, he took as many photographs as he could, wanting to enjoy his final moments in Prague, and to do so without apprehension or preoccupation.

On Monday, Karl checked out of his hotel, but not before there was one final incident. As he approached the front desk to settle his bill, the desk clerk asked how he would be paying, with American cash or Czech crowns. Karl, who had exchanged dollars for crowns with his schoolmate,

Miloš Nigrin, replied that he would pay with Czech currency. However, as he was pulling the bills from his wallet, the desk clerk asked him to produce his official receipt from a financial institution for the monetary exchange. Of course he had none. It was the final reminder that only government exchanges were valid. After a quick and curt negotiation with the desk clerk, Karl was able to settle his bill partly with American cash, and partly with his remaining Czech crowns. He caught a bus to the airport where he faced one last anxiety-ridden hurdle – passing through security.

"What was the purpose of your visit to our country?" the guard asked brusquely, as Karl relinquished his papers and willed himself to breathe deeply and slowly.

"My high school reunion," he replied, briefly describing the events that had formed the alibi for his visit.

"And how was it?" the guard asked, smiling now, almost friendly.

"Wonderful," Karl lied. With that, he collected his papers, boarded the plane and flew home to Toronto and to a welcome reunion with Phyllis.

POTVRZENÍ

Já níže podepsaný Ing Karel Reiser potvrzuji tímto, že jsem dne 27.května 1989 převzal od Dr Jana Pekárka,(bytem Bechyňova ulice č. 5, Praha 6)čtyři obrazy, které rodina Pekárkova skrývala po dobu okupace a uchovávala pro rodinu Reiserovu od roku 1945 až do dnešního dne.

Jedná se o následující obrazy:

1. Geoffroy : Ecolle maternelle
2. A. Ermole - Paoletti : Vor dem Ball
3. Rudolf Swoboda: Waldbrand
a čtvrtý obraz : Hugo Vogel: Die Hausfrau, který byl údajně slíben zesnulým panem Viktorem Reiserem jako odměna za ukrývání obrazů během nacistické okupace a který se stal předmětem soudního sporu mezi oběma rodinami.

Receipt from Jan Pekárek listing three of the paintings and then specifying that the fourth was the subject of legal proceedings between the familes.

I, Karl Reeser, Canadian Citizen and holder of Canadian passport
numbered RK 494805 issued in Toronto 16MAR89, do solemnly swear
that the Canadian Embassy and staff members are absolved from
responsibility of the four paintings mentioned below in case of
damage, loss and/or theft. Mr. Reeser is responsible for the
shipping and clearance necessary for the paintings departure from
czechoslovakia.

Paintings

1. "Ecole maternelle" by Geoffroy
2. "Vor Dem Ball" by A. Ermole Pauletti
3. "Waldbraud" by Rudolf Swoboda
4. "oil painting by Hugo Vogel *"DIE HAUSFRAU"*

declared at the Canadian Embassy, Prague Czechoslovakia, twenty seventh
day of May, nineteen hundred and eighty nine.

Mr., Karl Reeser

Richard VandenBosch
Consular Attache

Michel Lalonde
witness

A receipt from the Canadian Embassy acknowledging
the presence of the four paintings.

PART IV

THE HONEST
SMUGGLER

CHAPTER TWENTY-THREE

Toronto 1989

ON HIS RETURN, Karl dove into the task of trying to find a way to get the paintings out of the Canadian embassy in Prague and into Canada. It was a daunting proposition, and there were seemingly insurmountable obstacles at every turn. There was nothing fluid about the Czech laws. They were solid, sharp as a lethal knife, and unyielding. And while one could argue that there was a slight possibility that in relinquishing the paintings to the National Gallery and paying the tax, the government might agree to allow for their export, there was no way to know the outcome of this unless Karl openly came forward and acknowledged their existence. And once the paintings were known to the government, all control on Karl's part would be lost.

On top of these legal certainties, Karl was also aware that any disclosure of the paintings might endanger Jan Pekárek who could be perceived as having already defied the government by harboring the paintings in the first place, and for having turned them over to Karl and not to Czech officials. And, as Karl had already resolved, he did not want to do anything to jeopardize Jan's safety and that of his family.

As if all of this were not enough, Karl also knew that he could not disclose to the Czech government that the paintings were now being kept at the Canadian embassy. There was no question that the involvement of the embassy raised the profile of the paintings significantly. The secret police would likely be even more interested in them given that the embassy had thought them important enough to hide. Furthermore, there were possible implications for the embassy itself for having hidden the paintings. There could be consequences for the Canadian government and for those who had helped Karl in his mission – primarily Richard VandenBosch.

So there it was: a mountain of obstacles. Karl wished he could go back to Prague and carry the paintings out himself; find a way to conceal them in a case or crate. This would have been a compelling option, if it weren't for the fact that they were so big – that and the knowledge that Phyllis would never allow him to do anything as risky as hiding the paintings in his luggage and sneaking them across the border.

For weeks, Karl tried to fashion one solution after another. Each possible alternative disintegrated in the face of the stumbling blocks. Karl rode a wave of conflicting feelings and thoughts. He was frustrated that the paintings were so close to finally being in his possession and yet were still just beyond his grasp. He was angry at a government that still seemed to haunt and stalk his family years after they had fled the country. He felt fearful that nothing would ever come of his efforts and the paintings would never be returned to him. And in the midst of this emotional torrent, he would think of his parents, who had never stopped fighting to get their family out of Czechoslovakia during the war – and particularly of his mother and her brave attempts to keep the paintings together and retrieve them. Buoyed by the memories of his parents' strength and determination, he would once again resolve to find a way to recover the art.

"I know there has to be a way to do this; a solution somewhere in the midst of all of these barriers." Karl voiced this one evening as he and Phyllis sat having dinner with Hana and Paul. The two couples socialized together on a weekly basis. Recently their conversations had focused on Karl's trip to Prague and what to do about the paintings.

Hana shook her head. "I don't know what to suggest," she said. The truth was that Hana did not have the same burning desire to retrieve the art that Karl did. Even though she empathized with him and understood his longing, she had been largely indifferent upon discovering that the paintings had resurfaced in Prague. Perhaps it was because the events of the war and their family's escape from Europe had happened when Hana was still quite young. Her life had been more fully formed in Canada after their escape. Any attachment to their home in Rakovník and all of their possessions there had faded soon after arriving here. She did not share Karl's view that the paintings were a vindication of their mother's endless efforts to reclaim their property in Prague. She had been only mildly interested in her mother's attempts to retrieve the paintings years earlier. At any rate, she was at a loss as to how to help her brother.

"Your mother always talked about how wonderful it would be if the paintings could be returned to her – a restitution of sorts," said Phyllis. Karl's wife had been relieved beyond words to have him back safely. And while she empathized with his desire to regain the paintings, Phyllis's great fear was that Karl was going to undertake another trip to Prague. His first trip there had caused Phyllis many sleepless nights. A second excursion would be her emotional undoing. And yet she knew that if her husband resolved to do something, there would be no stopping him.

"Perhaps you've not yet exhausted every legal avenue to get the paintings out." Paul had been sitting quietly at the table watching the exchange take place, and now leaned forward to join the conversation. "Besides, you have no other choice but to follow the law." Paul was typically a reserved and cautious man, sometimes even appearing to be distant and aloof. In reality, he was a man of complex emotional character. Like many survivors of the Holocaust, Paul was hesitant to talk about his painful survival history, and reluctant to be outspokenly Jewish in general.

Karl frowned. He was not surprised to hear his brother-in-law make this cautious statement about following the law. He shook his head emphatically. "At this point, I'm prepared to do anything to get the paintings back," Karl declared. "I don't care what's involved. I'd beg, bribe, or steal them out of the country if I could find a way." The four of them fell silent. It was inconceivable to Karl that there wasn't an avenue open to him, legal or otherwise. "But clearly I can't do this on my own," he continued. "I wouldn't know the first thing about smuggling. Besides, I need someone who understands the political situation in Czechoslovakia."

"Someone who would know how to get around all those rules," added Phyllis.

"Exactly!" Karl replied, enthusiastically. "And preferably someone who understands fine art – how to transport something as delicate as the paintings. I'd be willing to pay for someone or some company who could do all of that."

"But even if you were to find such a person who was willing to be paid to bypass the laws, how would we ever ensure that they were in this to help us and not only themselves?" Hana posed this question and Paul nodded emphatically.

Karl stood from the table and paced anxiously across the dining room. "There must be something…there must be someone," he muttered, as much to himself as to the others.

"What we really need is an honest smuggler," Phyllis said, glancing up from her seat at the table.

Karl came to an abrupt stop, "Yes!" he said, nodding excitedly, "Someone who would be willing to go into the country and get the paintings out for us – but someone we could trust would bring the paintings back to us and not just abscond with them."

No one replied until Hana laughed softly. "If only there were such a person," she said.

Over the next few weeks, Karl made attempts to locate such a person. He began by extending his net of contacts and speaking to everyone he knew who might have a link to the art world in Canada and abroad. Political and legal contacts were next – those who might have dealings in Czechoslovakia or other Communist countries. When he had exhausted that list, he moved on to merchants who had conducted business abroad and were used to transporting goods. His research extended into the area of looted art in Europe during the Second World War, and he discovered that the Third Reich had, not surprisingly, amassed hundreds of thousands of valuable objects, including paintings and sculptures, from occupied nations. In 1943, the United Kingdom had joined with sixteen other United Nations countries to try to stop this plundering. A declaration was announced at that time making it clear that harboring property of this sort would not be tolerated. To support this, a set of non-binding principles was being developed that would assist individuals or their heirs who had lost art to come forward, identify their property, and then work toward achieving a just and fair resolution. Of course, the situation in Czechoslovakia was further complicated by the presence of the Communist government, which Karl knew would never adhere to these western principles.

Karl's days began to follow a particular routine. He would rise early, walk the dog, and have breakfast with Phyllis. And then he would head off to do his research. He was a frequent visitor at the reference library where he poured over telephone books and newspapers from every country, trying to track down possible resources. He wrote letters to every promising contact and used the services of a small downtown Toronto company that had an answering machine and fax service available for a small fee. Step by step, Karl's list of sources began to grow. With each contact he would begin by first asking for a lawful solution to his problem of retrieving the paintings. But when that avenue failed to yield positive results, he would quickly move on to asking if anyone might know a way to work around the law.

Several leads looked promising. There was a Czech expat, whom Karl had met while purchasing a painting for his home. This man had traveled extensively, buying art at auction houses around the world. He had done a substantial amount of business in Western Europe and frequently arranged for the shipment of this art back to Canada. But after a lengthy conversation with him, Karl again realized that shipping goods of value from countries like France or Italy and trying to get art out of Czechoslovakia were two very different ventures.

Next, Karl discovered several companies that organized industrial fairs at international expositions. These companies would import and display machinery and other equipment for these trade shows. Karl wrote to each of them, setting out his situation and asking for their assistance. One by one, they responded with the same verdict: *"We won't touch this project without the Czech export stamp."* One company even responded with a lengthy fax that gave a detailed description of the steps that foreign diplomats must comply with in order to gain permission to have personal property exported. No one was immune from the scrutiny of the Czech government, and, after several months had passed, Karl realized that he was no further ahead in his efforts to regain his property.

During all this time, Karl continued to have regular correspondence with Richard VandenBosch. In an early letter, Karl asked if Richard had any plans to return to Canada for a visit with his family, who resided outside of Guelph, Ontario. Karl hoped to be able to visit with him if he were planning such a trip. This would also make communication so much easier. In October 1989, VandenBosch responded, saying,

Dear Mr. Reeser,
I received your letter through the post on October 23. Unfortunately, I will not be able to come to Canada until probably July next year.

I was just composing a letter to you asking whether or not you have sorted out the problem relating to the shipment of your lovely paintings. Should you wish to discuss it further you can contact me by letter or telephone. I can make myself available during embassy hours.

Yours sincerely,
Richard VandenBosch
Vice Consul

There were numerous letters exchanged between the two of them from May 1989 to March 1990. And over the course of this correspondence the relationship between Karl and Richard VandenBosch began to take on a whole new dimension. They were becoming friends – separated by continents, but linked nevertheless. Despite the continued formality of their greetings and salutations, their letters moved from reserved updates on Karl's attempts to find a way to retrieve the paintings and Richard's confirmation of these efforts, to private accounts of their lives and families. The change in tone in their letters was an unspoken acknowledgment that they had shared a personal adventure of sorts. Richard seemed to have almost as much of a stake in the paintings and their fate as Karl did. There was no doubt that he was invested in Karl and his family.

In a letter dated November 28, Richard told Karl that he and his family were planning to vacation that coming Christmas in England. He suggested that it would be lovely if Karl and Phyllis could join them. He wrote:

> Just a quick note to say that I often to go Weiden, Passau, West Germany, for a quick relief from the Prague tension and I will be in England over the Christmas holidays. The embassy has my number if you require it. I would be happy to meet you around this place if you wish...

It was impossible for Karl to meet up with Richard in England. In his subsequent letter, he wrote:

> Thank you for offering to meet me in England during the Christmas holidays. Aside from the fact that the time frame was just too close, I would not want to intrude at this time into what for you must be a much-needed respite from the recent tensions of Prague. I may take you up on your offer during the first half of next year, or else, wait for your anticipated visit to Canada in July...

In the letter of invitation, VandenBosch also told Karl that he had decided that, for the time being, he would hang the paintings in the embassy offices. They were so big and impressive that he thought they deserved to be displayed. Besides, he knew they would add something special to the walls of the embassy, which were quite devoid of artwork. In addition, Richard wanted to make sure that the paintings would not sustain any damage while at the embassy, and he thought that hanging them was the best way to preserve them. The painting of the children in the bathhouse was mounted on the wall of his office. *Forest Fire* was hung in the receptionist's office. The housewife gazing at the sheet music went into Robert McRae's office. The fourth painting, the Spanish dancer, was stored in an upstairs room of the embassy. Periodically, Richard would rotate the paintings so that everyone would have a chance to enjoy them. He wrote that the paintings were providing great pleasure for himself and his colleagues, though it would please him even more when he knew that the paintings were finally hanging on the walls of Karl's home in Canada.

Karl was delighted with the news that the paintings were hanging in the embassy offices.

I read with much pleasure that two of my paintings are hanging in your offices.* At one time, all of the paintings had beautiful, ornately carved gilded frames. If there was some way of framing these paintings while they are in your custody, I would gladly assume the cost, and then perhaps all of them could be utilized to full advantage. But I would, of course, not want the paintings to leave the safety of the embassy.

I suppose that it comes across that the turn of events relative to these paintings has great meaning for me. It started fifty years ago when my mother hid them from the Nazis. Incredibly, two generations

* VandenBosch later confirmed that three paintings were hanging in the embassy offices.

later, an honest grandson of the original custodian has surrendered them. The fact that now, half a century later, these paintings grace the Canadian embassy, is a sort of a triumph for me: made possible by your understanding and actions taken during the few hours I spent with you last May. As this year draws to a close, I want to express my admiration and appreciation for your role. I presume that Ambassador Mawhinney and First Secretary McRae had prior knowledge in this matter, and I would like you to express to them my sentiments and greetings.

With best wishes for 1990, sincerely,
Karl Reeser

Though the many letters that passed between Karl and Richard had a warm nature, they also all alluded to the increasing tension and political unrest in Prague. Indeed, the situation in all of the Soviet Bloc countries was undergoing a dramatic change in the fall of 1989. Soviet President Mikhail Gorbachev was struggling with a faltering economy, the Iron Curtain was eroding, and countries on both sides of the divide were calling for reunification.

"It's happening all over," Karl proclaimed one night as he sat with Phyllis drinking tea and discussing these significant world events. "If someone like Andrei Sakharov can be elected to the new parliament of the Soviet Union, then anything is possible." Karl was referring to the dissident and Nobel laureate who had once been exiled from the country for his political views. "And look at what's happening in Czechoslovakia. Everyone thought that the student protests would end in violence, but instead of sending in the tanks, the Communists are resigning. They're even beginning to remove the barbed wire from the border with West Germany and Austria. It's being hailed as the most peaceful revolution in history."

"Let's just wait and see," Phyllis replied. Her voice was soft and somber. "Everyone believes that Václav Havel will become the next president, but he has his work cut out for him." The noted playwright and dissident was being hailed as the future savior of a new democratic Czechoslovakia, but Phyllis's view remained dark. "The country has lived in a fog of lies and meaningless rhetoric for decades. Communism has ruined the nation, quite apart from the extinction of civil liberties. The spirit of the citizens has been broken, industry is a mess, and technology is archaic. And then there's the history of harassment. The secret police aren't going to disappear just because the government has a new name."

Karl interjected. "You're right, of course. But it is a beginning – something to be optimistic about, wouldn't you agree with that?"

Phyllis was quiet and eventually she rose, cleared the dishes, and left the room. But when Karl read of the fall of the Berlin Wall on November 9, he was even more optimistic about the possibility of change within his former homeland. That wall, which had stood as a physical and political symbol of oppression for thirty years, was opened up in a single night. The events which followed in Czechoslovakia were immediate and rapid. On November 17, more than fifty thousand students who were part of the Socialist Union of Youth turned out for a mass demonstration. The date was significant, as it marked the fiftieth anniversary of the murder of a Czech student, Jan Opletal, by Nazi soldiers during the Second World War. His death was commemorated annually in what was known as International Students' Day. On that day in 1989, armed forces were on alert for what they anticipated would be an all-out riot. The students, and others who joined them, marched toward Wenceslas Square, where they were surrounded and eventually beaten by riot police. But the regime's decision to use force against the protesters would have consequences, and this demonstration was only the beginning. Within days, more peaceful marches were held and the numbers of protesters grew to over two hundred thousand. On November 27, a general strike was called, with workers demanding a new government. Millions of Czechs and Slovaks walked off their jobs. Under this intense pressure, the Communist Party of Czechoslovakia announced that it would relinquish power and step down. Gustáv Husák resigned on December 10, and on December 29, 1989, Václav Havel became the new president of Czechoslovakia. His political party, known as the Civic Forum, became a voice for revolutionary change in the country. In his "Declaration of the Civic Forum" speech, Havel proclaimed:

> The situation is open now, there are many opportunities before us, and we have only two certainties.

> The first is the certainty that there is no return to the previous totalitarian system of government, which led our country to the brink of an absolute spiritual, moral, political, economic, and ecological crisis.

> Our second certainty is that we want to live in a free, democratic, and prosperous Czechoslovakia, which must return to Europe, and that we will never abandon this ideal, no matter what transpires in these next few days.[11]

This overthrow of the Communist government became known as the Velvet Revolution, one that had miraculously happened quickly and without bloodshed. Graffiti appeared on the walls of buildings in Prague that said "Poland, ten years; Hungary, ten months; East Germany, ten weeks; Czechoslovakia, ten days."[12]

In Prague, a dissident was hurriedly released from jail so he could join the cabinet as the minister responsible for, among other things, the secret police! The unattainable was being achieved, and Karl watched these events unfold with great anticipation. A revolution was taking place inside his former homeland, and a peaceful one at that. A new democratic government was on the horizon, and with it, the promise of a complete restructuring of the political and social agenda.

Surely this would also eventually result in a lifting of the regulations governing the export of goods. Perhaps if he just waited a little longer, the paintings might become accessible to him without all this scheming and planning. More than fifty years had passed since his family had had possession of the paintings. Surely Karl could wait a few more months.

How jubilant it would have made his parents to think that the country might be opening up now, providing a route to regaining their property as it woke from its long coma.

But any hope of an immediate change in Czechoslovakia's policy of investigating and persecuting its citizens faded when Karl became suspicious that his mail was being opened and inspected. A letter which had been sent from his old friend, Miloš Nigrin, arrived with tape sloppily applied across the seal. And Miloš subsequently wrote to say that he too had received a letter from Karl which had been delivered opened. When Miloš went to the post office to casually inquire about this, he was told that the letter had indeed been inspected by the secret police. This sent Karl into a frenzy of worry. "No wonder everyone is paranoid there," he fumed bitterly to Phyllis as he held up the letter from Miloš, the evidence of what he believed to be police tampering. "Each time the citizens think they can taste freedom, the Communist goons remind them that they're still being watched – we're all being watched." His voice rose and shook with a sudden ferocity. Perhaps Phyllis had been right to be so circumspect about the news emerging from the country. Change would not happen so quickly.

"But what do you think it means?" Phyllis asked. "Are they really suspicious of you or is this just what they do to everyone?"

"Who knows?" Karl replied, shaking his head. "I'm most concerned about Miloš. He has nothing to do with this; he doesn't even really know why I was in Prague in the first place. I don't want him implicated in something that is my affair and mine alone. But if State Security is indeed suspicious of the business I was conducting while in Prague, then Miloš could be targeted just for having been seen with me when I was there. It's absurd!"

"And what about Jan?"

"Of course! He's just as vulnerable. More so!" Karl squeezed his eyes shut and shook his head, more convinced than ever that someone must have become suspicious when they saw him, Jan, and Richard carry the paintings out of Jan's apartment and into the waiting van – maybe the old man who had poked his head out the door of his flat, or the old women walking by on the street. They had appeared to be harmless, but no one, he reminded himself, no one could be trusted in a country that hunted for traitors and trained its citizens to do the same. And if Jan were arrested, it would be a short path to the whereabouts of the paintings. Ranting didn't help, Karl knew. But he felt so powerless and deceived. What good was a new democratic government when, at the end of the day, it still resorted to its old tricks? A wolf in sheep's clothing, that's what you could expect from Czechoslovakia, old or new.

Karl became increasingly concerned about the frank correspondence he had been having with Richard VandenBosch, in which they had both openly discussed the paintings, their current whereabouts, and the plans for their future. When he received a letter from Richard that appeared to have been opened and then resealed with tape, he knew with certainty that his mail was being scrutinized. His subsequent letter to VandenBosch cautioned him as follows:

> Many thanks for your letter…which by the way arrived resealed with transparent tape. I mention this, because I experienced repeated instances of non-delivery of mail to two of the persons with whom I met while I was in Prague last May. That is one of the reasons why I would like to meet with you privately, even if it must wait until you visit Canada in July of next year. If by chance you may be somewhere in Central Europe before then, I could probably arrange to meet you there…

Now, more than ever he needed to get the paintings out of the country. But a plan still eluded him. He even asked VandenBosch for help in locating someone to assist him. Richard replied by saying:

> I must apologize for my tardy reply to you in recommending any lawyers. The Canadian embassy from time to time uses the lawyers at Advokatni Poradna 1, Narodni 32 (dum Chicago), Prague 1… Unfortunately, we cannot attest to their competency in this field. I hope this will be of some help…

This did not appear promising. But that same letter contained some news which was even more distressing. In it, VandenBosch indicated that, in light of the changing political scene in Czechoslovakia and elsewhere, the embassy would be undergoing a massive staff turnover in the coming months. He personally would remain in Prague for another year. But the changeover in staff would probably necessitate the removal of the paintings from the embassy and their relocation elsewhere. His letter had a tenor of urgency when he wrote:

> On another note, have you had any success in obtaining exit permission for your paintings? The staff will be changed over this summer and will probably result in the removal of your paintings elsewhere for storage. I would be somewhat relieved if they could be in your possession before this summer. I shall be here for a further year and, if possible, shall be available to assist you...

"The paper says that Prague citizens are popping champagne and dancing with joy on Wenceslas Square."

Karl, Phyllis, Hana, and Paul had once more gathered for dinner in the Reeser home. Their conversation was filled with news of the changing political events in Czechoslovakia and other countries. Phyllis held a copy of the *Toronto Star* in her hands and was pointing to a column which declared:

> Sirens wailed, horns honked and bells pealed...in Prague and other cities to mark a dramatic opposition victory that ended the Communists' 41-year domination of the government.[13]

"The people there have been deprived of political expression for so long they don't know what to do with themselves," she said. "These are extraordinary events! The entire Communist party leadership structure has collapsed. And not just in Czechoslovakia. Gorbachev is signaling that he is willing to end the Communist party monopoly on power in the Soviet Union. Hungary and even Bulgaria are hinting at free elections.

Lithuania and Estonia will follow suit. You must admit, it sounds like a hopeful future."

Hana nodded, though she remained silent.

Karl frowned. This time he was not being quite so optimistic. "I'm concerned about the men who will replace those who have resigned. The Communist party veterans are not going to walk away so easily. They'll want a place in this new government. And, as you have suggested more than once, a Communist with a new title is still a Communist."

He spat the words out and then went on to detail the letters that he and Richard VandenBosch were exchanging. "With the fall of the Communist government, the entire Canadian embassy is restructuring. The paintings may have to be moved elsewhere. I still don't trust that a new government will be any more likely to open up the borders to allow valuable property to be exported. And I'm terrified that if our artwork is moved, it will be exposed in public and subject to investigation." He went on to describe how his recent letters had been opened and likely inspected by whatever was left of the secret police. "Nothing is changing quickly, in spite of what we read of free and open elections."

There was a long moment of silence at the table as each person digested this pronouncement. Finally, Karl spoke. "At least VandenBosch is getting to enjoy the paintings. I just wish they were hanging on our walls." Another long pause, and then, once again, he voiced the need for an honest smuggler.

At this, Hana sat up in her chair. "Oh, how could I have forgotten to tell you this," she said, suddenly animated. Hana explained that she had told some Czech friends about the paintings and the problems her family was facing getting them out of Prague. "Someone mentioned a contact, a man who has brought art from Czechoslovakia to Canada on several occasions."

Karl was out of his seat in a flash. "Who is he?" he demanded. "How do I get in touch with him?"

"I'll find out his name and how to contact him," Hana replied. "My friend was a bit vague with the information, but I'll follow up."

A day later, Hana telephoned Karl. "His name is Theofil Král," she said. "That's all I have – a name and not much information. But you won't believe this. He lives here in Toronto and practically around the corner from your house!"

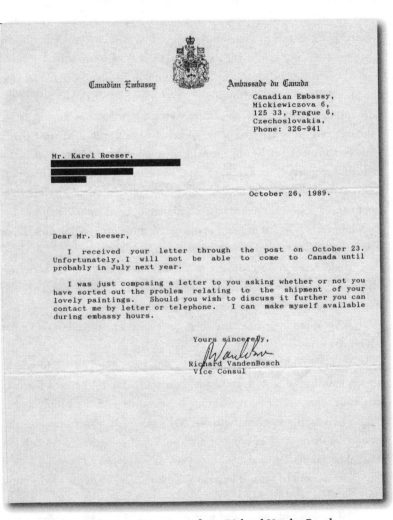

One of the many letters sent from Richard VandenBosch
in Prague to Karl in Toronto.

CHAPTER TWENTY-FOUR

Toronto, February 14, 1990

THERE WAS NO SNOW falling outside the front window of Karl's home that February evening. Tiny flakes of ice crystals practically danced off of tree branches, and then hung in the gray twilight of the setting sun before disappearing, swallowed up by the swirling wind. Karl, Phyllis, Hana, and Paul sat in silence, staring at the frost-covered streets, awaiting the arrival of Theofil Král, the man who had quickly become known simply as "the smuggler." Karl had had a short telephone conversation with him several nights earlier, after Hana had managed to track down his contact information. In that conversation, Karl had talked briefly about the paintings and the need to get them out of Czechoslovakia expeditiously. Král had expressed interest in the project, promising nothing and giving little information about himself. He had agreed to meet with Karl and his family.

"He didn't say that he'd do it, did he?" asked Phyllis. "I mean, he didn't actually commit to going to get the paintings."

Karl shook his head. "But he didn't say he wouldn't do it, either – not like all the others contacts I've made."

"Did you tell him everything?" asked Hana. "I mean about the Canadian embassy and VandenBosch?"

"I only gave him the basics, but think I told him enough," Karl shrugged. "At least this fellow has agreed to talk with us face-to-face. That must be a good sign, don't you think?"

The others nodded tentatively. It was far too soon to get their hopes up. Karl rose from his chair and looked out the window, checking for the umpteenth time to see if there was any sign of their guest. The biggest surprise, of course, was that this smuggler lived in Toronto and close to the Reesers. After having scoured the globe for months, who would have ever imagined that the man offering the best prospect of getting the paintings out of Prague lived within a stone's throw away – was practically a neighbor?

"That must be a good sign too, wouldn't you say?" Karl asked. "Perhaps an omen that this man is the one who will help us."

The doorbell rang suddenly and the dog let out a soft growl. "Quiet, Quinta!" Karl commanded. He rose quickly, as did the others, and moved to welcome their guest. Introductions were made and then Theofil Král settled on the long sofa facing Karl and the members of his family.

Karl quickly sized up his guest. Král was a young man of medium height and build and engagingly good looking. Karl guessed him to be in his early thirties, though he might have been younger; he had piercing blue eyes, disheveled blond hair, and the kind of face that could find a place in several generations. His clothes were expensive but thrown together, as if he didn't really care one way or the other about his appearance. And yet his strong frame carried the look well.

Theo Král graciously accepted tea and cookies from Phyllis. "Thank you," he said warmly. "And please call me Theo. I appreciate your hospitality. I'm not often served in this way."

That's probably a lie, Karl thought wryly. Theo looked like the sort of man who had people waiting on him all the time. But he *was* charming, and completely composed, and Karl appreciated that. In fact, as far as first impressions went, Karl liked what he saw in front of him, a young man of radiant confidence and casual elegance. This was someone who knew his way around the world and probably could hold his own in all kinds of company.

Theo sat back in his chair and in the spotlight of the family's gaze, allowing himself to be appraised, almost like a piece of artwork. He seemed accustomed to the scrutiny – perhaps he reveled in it. A few more minutes passed with informal chitchat about the weather and the odd coincidence of Theo's proximity to the Reeser home. Karl was the first one to launch into the interview.

"What part of Czechoslovakia are you from?" he asked. Although Theo's Czech accent was refined from the years he had spent living abroad, his roots were undeniable.

"I'm from Prague," he replied. "I haven't lived there in years, though I do go back as often as my business requires."

Karl paused. They would get to Theo's business dealings soon enough. There was much to learn about this man and his intentions. Slowly but surely, and under the examination of Karl and the others, Theo began to fill in the relevant pieces of his life. He had been born in Prague in 1952, the son of affluent parents, and raised in a life of privilege.

"My parents still live there, which is another reason I return often."

"I'm sure you, like so many others, were happy to get out," Karl said.

Theo shook his head. "It was not so difficult for me. I was a member of the Communist party. Everyone was," he added. "It was the only way to live a relatively easy life, and it came in handy over the years. The secret police were not really an issue for me as they were and are for others," he said easily.

At this, Karl set down his coffee cup with a bang. "The secret police are more than just an irritation for those who are subjected to their methods of interrogation and terror," he declared. "People are always looking over their shoulders to see who is following. They wait for the pounding on the door late at night, for men in long leather coats to search their homes without warning. Everyone watches their back. No one is trusted."

"This is not a life," commented Paul bitterly. It was particularly hard for Karl's brother-in-law, after having experienced the horrors of Hitler's concentration camps, to be lenient about the current Czech regime – or of anyone who might be part of it, no matter what their motive or background.

"Yes, of course," Theo replied. "The Communists learned a lot from Hitler. Wasn't it Joseph Goebbels who once said, 'If you tell a lie big enough and keep repeating it often enough, people will eventually come to believe it.' That was and is the mantra of the party – spreading propaganda, inducing fear, controlling the masses."

"Surely you don't condone the activities of the Communists," said Karl. "The party has stripped the country of its freedom and created zombies of its population."

Theo shrugged. "I believe in doing whatever one must in order to get by. Surely you, of all people, understand that, Mr. Reeser. How else would your family have gotten out of Europe before the war?"

Karl reacted quickly and vehemently to this. "It's one thing to use one's resources in order to survive," he replied. "But I would never have joined forces with the enemy. Not that we as Jews would have been given that chance."

"I can't say I believe in what the Communists have done," Theo replied, choosing his words carefully. "Let's just say that I have used my party affiliations to my advantage."

Karl weighed Theo's response, once again taking stock of the man who sat in front of him. It didn't surprise him to learn that Theo had been a member of the Communist party. Nor did it shock and horrify him. If you lived in Czechoslovakia, you were either part of the system or persecuted by it. But could he trust Theo, a man who clearly harbored his own interests above all others? Then again, perhaps Theo was the perfect man for the job – someone who knew the workings of the Czech regime from the inside.

"What did you do in Czechoslovakia?" Hana asked. "What kind of job did you have?"

Theo smiled. "I studied film at the film academy in Prague, and worked for the Czech film studio. It was a good job, complete with many perks that came from being a trusted party member."

"The Communists have eyes everywhere," said Karl, ruefully. He surmised from Theo's cryptic response that, within this position, Theo had likely acted as an informer for the government. Theo smiled again but did not reply.

"Then why did you leave?" asked Phyllis. "It sounds as if you had a good life back there."

Theo turned his attention to Karl's wife. "Some left to pursue freedom. I left for adventure," he replied. "It was time for some. My life was good, but when a friend of mine proposed that we try to make our fortune in Canada, it sounded like a good idea. And I was ready for something different. I jumped on a Czech airline plane and flew to Toronto, arriving here about twelve years ago." Theo paused, recalling the difficulties he had had in the early days after leaving Prague.

"My first job here in Toronto was as a broker for an insurance company." He shook his head, laughing softly. "A desk job was certainly not what I was cut out for." It was tedious, and Theo yearned for the social connections and easy life that he had abandoned. "So I eventually left the insurance business and returned to the arts community that I had left behind in Prague. That's when things took a turn for the better."

"And now?" asked Karl. "What is it that you do here? I mean, what actual business are you in?" He was still skirting the issue of art smuggling. That discussion would come soon enough.

"I work for a small private art gallery here in Toronto," Theo replied. He went on to explain his role as coordinator of the exhibits. In the early 1980s, art was once again becoming profitable, and Theo began to thrive in a community of artistic intellectuals who loved fine wine, good books, and beautiful people as much as he did.

He spoke easily and confidently. His eyes moved across the people in the room, resting momentarily on their faces, engaging each one in his gaze before moving on to the next. He chose his words carefully, but did not skirt the questions that were thrown his way. He was honest about his past Communist affiliations and candid about his history and his current situation. There was nothing for Theo to hide. He documented the events of his life with the flourish of a seasoned storyteller. "I can tell you that my art openings are known across the city. Musicians, poets, and even businessmen and politicians flock to the gallery," he concluded, adding that he loved moving within high society's inner circle. "It reminds me of Prague without the political irritations and tedium." At that he chuckled irreverently. It was only after he had achieved this success within the Toronto arts community that Theo had thought about returning to Czechoslovakia.

"I knew that I could find art there that was inexpensive," he continued. "I figured that if I could bring it to Canada and have it restored, it would sell for a good price. That's exactly what began to happen."

It was not easy to enter Czechoslovakia as a former citizen who had chosen to leave. In order to travel there in the early 1980s, Theo first had to cancel his Czech citizenship and then apply for an entry visa. He traveled to the Czech embassy in Montreal with his old passport, where he filled out the appropriate forms and was quickly stripped of his Czech citizenship. Next, he applied for a pardon from the government. This was granted immediately. Finally, with his pardon in hand, he applied for a visa, which was also granted. Given the circumstances of his expulsion from the Communist Party, Theo had been surprised at how easy it had been to get accepted back into the fold. Perhaps his brother-in-law, still a top-ranking member of the government, had pulled some strings.

"Art was cheap then," continued Theo. "And I knew what I was looking for, old classics that were in high demand with Canadian art collectors."

"But how did you ever get the paintings out?" asked Karl. "Surely the Czech government and the National Gallery wanted their cut." He did not have to explain to this man the hoops that one needed to jump through in order to export goods of value.

Theo nodded. "I knew what to choose," he replied. "Things that the gallery would easily grant approval for. And I made friends," he added. "Without saying too much, I can tell you that this is where my strength lies. And friendships in the right places can mean more than position or even money, though that sometimes helps." Theo smiled easily and looked up to meet Karl's eyes with a level gaze. He settled back in his seat, once again allowing the family to study him.

There was that charm again, Karl thought as he returned Theo's smile. Charm and confidence were riveting character traits. They drew you in and held you captive in spite of yourself. This man had that power, Karl realized. Even in the silence of the next few minutes, all eyes were on Theo, magnetized by him and his charismatic personality.

"Now, I think it's time that we talk about your situation." Once again it was Theo who took charge of the conversation. "Tell me more about the art that you are hoping to get out of the country."

As he had done with so many others, Karl began to fill Theo in on the history of the four paintings. Theo interrupted Karl on a few occasions and asked specific questions about the exact whereabouts of the paintings and their size. Karl produced the photographs he had taken of the paintings and outlined their dimensions. Theo whistled under his breath as Karl remarked that the largest of the four, the painting of the forest fire, could fill almost half of one wall of his home. After having clarified their measurements, Theo moved on to establish who else besides Pekárek and VandenBosch knew about the paintings.

"You're sure about this?" he asked. "No one besides these two gentlemen has any information about the paintings?"

Karl shook his head. "There's a Canadian security guard at the embassy who signed the document verifying my ownership of the paintings. And the ambassador and chargé d'affaires, of course. They have full knowledge of our case. But other than those people, no one else knows." He hesitated and Theo looked at him questioningly. "I should probably tell you that I suspect that my correspondence with the vice consul may have been opened and examined." He went on to relate how a letter had arrived resealed, and how his friend's letters also appeared to have been tampered with. "I can't say for sure whether the secret police are inspecting our mail, but you should know everything there is to know."

Theo mulled over this information for a moment, recalling his own gifts and letters that occasionally arrived from Prague torn apart and hastily repackaged. "It doesn't surprise me, though I imagine the Communists may be more interested in mail that is leaving the Canadian embassy, and not what a private citizen such as yourself is sending there. It's good to know, at any rate."

Other than those questions, Theo remained relatively quiet during Karl's recitation, listening attentively and trying to take in all of the information.

"So you've thought of and explored every legal way to get the paintings out?" Theo finally asked when Karl had finished talking and had sat back in his chair.

Karl nodded. "I've tracked down possible sources from around the world. But I have had no success. Most people have refused even to meet with me. Until you."

"Can I ask what the paintings are worth?" asked Theo.

Karl hesitated. As far as he was aware, the paintings had never been formally appraised. Karl estimated that they might be worth a half a million dollars today, perhaps more. But that was not how he valued them. He explained this to Theo. "After everything my family has been through, the paintings represent so much more than money. My mother loved them right from the beginning. After the war ended, her first thought was to retrieve our family home and property. When she realized that that was impossible, she turned all of her energy and attention to these four paintings. To her, they represented our entire estate, and everything our family had lost during the war. My mother believed that if she could retrieve the paintings it would symbolize a restitution of all that the Nazis had stolen. Since the paintings resurfaced last year at Pekárek's, they've become rather an obsession for me, too." He paused and stared somberly at Theo. "They may be worth some money. But that's not what is important to us. If we can somehow manage to get them out of Czechoslovakia, it will be a vindication of sorts for everything my family had to sacrifice. My mother never wanted them separated just as she never wanted our family members to be apart from one another. To us, they have become quite simply priceless. Can you even begin to understand that?" His voice trailed off.

Theo nodded slowly. It's true that he was a businessman first and foremost, and he lived a life of calculation and risk, exploring new financial opportunities and determining what was in it for himself. This was something quite different. Here he was being asked to take on a project that centered on a personal quest, a mission of family reunification. He would have to put himself aside for this venture, and putting the needs of others above his own was by no means second nature to Theo. And yet, beneath the armor of finance and conquest, there was a humane and even selfless heartbeat. Righting the wrongs that had beset this family would require a magnanimous and noble gesture from Theo. And that, too, was somehow appealing. Besides, this chance to go to Prague and rescue this family's treasures was an exciting prospect, filled with the kind of adventure and danger that Theo frequently sought. Excitement and family restitution – an intoxicating combination.

"Can you help us?" asked Karl. He had reached the end of his rope. If this man were unable to offer assistance, Karl did not know what else he would do. He feared that the paintings would remain trapped inside Czechoslovakia, lost to his family forever.

Theo exhaled slowly and sat forward in his seat to face Karl. "It seems to me that there are two ways to get the paintings out of Prague. There's the legal way, of course. As you've described, it appears that you have exhausted that avenue. Then there is my way." Theo paused and looked around the room, his gaze taking in the members of the family one by one. "For that, you will have to trust that I am capable of doing this. I have a way to get your property out. I have the resources and I have the connections. I will bypass the legal channels and I will smuggle the paintings out for you."

There it was – the solution that Karl was looking for. For a moment no one spoke. Finally Karl broke the silence. "Is that really a possibility? How will you ever be able to do such a thing?"

"Let's just say that I have had experience with similar situations," Theo answered. "But that's all I can say. Better not to know too many details. Here is what I'm prepared to offer." Theo went on to explain that he had a trip planned to Czechoslovakia in a few weeks' time. "Some other business that I must attend to. I am prepared to combine my trip there with an excursion to rescue your paintings. It will cost you three thousand, five hundred dollars up front and thirty-five hundred more when I successfully deliver the paintings to you."

"And what if you fail?" Hana spoke up. Her eyes were narrow, and her voice had an unmistakable note of accusation and mistrust.

"The deposit is nonrefundable, if that's what you're asking," Theo replied evenly. "But I'm quite confident that I will be successful and you will have your paintings."

Again no one spoke. Karl turned eagerly to look at the faces of Phyllis, Hana, and Paul. Finally, someone was offering a solution – the only solution thus far to getting the paintings out of the country. He was ready to extend a handshake to Theo and seal the deal. Yet there was something in Hana's face that stopped him. Karl stared intently at his sister.

"Perhaps we should talk about this," she finally said.

Before Karl could utter another word, Theo jumped in. "Yes, by all means, discuss this as a family and let me know your verdict. I'm not leaving until mid-March. So you still have a few weeks to decide what you want to do. As soon as you've reached a decision one way or the other, you can be in touch with me. You have my contact information." He stood, signaling the end of the meeting and turned once more to Phyllis, bowing formally and reaching out to take her hand. "I thank you again for your hospitality," he said warmly as he left.

"I don't trust him!" Hana blurted as soon as the door closed and they were once again alone in the living room. "Who is this man, after all? And why would he be willing to take this risk for us? What's in it for him – besides the money?"

"He's a card-carrying Communist," added Paul. "You heard it from his own lips."

"And he's proud of it," Hana continued. "This is the man we're going to trust to bring out our belongings?" There were many things about Theo that put Hana off, including his sense of privilege and entitlement. "I don't find him charming at all," she added in response to Karl's appraisal.

"I find him arrogant. And who knows what might happen to Pekárek or even to VandenBosch if we involve this smuggler. We don't want to jeopardize either of them, do we?" To Hana, Theofil Král came across as overly confident – too charismatic, in fact, from his obsequious handshake, to his phony deference and his smooth, flattering demeanor.

Her husband was equally hesitant. "I also don't know if we should put our faith in his hands," Paul said. "For all we know, he could take the money and the paintings. You might never see either of them again."

"But what other choice do we have?" Karl asked in a hollow voice. He looked and felt worn out, exhausted from the emotional strain of having searched for a way out of this predicament for months now. Time was running out, and with it, all chances of being reunited with the art. Marie's dream of family restitution was slipping away. Theo Král was offering a solution, even if it was fraught with uncertainty. Karl knew it was a leap of faith to trust him. But Karl was willing to take the chance.

"Why can't you simply continue to pursue finding a legal avenue to retrieve the paintings?" Paul asked. "Perhaps we haven't exhausted every channel. With the fall of the Iron Curtain, it will only be a matter of time before the rules are relaxed. Why don't we just wait until that happens?" The cautious side of Paul emerged once more. But this time Karl would have none of it. He sprang from his chair and paced the living room.

"And how much time will that take?" he asked, fighting to control his growing agitation. "Another year? Two? Five? And what assurance do we have that things will change enough for us to be able to retrieve the paintings even if the border restrictions are loosened? I'm not getting younger – none of us are. Besides, who knows what will happen to the embassy in the next year, or where the paintings will end up if things are restructured there, as VandenBosch is suggesting." He paused and faced the others, reaching up to rub his eyes, weary from walking the tightrope he had been on since discovering that the paintings were there in Prague, waiting for him. "I have explored every conceivable alternative with no success. We have no more options. I say we go with this one." No one answered and, in the end, Hana and Paul left without the family having reached a resolution.

Karl was beside himself. He paced in the living room like a caged tiger long after Phyllis had gone to bed. Even Quinta tired of watching her master, and lay curled up on a corner of the sofa. But Karl could not be still. The conversation with Theo looped over and over in his mind like a movie reel replaying itself. It would certainly have been his first choice to find a legal way to retrieve the paintings from Czechoslovakia. But that was not an option. Theo's offer was the only viable solution, and Karl was ready and willing to put his trust into this stranger's hands. He had no basis for this faith. Why should he trust a man with whom he had no relationship? The fact that Theo was arrogant didn't matter to Karl the way it did to Hana. In fact, arrogance was probably a virtue in this case. It would take a fearless man to do the kind of work that Theo was clearly accustomed to doing. He knew nothing of Theo's background, and he had no idea if Theo was honest or deceitful. He was a self-proclaimed spy and a smuggler! That should have been warning enough. And yet Karl believed that this was the only path left to him, and Theo was the only man for the job.

This belief wasn't rational, he knew, and Karl was a logical man. His intuition here was spontaneous, and perhaps even reckless. But had his mother not been spontaneous when she hustled the family out of Czechoslovakia at the start of the war? If she had waited, if she had moved more cautiously, where would the family be now? Probably in the piles of ashes left from the death camps of Europe. Marie had acted on gut instinct. And Karl's gut was telling him that this was what he needed to do to fulfill his mother's mission. Yes, he was putting his trust in the hands of a total stranger. Yes, he was taking a big chance. But this simply felt right. By the time Karl went to bed, light was beginning to cast a soft glow on the horizon. He knew what he had to do.

After only snatches of restless sleep, Karl arose, being careful not to wake Phyllis. He dressed quickly and walked downstairs to his study where he sat down at the desk to compose a letter to Richard VandenBosch.

Dear Mr. VandenBosch:
The bearer of this letter is [Theofil Král], with whom I have entered
into an agreement to arrange for the shipment of the four paintings,
which I left in your custody last May.

Please accept this letter as your good and sufficient authorization to
hand the items over to [him].

Sincerely yours,
K. Reeser

Karl sealed the letter in an envelope and then left the house, locking
the door quietly behind him. He headed for the bank, where he withdrew
three thousand, five hundred dollars in cash. With the money and the
letter of authorization burning a hole in his pocket, Karl walked over to
Theo's apartment and knocked on the door.

"Mr. Reeser!" Theo greeted Karl warmly and invited him in.

Karl entered and stepped carefully over piles of books and clothing
before taking a seat in the living room. "I have your money and will pay
you the balance when you've brought me my paintings," he said.

Theo smiled and leaned forward. "Are you certain about this?" he
asked. "Not everyone in your family seemed eager to engage my services."

Karl nodded. "My sister is cautious. So am I, usually. But with respect
to reclaiming these paintings, I have never been more certain of anything
in my life. The answer is yes. I'm ready to go ahead with this and ready
to hire you for the job." He held Theo in a cool and confident stare and
then proceeded with the business at hand. "Let me explain again where
the paintings are and who you must meet with." He handed Theo the
letter of authorization and gave him the information regarding Richard
VandenBosch and his position at the embassy. Theo listened carefully,
noting the information and adding it to the growing list of details and
contacts that he was already beginning to amass for the journey. Suddenly,
he stopped and looked up at Karl.

"The Canadian diplomat – what did you say his name was again?"

"Richard VandenBosch." Karl spelled the name for Theo. "He's the vice consul at the embassy. I owe a huge debt of gratitude to him already for everything he's done to help me. He's become quite a hero to me."

Theo paused again, staring off in a moment of reflection. Then a smile slowly crossed his face as he turned his gaze to meet Karl's. "VandenBosch," he repeated. "I assume he's Dutch."

Karl nodded. "His family is. Why? Do you know him?"

"Not exactly," Theo replied, slowly and deliberately. "But there's a connection here that is quite simply wonderful. You see, I happen to be a huge fan of the work of the Dutch painter, Hieronymus Bosch. He's a hero of mine, in fact. Don't you see?" he asked in the face of Karl's quizzical look. "Vanden*Bosch* and Hieronymus *Bosch* – our two heroes. These men share a common last name – Bosch! Perhaps this is an omen," he added jubilantly. "A sign that I was destined to take on this project."

Karl thought about this for a moment, and then smiled, nodding his head. "I believe in omens as well," he finally replied. "Let's hope it also means that you are destined to succeed."

There was only one last thing to do. Karl reached into his pocket once more and withdrew the envelope of cash. With no hesitation, he extended his arm and placed the money in Theo's hands. "These paintings became the focus of my mother's attempts to regain our property when everything else was unattainable," Karl said. "She did everything she could to achieve that goal and she was unsuccessful. Please don't fail us now." Theo accepted the payment and laid it on the coffee table between them, waiting for any further instructions.

"You understand what this means to me and to my family?" asked Karl.

Theo nodded.

"When will you be back?"

"March 21," Theo replied. "I will call you then."

CHAPTER TWENTY-FIVE

Toronto, February 15, 1990

THEO CLOSED THE DOOR behind Karl, picked up the money from the coffee table, and walked into his bedroom in the back of the apartment. He counted the cash that Karl had given him, replaced it in the white envelope, and then deposited it into his bedside table, closing the drawer with a soft thump while his mind mulled over the job ahead of him. Thirty-five hundred dollars was a decent advance for the kind of assignment that he was about to undertake, although, in truth, most of it would be used to fund this venture. The thirty-five hundred waiting for him at the end of the job would be even sweeter, though he couldn't think about that just yet. There was too much to do, too many details to work out before he could imagine enjoying the final reward. Yes, he had taken valuable artwork out of Czechoslovakia for some time, under the noses of State Security and the National Gallery. But the paintings that this family was trusting him to retrieve sounded bigger and certainly more valuable than any he had smuggled to date. He would have to make sure that all of the elements for this project were perfectly lined up, all of his trusted contacts in place, all of the equipment ready for the transport.

There was a lot to do and not much time before he was due to leave for Prague. How convenient, he thought, that this business trip was already in place. His passport was up to date, and he had already secured a visa. No one would suspect his other motive for this particular venture. He was already a familiar face in the Czech art scene. It had become an effective cover for adding those extra pieces of artwork to his shipments – those that would not pass the scrutiny of the National Gallery. The paintings that the Reeser family had talked about certainly fell into that category.

Theo went over the conversation he had had with the family. He liked Karl. He was sincere, passionate, and clearly driven to right a wrong that had been imposed on his family. There was more at stake here than just four valuable paintings. Karl had called it family restitution and Theo admired him for devoting himself to reclaiming what was rightfully his. He sensed that Karl respected him in return, though he certainly didn't get the same feeling from Karl's sister or her husband. At that, Theo shrugged. It appeared that Karl was the one driving this mission, his employer, in a sense, and that was what mattered most.

The telephone rang shrilly, and Theo moved to the bedside table to answer it. "Hello," he said, distracted.

"I thought you were avoiding me." The voice on the other end was low and seductive, but unfamiliar.

"Darling!" Theo exclaimed. "Why do you think I would ever avoid you?" He closed his eyes momentarily, wracking his brain to place the voice.

"Oh, I don't know. Perhaps it's the fact that you haven't called in several weeks, not since the night you took me to the opera. Ring a bell? As I recall, you said I was the most fascinating part of the evening."

Ah, now he remembered! He had met this woman at a dinner hosted by another friend in the arts community. Theo had been seated next to her at the dinner table. She had cat-like green eyes that shifted in the dim candlelight like a kaleidoscope held to the light. Theo had been taken with her exotic beauty and she in turn had fallen victim to his charm. By the end of the evening, he had invited her to the opening night of the opera with tickets his host that night had provided. He recalled entering the theater and sinking into the plush red velvet seats. As soon as the lights dimmed, he felt his head begin to nod and his eyes grow heavy. Before long, he was dozing and the music blended into a background of sounds that drifted in and out of his consciousness. His date woke him at the end of the performance. The evening, however, had not been a total disappointment. He had managed to convince this woman to come back to his apartment.

"It's wonderful to hear your voice," Theo replied. He chose to ignore the reprimand, focusing instead on his memory of the passionate night they had shared. He had not deliberately abandoned her after that. Things had gotten busy at the gallery, though that was never an excuse for Theo to neglect a romantic diversion. It was simply that in the meantime he had met his current companion – the woman from the gallery opening.

"You won't think it's so wonderful when you hear what I have to say." The tenor of her voice had taken a turn. Theo heard the sharp edge creep into her tone and he braced himself slightly for what was to come. Anger? Tears? Admonitions? He had seen and heard them all, and had dealt with every conceivable fallout from the relationships he had left in his wake.

"Five thousand dollars. Sound familiar? I lent you the money and I'm still waiting for you to repay me." By now her voice dripped with sarcasm and disdain.

It was all coming back to him now. After their night together, he had convinced this woman to loan him money that he had said he needed to restore another painting at the gallery. He had promised her that the loan was short term, a brief cash flow problem that would soon be remedied by the sale of this particular work of art and the profit that he expected to make. While some of the money had indeed been used for the refurbishment of the painting, the bulk of it had been used for a number of other activities, including the restocking of his wine cabinet. It also helped to have some of that cash on hand for his upcoming trip to Prague.

"In fact, I was just thinking about you," Theo lied. It was time for some quick thinking and quicker talking. He understood that the sting this woman was feeling for having been abandoned by him was sharper for the fact that he had also milked her for a substantial amount of money. "You'll be happy to know that the restoration of that painting we discussed is almost complete. It took longer than I had anticipated, so in fact that particular work of art hasn't yet come up for auction." He couldn't actually remember whether the painting had already sold or not. It didn't really matter one way or the other. "So I'm hoping you'll be patient for a little while longer. I haven't forgotten about you, so please don't be angry with me." His voice was honey now. "We shared a wonderful time together, and you *will* be repaid. You just have to trust me on this."

"You expect me to trust you? I think that was my mistake the last time."

It was time to end this call. Theo had too many other things to do. "I'm leaving for a trip in a few weeks. I'll be gone for about a week. You'll have your money when I return." With that, he said good-bye, cutting off any final protests, and hung up the receiver. Then he quickly dialed another number and waited for a voice to pick up on the other end. "Hello, it's Theo," he said when the line was answered. "Listen, I have a favor to ask – a loan of a few thousand dollars, if you wouldn't mind." He paused and listened for the response. "No, it's not for me. It's for another friend – a charming lady I know."

It was tempting to ignore the woman's demand for the return of the money he had borrowed. In other circumstances he might have done just that, simply playing for time and letting so much of it pass that the loan and the fury associated with it would disappear. But this woman was someone who might come in handy again, he reasoned, and this was a relationship that was worth salvaging. Who knew when extra cash might become necessary? So Theo did what he often did in these circumstances. He sought out another friend to repay the first debt, borrowing from Peter to pay Paul, as the saying went.

"That's wonderful!" Theo replied to the good news on the other end of the line. "I'll pay you back. I promise. And when I get back from my business trip, we must go out for a drink. It's on me." He laughed out loud and hung up the phone, sitting back for another minute before reaching over to dial the telephone once more. He needed to begin to inform colleagues and clients that he would be going away in March.

As he connected with one colleague after another, he reflected again on the details of his upcoming trip. There was one part of the Reeser family saga that troubled him deeply, though it was something that he had not mentioned to Karl. The involvement of the Canadian embassy complicated things in many ways, some of which Theo himself couldn't foresee. If the paintings had still been hidden with Jan Pekárek, Theo knew that he would have been able to go into Prague, secure them from Jan, and get them out of the country using the resources he frequently mobilized for these ventures. It would not be so simple, however, to slip the art out of the embassy. Theo knew all too well that the secret police and other watchdogs had regular surveillance on embassies throughout Prague, alert to any material or information that was coming or going. It wasn't the paintings themselves that might be under suspicion, though their value would certainly make them desirable. What heightened the danger here was the possible belief on the part of the Communists that the paintings might be a front for some elaborate espionage ring – that they might be a cover for other more important documentation that might be smuggled out of Czechoslovakia and into the hands of the enemy. America was already considered to be a foe of the state, and Canada was not far behind the U.S. in terms of the suspicion attached to it.

The Communists would very likely assume that hidden somewhere within the canvases were microchips containing information about their government. That was why the embassy would be a difficult site from which to extricate Karl's property. Any movement of goods would be watched and subject to seizure. And even if the secret police found nothing concealed within the paintings, the artwork itself would be destroyed in the search, and Theo would certainly be jailed for his involvement. The stakes here were higher than Theo had ever faced, and he would have to be more alert and more vigilant than ever before.

He wondered briefly about the fact that Karl had suggested that his mail might be tampered with – that letters had arrived resealed. Should he worry about that? Probably not, though it was worth keeping in mind. The one thing that reassured him in all of this was that as dangerous as the Communists could be on the one hand, they were also bumbling fools on the other, easily seduced with the promise of money or favors, and Theo could muster plenty of both. He rose from the bed and glanced again at the bedside table where the advance from Karl was safely tucked away. For now, all he wanted to do was put his worries aside and focus on his plans for the upcoming trip. It was worth all of his attention.

CHAPTER TWENTY-SIX

Prague, March 15, 1990

THEO'S PLANE touched down in Prague one month after his first meeting with Karl in Toronto. He gathered his belongings to disembark in the city of his birth, joining the column of foreigners passing through customs inspection. He glanced to one side, noting the conspicuous presence of several men in dark coats eyeing the line of travelers, their faces impassive and yet intrusive at the same time. There was no mistaking the secret police. *No wonder people here sleep with one eye open*, Theo thought as he shifted his carry-on bag to the other shoulder and prepared his Canadian passport and the other necessary documents as his line wound closer to the official at the front. When he was finally motioned forward, he greeted the customs guard in his native language, speaking Czech naturally and with ease. The border official raised an eye curiously.

"What is the nature of your trip?" he asked, his voice and stare penetrating.

There is nothing subtle about these guards, thought Theo. *They enjoy using their position of power to intimidate citizens and visitors alike.* Theo returned the stare, though being careful to show a measured respect for the man. *No need to provoke.* "I'm here on business," he replied, evenly and cordially.

"And the nature of your business?"

"Art. I'm here to purchase paintings for some clients in Canada – with the permission of the National Gallery, of course. Canadians love European artwork," he added, leaning in and smiling slightly as he turned on the charm. "They have nothing in the West that compares with ours."

The guard paused briefly and then nodded his head in agreement. *Bait extended and received*, thought Theo happily as the official stamped his passport and motioned him through. "Enjoy your stay," he added.

Theo returned the welcome with an exaggerated and derisive salute. The guard didn't seem to notice.

Luggage in tow, he hailed a cab to take him to the Aria Hotel, a beautiful historical residence in the Castle district, and the place he regularly frequented on his trips to Prague. En route, he glanced out the window, taking stock of the city. There was a mystical quality here that always seized Theo in the initial minutes of his arrival. Prague was a city built on legends and magic. Horror films often mentioned Prague as the birthplace of vampires. Every street in the old town had its ghosts, every castle was haunted, every church claimed a poltergeist. The people of Prague often asserted that the streets moved around. Gates would suddenly appear in a wall leading to a never-before-seen garden. Spires were alleged to materialize on the top of towers. There was even said to be a house at the end of Golden Lane in the Castle district that appeared only on certain nights and marked the bridge between what could be seen and what was invisible. Theo never for a minute believed that the streets of Prague could really move. Prague was, after all, a city full of alleyways, manifold steps, and little-known detours. The most seasoned traveler could easily become disoriented in the maze. But the mystery of this place did captivate him and fed his belief in all things spiritual.

"Ah, Mr. Král. Welcome back!" The desk clerk of the hotel greeted Theo like an old friend.

"It's nice to see you again," replied Theo. "Is my usual room ready?"

"Of course," the clerk said, nodding courteously. "And I've provided a nice bottle of red wine for you as well," he added, knowing that there would be a substantial tip waiting for him at the end of Theo's stay if all was in order. "How long will you be with us this time?"

"A week, if all goes as planned," Theo said. "I'll need to rent a car while I'm here."

The clerk nodded. "I'll arrange to have one here for you tomorrow morning. Let me know if there is anything else I can get for you."

At that, Theo chuckled. There was usually little to be had in Prague unless you had sources in the black market – which he did. With money and connections, anything was attainable: fine wine, good food, even beautiful women. But that would have to wait until his business was done.

He deposited his luggage in his room and sank down onto the bed, reaching into his pocket to remove a small address book. Flipping through the pages, he finally reached the name he was looking for. Then he lifted the telephone receiver and asked the front desk to dial the local number.

"Hello! It's Theo Král," he exclaimed when the line was answered. "Yes, I'm here for a few days and would like to meet. Shall we say four this afternoon? I have an interesting project I'm working on." He paused, listening to the reply. "Yes, I knew you would find that intriguing. See you soon."

He had a few hours to kill before his appointment and he lay back on the bed to rest, closing his eyes and taking a long, deep breath. But sleep would not come. There were too many details facing Theo over the next few days – a labyrinth of minutiae that his mind was working through, challenging even *his* penchant for order. Dizzy with facts and particulars, he finally sat up. Perhaps a walk would be a better way to clear his head.

It was cold outside and so damp that the air felt wet against his face. Instinctively, he pulled the collar of his coat up to protect his neck and bent his head forward against the moist wind. The city seemed endlessly bleak beneath a blockade of low, dense clouds. But, despite the dreary weather, there was a sense of fresh developments here. You could see it in the new constructions which had picked up since Theo's last trip to Prague.

And you could sense it in the anticipation on the faces of the citizens who raced past on the city streets. Czechoslovakia was gearing up for its first democratic elections since 1946. But it was hard to imagine how the country would achieve full democratization. The Communist hold on the country was extensive. Social, economic, environmental, and other problems had accumulated over forty years of oppressive rule. Things felt uncertain, as if people didn't know what to expect but hoped for the best. But Theo couldn't be distracted by any of this. He had a job to do. Besides, it really didn't matter to him one way or the other how the politics of the country might evolve.

He checked his watch. It was almost time for his rendezvous and he quickened his pace, finally arriving at a small café almost hidden from view down a narrow cobblestone laneway.

"Mr. Král! Why so long since your last visit?" The owner greeted him warmly as soon as he stepped through the front door.

Theo returned the welcome. "Is my usual table available? I'm meeting someone and want a bit of privacy."

"Of course. This way," the restaurateur replied, leading Theo to a small table in a back corner. Cigarette smoke darkened the room like a black cloud passing across the sun's face. Without asking, the waiter brought over an espresso and a slice of cake layered with chocolate butter cream and topped with thin caramel slices – a local specialty. Theo smiled gratefully and sat back to await the arrival of his colleague. Minutes later, a familiar figure burst through the door. He spied Theo at the back and made his way over to greet him.

"I see you've started without me," the man exclaimed, indicating to the waiter that he would have the same as Theo.

"It's good to see you, Adolfo," said Theo, standing and reaching out to grasp the hand of the man who faced him. "I see you haven't stopped enjoying the wonderful desserts that Prague has to offer."

Theo's guest sat down and smiled, patting his rather ample middle. "These tortes will be the death of me," he said. "But what a way to go."

Adolfo Flores was as young as Theo, though one would not have guessed from his badly out of shape frame and thinning hair. He pulled out a package of cigarettes, offering one to Theo, who declined. It was one habit he was glad he had never taken up. Adolfo dragged deeply on the cigarette and coughed loudly into his jacket sleeve. "I thought our Spanish cigarettes were bad. But these Czech ones are truly disgusting. I vow everyday to give them up, but..." He shrugged, shaking the ash off the tip into an already overflowing ashtray. "At least they're cheap, whether you buy them on the black market or not."

"How are things at the Peruvian embassy, my friend?" asked Theo after Adolfo's order had arrived and they had settled down to exchange pleasantries. Adolfo was a low-level diplomat whom Theo had met at a gathering during one of his earlier trips to Prague. The evening had been hosted by a friend of the family who had connections with embassy diplomats across the city. In making the rounds, Theo had been introduced to Adolfo, and had discovered that he had a curiosity about art that matched his own. He had also ascertained Adolfo's interest in making some extra money on the side, provided that it wasn't too risky. "I have some benefits as an embassy official," he had told Theo. "And I'm happy to extend them to you for the right project." Adolfo had been helping Theo move art since that initial meeting. Their association had been profitable for both.

"All of the embassies are up in the air about what will happen over the next months, or what our roles will be if and when the election takes place."

"Amazing to think it's all changing," interjected Theo. "It took forty years for Communism to take root in this country and ten days for it to fall."

"Don't fool yourself into thinking it's over," cautioned Adolfo. "Some people think it's all a conspiracy – that this so-called peaceful revolution was engineered by the secret police here and the KGB in Moscow."

"Some people are just paranoid," Theo replied, though his mind flashed to an image of the men in dark coats standing by at the airport to *welcome* visitors.

"Do you blame them for their mistrust?" Adolfo placed a forkful of torte into his mouth. Cake crumbs and flecks of cream flew as he brandished his fork in the air. "When we step out onto the street after our little social get-together here, look to your left. There's a car parked there with blackened windows. When I passed it earlier, I was certain that I saw the shadow of a camera on the inside pointed this way."

Theo shrugged. "Luckily, they can't do anything to you. And I'm sure they're not interested in me."

Adolfo stared. "Don't be so cocky, my friend," he cautioned. "At any rate, I'm still here for a short while – a few more months at least. But after that, who knows?" He shrugged once more. "You mentioned a business proposition that might intrigue me. Well, let's hear it. It may be the last one we work on together."

Theo smiled. "As usual, I need you to transport some cargo for me out of the city." Instinctively, he lowered his voice and glanced around. The walls often had ears, and while he knew his way around the Communists and their police watch dogs, there was no point in being reckless.

"Have you found something of value?" asked Adolfo.

"I think so. Actually, I am doing a favor for a family," Theo replied. "This time, the paintings aren't for me." He briefly filled Adolfo in on the details of Karl's story and the resurfacing of the paintings. "I haven't seen them yet – only photographs – but I understand they are quite valuable – *and* rather large," he added. This would be an important factor in determining how and when they might be transported. "This family in Canada is desperate to have them back."

Adolfo frowned. "Doing a favor for a family? Don't tell me that you're going soft on me," he joked.

Theo shrugged. "I like the man who has asked me to help," he said. "And if I can assist his family, then why not?" he asked, turning his attention back to Adolfo. "Besides, you know I'm a sucker for some thrills, and this project offers plenty. But don't worry, my friend," he added. "You and I will benefit from this business deal. I promise you that."

"Now that's what I like to hear," Adolfo replied.

The two men huddled together to discuss the details of the retrieval and transport of the paintings. "I'm hoping to return to Toronto by the middle of next week," Theo said. This would give him six days to complete his work here. It would be tight and would depend in part on Adolfo's availability.

Adolfo nodded thoughtfully. "I can manage that. I'll arrange with my embassy to take a drive across the border into Germany. I'm assuming that's where you will want me to take these paintings?"

Theo nodded. One of the reasons that Adolfo Flores had become such an integral part of these operations was that, as a member of an embassy in Prague, he had access to a vehicle with diplomatic license plates. The plates would ensure that whoever was driving the car would be able to leave the country without being searched at the border. There was of course the possibility that if border officials suspected anything amiss, the car might be turned back and not allowed to cross into Germany. But the Peruvian embassy was fairly low-profile in Prague, and would not likely be considered a threat to the government. There were other embassies that were on the radar of the secret police, but not this one. Theo had known this when he had chosen to make Adolfo his accomplice. Besides, at this point, he couldn't think about the possibility that the car might be stopped at the border. First things first: he had to have the car with the right plates, and Adolfo was the one who could provide that.

"By the way," Adolfo said, reaching for another cigarette. "Where is this valuable artwork right now?"

Theo hesitated, weighing his response. There were some things that even this accomplice might not need to know. Finally, he shrugged and replied, "They're at the Canadian embassy. There is a diplomat there who is helping out with all of this."

Adolfo whistled softly under his breath. "Could be a problem for you, no? If you think they're watching everyday citizens, just imagine the surveillance on the embassies. If you move something out, they'll be on you like vultures on a carcass."

"That's not your worry," replied Theo. "I'll take care of getting the paintings to you. Your job will be to get them out of the country." He reached into his pocket and pulled out his wallet, extracting five hundred dollars in new American bills and sliding them across the table to his accomplice. Adolfo glanced around, and then reached for the money, pocketing it quickly.

"And the other half when I meet you on the other side, my friend," continued Theo as Adolfo placed the last piece of cake into his mouth. "I'll call you when I have the artwork and we can arrange for its delivery to you. Here's to a successful transaction."

The two men finished their coffees, shook hands, and went their separate ways.

The next day, Theo rose early to the sound of construction workers and traffic outside his hotel window. He gulped down a quick breakfast and left the hotel to find the car he had asked for waiting for him outside the front doors. He climbed in and headed out of the city center to meet with a contact in the area of Kubánské Square, a quiet residential part of Prague.

Parking his car close to the busy intersection, he quickly located the small dry goods store at one corner. Entry to the apartment was through the store and up some stairs at the back. Theo didn't know the proprietor of the store, though he had seen him in his previous visits here. The man was a gatekeeper to the apartments above, and Theo assumed that his contact upstairs paid him a kickback of some kind to let visitors through and not ask any questions.

Notwithstanding the early hour, there was already a long line-up of people waiting to get into the shop. Theo bypassed the line, ignoring the angry glares of would-be shoppers, and entered the dimly lit store. The owner was in a heated discussion with an elderly gentleman who held some worn wires in his hand, obviously desperate for some supplies that were not available. In fact, the shelves of this store were completely devoid of goods, a consequence of the Communist government and its regulated shopping. Not only was it empty of supplies, but even the shelves and display cabinets themselves looked as if they were leftovers from another era. Dust filled Theo's nose. The building was worn and dirty, as if it had been neglected for years.

He moved quickly through the store, catching the eye of the owner who was trying unsuccessfully to appease the disgruntled shopper. The man raised his head and stared suspiciously at Theo. Then, recognizing him, he nodded briefly and returned to his discussion with his customer. Theo entered a dark staircase at the rear. As he climbed the steps, he thought back to the telephone conversation he had had earlier that morning with Richard VandenBosch. He had been put through to VandenBosch's office immediately.

"Mr. VandenBosch, my name is Theofil Král. I am a friend of Karl Reeser in Toronto, Canada." He had waited, half expecting to hear a click on the telephone indicating that the line was being monitored. "I am here at Mr. Reeser's request to pick up some things that I believe he left with you." He chose his words thoughtfully, being careful not to mention the embassy by name.

There was a momentary pause and then the voice of a jubilant Richard VandenBosch had boomed back in Theo's ear. "It's good to hear from you," he had exclaimed. "I've been waiting for this moment for some time." He too was vague and prudent in his reply. "When can you come here? The sooner the better," he added.

Theo had thought for a moment, weighing how much time he would need to gather the necessary materials to make the bundling and transport of the paintings possible. "I have a bit of business still to do here in the city," he had finally replied. "I can come to meet you on Tuesday, March twentieth." He knew this was cutting it close if he still wanted to leave that same night to be back in Toronto on the twenty-first. But it would be better not to hold on to the paintings for any longer than was necessary. Pick them up at the embassy, deliver them to Adolfo, and get out of the city. That was his plan, provided that there were no hitches.

"The twentieth it is," VandenBosch had replied, and the two men had hung up.

There were four doors at the top of the staircase. Theo approached the second one on the left. He knocked lightly and, a moment later, the door opened and a wizened old man greeted him and ushered him into a small, sparsely furnished one-bedroom flat. Despite the cold outside, it was stifling in the room. An old floor fan whirred noisily from a corner, but it didn't help. The air was hot and stagnant. The man motioned for Theo to sit, and Theo perched himself on a wooden chair, nodding to his host's wife as she scurried past. She was a small, doughy woman, with an ample bosom and wide hips that wobbled as she walked across the floor of the room. She returned Theo's nod, and headed out the door.

"Is it busy downstairs?" the man asked. His ruddy face was as shriveled and dry as leather, but beneath the worn and faded clothing, there was a body hardened by years of labor. Theo gestured out the window at the growing horde of people lined up to get into the store below. "They line up every day, and for what?" the old man snarled. "A few screws, some laundry detergent, a light bulb if they're lucky. Maybe after the elections, when the country is finally able to privatize, things will be better and we'll actually have proper stores with a decent assortment of supplies." He shook his head in frustration and then turned back to Theo. "But enough of that. It's been a while since I've seen you. What can I do for you?"

"I need the usual transport containers," Theo replied, getting down to business. "Five of them." He pulled a scrap of paper from his pocket and began to jot down the dimensions of the containers he needed, spelling them out as he wrote. "One will be two meters long and about a half a meter in diameter."

"Bigger than usual," the man interrupted.

Theo nodded, thinking again to the size of the paintings that Karl had described. "The four others are regular size, a meter and a half high and also a half a meter in diameter. Make sure the aluminum is strong."

He handed the sheet over to the old man who reached out to take it with hands that were even more wrinkled and hardened than his face. Tiny beads of sweat lay on his forehead. He squinted at the scrap of paper, removed his glasses, and began to clean them with a worn handkerchief he pulled from his pocket. He rubbed the glasses methodically, holding them up to the light, and, finally satisfied, replaced them on his nose.

Theo watched and waited patiently through this ritual. This man had been supplying him with containers to transport art since Theo had begun doing business in Prague years earlier. They had met through a relative of Theo's, one who had Communist party connections. The man was a skilled blacksmith who worked for a company that manufactured eaves troughs for houses and also made electrical tubing. Theo had been looking for someone with access to these supplies and considered himself lucky to have found this capable craftsman. He knew nothing of this man's life – he didn't know his full name or age, though he looked ancient. They met here at his apartment each time Theo needed containers, so that they could discuss the details of the made-to-measure orders. It was safer to meet here rather than at the factory, where other workers or a nosy company boss might become suspicious of their discussion. Here in this man's home there was anonymity. No personal information needed to be exchanged, just business.

The man finished reviewing Theo's specifications, nodded, asked a few more questions about the size of the containers, and jotted some additional notes alongside Theo's scribbles on the piece of paper. No questions about their purpose; that was something he had never asked. What was important to him was that he knew he would be paid well for providing the materials and keeping his mouth shut.

"The four regular-size tubes will be delivered to the National Gallery," continued Theo. "The other one…" He paused. "I will pick up the other one myself."

The man shrugged and again said nothing.

"When can you have these ready for me?" asked Theo, thinking ahead to the meeting he had arranged with VandenBosch for the twentieth.

"It could take a while," the man replied. "It's the material. I can get it, but I have to be careful."

"Come on, my friend. I'm sure you can make this happen quickly," Theo said. "You've never let me down before."

The man shook his head. "You know that I have my own sources, but even they are stretched to the limit. I have to get the aluminum you're requesting, cut it to these sizes, and have it welded into the tubes. It all takes time if you want it done correctly. Is it urgent?" he asked, noting the look on Theo's face.

"The sooner the better," replied Theo, evenly, "but before the twentieth for sure. Don't forget how much I appreciate it when things are delivered on time." He raised a knowing eye and extended his hand. "You won't let me down, will you?"

The man sighed and grasped Theo's outstretched hand. "I'll make sure the work is completed to your specifications. And I'll call you at your hotel when it's ready to be picked up."

CHAPTER TWENTY-SEVEN

Toronto, February 1990

BACK IN TORONTO, Karl had finally confessed to Phyllis that he had withdrawn money from the bank to pay Theo Král to retrieve the paintings. Upon hearing that he had put his faith and resources into the hands of this art smuggler, Phyllis had thrown her hands up into the air. "I knew you would do whatever you wanted," she cried.

"Don't be angry with me," Karl replied, trying to placate his wife. "We can afford it."

"Do you think I care about the money?" she said. "It's not that."

"Then what?" asked Karl.

Phyllis shook her head in frustration. "It's this endless mission to get the paintings. You're consumed by it. When will it stop? When will you realize that you've done all you can do, that maybe they are simply unattainable."

Never! he thought, though he couldn't say that to Phyllis. He couldn't bear the notion – wouldn't acknowledge the possibility – that he might never retrieve his family's property. There was a long pause, and then Phyllis spoke, more gently this time.

"All of your determination," she began. "You know I think it's admirable. I just don't want you to be disappointed if this plan doesn't work."

Of course he would be disappointed, devastated in fact. But again, this was a possibility that he simply could not entertain. It was his certainty about this journey that kept him energized. It was the hope. Take that away from him, and there was nothing. He could not stop believing that he would get the paintings back. Still, Karl needed his wife's assurance and support – now more than ever.

"Please tell me you think it was the right decision to give Král our money," begged Karl.

This time, Phyllis laughed out loud. "I've always said that if it had been up to me, you would have never made the trip to Prague in the first place, you would have never gone to meet with Richard VandenBosch, and you would have never arranged a meeting with Theofil Král. You have more guts than anyone I know. Was this the right thing to do? Time will tell."

Explaining his decision to Hana and Paul was more difficult. Karl called his sister and arranged for her and her husband to come over. They gathered in the family room, where Karl once again confessed that he had paid Theo Král his advance asking price of three thousand, five hundred dollars.

Hana was astounded. "You actually paid him in cash?"

Karl nodded. "Král has gone. He says he will return on March twenty-first with the paintings. I'll pay the balance when he comes back."

"*If* he comes back!" interjected Paul.

"And *if* he brings the art," continued Hana. "You realize of course that he could return to Toronto and simply lie about all of this. He could say that he tried and failed to get the paintings. And he would still have half the amount of money and we would still be without our property!"

This was certainly true, thought Karl. And yet, he still felt strongly that he had done the right thing by entrusting Theofil Král with this mission. Hana opened her mouth to speak again, but no words came out. She clamped her jaw shut, sucking back any further reproach and sat, silently shaking her head. Paul was equally stunned and quiet.

"Hana," said Karl, moving closer to his sister, trying to articulate his thinking. "Please try to understand. I have a feeling. It's hard to explain what it is. Something tells me – my gut or my instinct – that this man is the one to make this happen. I like him." Hana looked away. "I know that seems ridiculous," continued Karl, "because I don't even know him. But it's true. He is straightforward – honest, if you will. I appreciate that."

"He's a thief!" exclaimed Hana. "Probably a con artist as well. That wasn't honesty, Karl. That was pulling the wool over our eyes. How could you be fooled by that?"

"I'm not asking you for any money, Hana," Karl continued. "This was my decision, my risk."

Hana was silent for another moment, and then she asked, "Did you at least get a receipt for the thirty-five hundred dollars?"

Karl paused and then burst into laughter. "Hana," he finally said, when he could catch his breath, "the man's a thief! You said it yourself. What good would a receipt do?"

The question hung in the air and then Hana started to chuckle. Paul joined in and then Phyllis, and soon the four of them were doubled over in laughter. The release felt good. It was something they all needed. In the end, Hana and Paul agreed to split the cost of the venture with Karl. "I may not agree with what you've done," said Hana. "But you know I support you one hundred percent. This can't be just your risk. It's for our family – for Mother and Father as well. We're in with you on this."

Karl nodded, too overwhelmed to speak, grateful to have his sister as an ally, even though she did not agree with his tactics. That was a tribute to their devotion to one another. It also added to the burden of responsibility. And Karl felt that resting even more heavily on his shoulders. He had put the wheels in motion and now he had nothing to do but stand aside and wait for events to unfold. March 21 – that was the day that Theo had said he would return. It was not that far away, and yet it seemed out of reach, as distant as the paintings themselves.

CHAPTER TWENTY-EIGHT

Prague, March 16, 1990

THE MOST IMPORTANT thing for Theo to do while in Prague was to go about his business as usual, and not to dwell too much on the four paintings. It was only when one broke with routine that the secret police and their goons became suspicious. Theo was here in Prague to buy art, and that's what he intended and needed to do. On the day of his visit to meet with the old man who would build his transport tubes, Theo had also made arrangements to meet with several families in the city. Over the last two years, he had cultivated a list of contacts here in the arts community. It hadn't been difficult. He had simply put out the message that he was interested in purchasing art, and those in that circle had responded. This trip was no different. Prior to leaving Toronto, Theo had circulated letters to his arts colleagues, informing them that he would be in Prague for a week and wanted to meet with private citizens with art to sell. A number of contacts had responded and Theo's list of potential clients had grown.

His first stop was at the home of a wealthy family who lived in the Nové Město, or New Town, district of Prague. The name was somewhat misleading. The area, close to Wenceslas Square, had actually been established in the fourteenth century, and was home to a diverse collection of luxurious homes, cafés, and shops. Theo parked his car in front of an old, impressive brick building and walked up the stone steps to the front door. He grasped the brass knocker and tapped lightly on the door. Hearing no sounds on the other side, he knocked again, louder this time. There were muffled footsteps on the other side of the door, and then it opened to reveal a middle-aged woman, elegantly dressed and nervously smoking a cigarette that dangled from her jewel-encrusted hand. Theo introduced himself, and she moved aside to allow him to enter. He stepped into a large, tiled entrance hall. Classical music played in the background. A crystal chandelier hung from the vaulted ceiling high above Theo's head. A large circular staircase faced him, secured by an ornately sculpted banister. The home reeked of wealth, an atmosphere that Theo was accustomed to. The woman had been joined by her husband and they led Theo to an adjoining sitting room where high windows were topped by smooth stone lintels. The walls here were covered in paintings of every size and style, an impressive array of watercolors, oils, and pencil drawings.

"We're trying to liquidate some assets," the man explained.

Theo didn't ask why. It wasn't his concern, and, in truth, he didn't really care about this family's motivation to sell their artwork. Their wealth identified them as loyal Communists in the inner circle, probably close to government officials. But he knew that families like this one were always desperate for more money, always looking for ways to improve their lot in life and climb even higher on the social ladder. Greed ran rampant among the wealthy in Prague. They wanted newer cars, bigger homes, and more possessions. In this sitting room alone, Theo noted the presence of Baroque furniture, crystal vases, and fine art that would impress a museum. But for families like this one, Theo knew, it would never be enough. And he could offer some cash to supplement their bank account and enhance their already excessive lifestyles.

"We're told that you have *connections* – a way to help us sell some of our art," the man continued. His wife remained silent, smoking furiously and watching the exchange from one side of the room.

At that, Theo smiled broadly. "I'm delighted to help you," he said warmly. "You must have so much on your mind these days. Why bother with government bureaucracy when I can take care of that for you?"

The man nodded enthusiastically, taken with Theo's assurances. "They do make it difficult at times, don't they?" he asked. "All that red tape, just to sell our own paintings abroad. We're desperate to buy a new car and we're having some difficulty raising the cash. Foreign cars are so bloody expensive and impossible to come by," he offered by way of meager explanation. At the time, there was only one company in Prague that could arrange for the import and sale of foreign, usually German, automobiles. A Mercedes-Benz was a highly coveted possession and a mark of wealth and position.

"And that's why I'm here," continued Theo. "I'm your middle man, if you will. I'll take the paintings off your hands and pay you a fair price to do so. It's as simple as that." He glanced over at the woman, who nodded gratefully and then went back to her cigarette, which was by now almost entirely consumed in ash. "Besides, I'm actually doing you a favor by buying your artwork," he continued as he gestured around the room. "Once these artists are listed in the catalogues of art houses around the world, the value of these paintings and the others that you have will only increase. So, over time, the worth of your estate will continue to rise."

With that, Theo went to work. He approached the walls, scrutinizing each painting, straining to see the artist and year that the work had been done. Sketches and watercolors were quickly rejected in favor of the oils. And only specific ones were on Theo's radar screen. He paused in front a painting, dated 1750, of a nymph-like woman lounging in a garden. The painter was German. This one would do, he thought, and so would several paintings by Czech artists of ladies and gentlemen socializing in various pastoral settings. There was a painted view of Venice from the same time period, as well as one by another Czech painter from the early nineteenth century. This one was more architectural; straight lines had supplanted the sensual shapes of the previous time period. There were several paintings of Christ and his disciples that Theo walked right by. He dismissed anything that was religious, having learned that these were less likely to sell to his Canadian clientele. He worked quickly, indicating with a nod of his head whether or not he wanted to consider a piece. By the time he had finished examining the walls of the room, he had selected half a dozen works. Each was of moderate size, dated back to the eighteenth and nineteenth centuries, and was painted by an artist that Theo knew would pass the inspection at the National Gallery. Finally, he turned to face the couple who stood anxiously awaiting his decision.

"They are all wonderful," he began. "I see that you have amassed quite the collection of fine art."

"But we're willing to give them up for the right price." It was the woman who finally spoke this time. She tugged nervously at a large cameo at the nape of her blouse. "It's simply impossible to move ahead in the world these days. Not that I'm complaining, of course. I'm just a nervous wreck over this." Her husband stroked her arm, hushing and soothing her.

"It's indeed difficult," Theo said sympathetically, marveling at how greed could consume a family. "But take heart in knowing that some families in Canada will derive great pleasure from your beautiful paintings. I know I can find good homes for them."

At that, the couple beamed. "We so appreciate your understanding," the man said. "Which ones would you like?" He was eager now to complete the transaction. Theo indicated the paintings he wished to buy and offered the couple a price. "I'll pay you in American dollars – an additional incentive of course." American cash was essential when it came to buying foreign cars, and much more desirable than the devalued Czech crowns.

"But it's so little!" the woman exclaimed. "They are worth ten times that."

Theo nodded. "Of course. But again, please remember that I am providing a service to you as well. The government will tax you heavily on these paintings if you wish to sell them overseas, and, at the end of the day, may not even release them. I'm willing to take them off your hands for cash, and try to pass them through the government red tape myself. But there are no guarantees for me either. I take a risk each time I purchase art. And I must take that into consideration with the price that I offer."

There was silence in the room, and then the couple bent their heads together and began to whisper feverishly. Theo waited patiently. How different these people were from Karl Reeser, he thought as he watched their animated exchange. It was self-indulgence that had motivated them to buy art in the first place, and it was avarice that was driving them to unload it now. Karl had neither of these qualities. He was strong-willed, of that Theo was certain. But there was nothing selfish about his desire for restitution. Karl's motivation was passionate and personal and generous. It was true that Theo identified more with the couple standing in front of him than with the man who awaited his return in Toronto. Nevertheless, one made him dig in his heels and go for top dollar, while the other inspired him to take greater risks for smaller gain.

The man and his wife were still muttering, their voices rising and falling as they gestured at the walls of their home and then at Theo. He had been through this same scenario many times and knew it was just a matter of time before they would relent, just as most of the others had. But to be on the safe side, he stepped forward slightly and threw his last card on the table. "I know how difficult this must be," he said in a voice dripping with false compassion. "Please don't think I am pressuring you. If you think you can do better elsewhere, then I will step aside and wish you luck." He turned as if to leave.

"No!" The man responded quickly and exactly as Theo knew he would. "No," he repeated. "We accept your offer. There are too many other things for us to worry about now." This he said as much to his wife as to Theo. "Please come into the study and I'll draw up the paperwork."

Theo nodded slightly and followed the man into his office. There, he reached into his breast pocket and removed a leather wallet, counting out the agreed-upon amount in American dollars and handed it over to the man. In return, he received a handwritten letter listing the paintings and a signed agreement releasing them to Theo.

"A colleague of mine will come by later today to pick them up," Theo said as he finished his business and was escorted back to the front door. He bowed courteously to the couple and reached out to shake the hand of the woman. "Once again, I wish you the very best of luck." She smiled faintly and Theo left.

Once on the sidewalk, he could barely contain himself. The woman had said that the paintings were worth ten times what he had just paid. In truth, once they were cleaned and restored in Canada, Theo knew he would be able to sell them for at least fifty times that amount. The day was going well. By the time evening rolled around, Theo had visited five such homes and had bought more than fifty paintings. He contacted the National Gallery to confirm his meeting with them Monday morning. Then he made a quick call to a young nephew of his who agreed to make the rounds of the homes he had visited and collect the selected art.

That night, Theo arranged to meet some old friends for dinner and drinks in a secluded bar in the old city. He had earned this celebration, he thought, as he bought a round of drinks for his group and silently toasted the profits that he knew would come from this business trip. Early next week, he would deal with the hurdle of securing Karl Reeser's paintings. And, of course, he still had to meet with the staff of the National Gallery and get their approval to transport the artwork he had purchased that day. But the weekend would be for his own pleasure, and Theo was looking forward to reentering the Prague social scene.

He spent the next two days and nights going to bars, restaurants, and clubs. He met with old friends and sat at outdoor cafés, downing espressos and sipping wine. He dropped money like a gardener scatters seeds, and his friends and acquaintances scrambled to pick up the crumbs, basking in the pleasure of being wined and dined. Women flocked to him, and he chased several of them with the same passion that surfaced in his pursuit of fine art, selecting only the best from the group and adding them to his list of acquisitions. He had few thoughts of Toronto and the freedoms to which he was accustomed there. Theo understood and was equally at home in Prague society, despite the oppressive atmosphere.

He knew he was being followed during that weekend. Early Sunday morning, when he left his hotel to escort his date from the previous night back to her home, he noticed a black car parked across the street. He wondered if it had been there the day before. Shadows in the bushes, phantom figures emerging from behind brick facades, cars that were there one minute and gone the next – maybe the ghosts of Prague were real, Theo thought. They were the secret police. The goons were not that good at concealing their surveillance tactics. You knew you were being followed when the same face would appear behind you three or more times a day! Or, more likely, they didn't care to hide their presence. There was nothing subtle or discreet about State Security. It excelled in intimidation and coercion. And nothing heightened one's paranoia more than the *thought* that one was being followed. The police knew that and used it to their advantage.

Briefly, Theo wondered again about the information that Karl had shared about his mail being tampered with. Were the police here because they knew about Karl's paintings and had somehow linked Theo to their retrieval? Did they know that the paintings were at the Canadian embassy, and were they already plotting to intercept them? His phone at the hotel was probably being tapped as well. But as quickly as any of those thoughts entered his mind, they were dismissed. His eyes were more watchful than those of the authorities, and his senses were keener. They were idiots, he continued to tell himself, puppets of a regime that was dying and yet desperate to make its last stand.

Early Monday morning, the telephone rang in Theo's hotel suite, arousing him from a deep sleep. It was his blacksmith friend calling with the news that the aluminum tubes were ready.

"I've delivered four to the National Gallery, as you requested," the man said. "The other one is waiting here for you. That's what you wanted?"

"Yes, that's correct," Theo responded, sitting up in bed, alert now.

"And when will you come and pick it up?"

Theo quickly went through his agenda in his mind. Today was his meeting with the officials at the National Gallery. Tuesday morning he was due to meet with Richard VandenBosch. "Tomorrow," he replied. "I'll come by your flat early in the morning."

"It wasn't easy," the man continued, carefully choosing his words. "I pulled a lot of strings to get my suppliers to deliver."

"And I'm grateful, as always to you, my good friend," Theo replied with equal care. "We'll settle all of this when I see you on Tuesday." He hung up the telephone and then picked it up again to make a call to Adolfo Flores.

"You're up early!" Adolfo's thunderous voice greeted him as soon as he identified himself. "I expected you would be partying all weekend and be in no shape to get up today."

"It was indeed a good weekend," Theo replied, easily. "I'd forgotten how much there was to do in this city."

"Not too hung over, then?"

Theo ignored the remark. "Can you get away? Come meet me here at my hotel. We'll have coffee in the restaurant downstairs." Theo rubbed his hand across his temple and squeezed his eyes shut. "I guess I could use some."

A half hour later he was waiting in the hotel café, now fully awake, sipping an espresso and reading a local newspaper while he waited for Adolfo. Several stories caught his attention. American Ambassador Shirley Temple Black had recently been named as envoy to Prague, one article said. The former child star had taken up residence in a sixty-five room palace filled with antiques. "The Czechs are polite, industrious, very clever, intelligent people," she had been quoted as saying about her hosts. "I think they are going to perform miracles."[14] Theo chuckled, wondering about the artwork that he might have acquired from such a home.

"You look better than I thought you would." Adolfo eased himself into the booth across from Theo and nodded to the waiter to bring him a coffee.

"I'm here on business, Adolfo. Have you forgotten that?"

Adolfo laughed softly, waiting for the waiter to pour his coffee before continuing. "So what's on your mind, since you seem to be all *business*?"

Theo glanced around. The coffee shop was full of customers on this Monday morning, mostly tourists with cameras dangling from their necks, noses buried in the pages of guide books. Here and there, lone businessmen were wolfing down breakfast. No one seemed to take notice of him, but he instinctively lowered his voice and leaned forward. "I will have the package we discussed ready for you on Tuesday – tomorrow. I should be able to deliver it to your embassy before noon." He heard Adolfo draw in his breath and paused. "Will that be a problem?" Everything hinged on Adolfo's availability to drive the paintings into Germany.

"No, no, that should be fine," Adolfo finally replied. "I'm due for a trip across the border. I can leave right after you get there."

"Good," Theo replied. "I'll have the artwork packaged as usual. I'm not sure yet how big the bundle will be, but I'm hoping it won't be too conspicuous."

"I'll cross over at Waidhaus," Adolfo continued, already thinking ahead to the journey. "And meet you at our usual spot. We'll make the exchange there."

"And I'll have your final payment with me. Have you thought about what you'll do if anyone stops you?"

"I'm protected, remember?" Adolfo replied easily. "I should have no trouble. But what about you? You could be searched, you know."

"I won't have anything in my car worth searching for," Theo replied.

"I'm not talking about being stopped at the border," Adolfo went on. "I'm talking about being stopped when you leave the embassy with your *acquisition*." This time Adolfo was the one to glance around and over his shoulder.

Theo nodded slowly and pressed his lips together in a tight smile. When he finally spoke, he was somber and grim-faced. "You can be sure, my friend, that if I so much as smell trouble, I will pull out. If you don't hear from me by one o'clock tomorrow afternoon, you can assume it's off." A few minutes later, the two men rose to go their separate ways.

Theo headed outside to pick up his car. All around the hotel, posters bearing the image of Václav Havel were plastered on windows and walls. Hawkers lined the pavement peddling campaign buttons for Civic Forum, the political party that Havel led and that had brought down the Communist regime in November. Only months earlier, at his presidential address, the new leader had proclaimed, "The future is again opening for us. Our home may once again become a favorite and sought-after place in Europe."[15] The posters reminded Theo once again that changes were on the country's horizon.

Prague had always been known as the golden city, full of castles and churches, statues and monuments. Even when its buildings had fallen into disrepair under Communist rule, it had remained one of Europe's most architecturally alluring cities. Now the dirt and the brooding gloom were being lifted. In and around Theo's hotel, buildings were being renovated at a breakneck pace, trying to make up for the years of neglect as the country was repositioning itself as a free-market state. The Communist nightmare was ending, but the country was far from being able to shake off its effects. Even the fact that Theo had to contend with the National Gallery's rules for the export of valuable goods was evidence that the country was still in a gridlock, trying to move forward with a new government and new autonomy, and still stuck in its old political rut.

The meeting with the officials at the Gallery had been arranged for ten o'clock that morning. Theo arrived early to ensure that the paintings he had bought from local families had indeed been delivered there, and that the transport tubing was also on hand.

The National Gallery was housed in different buildings within the city, the largest being the Veletržní Palác. He parked his car close to the building, entered, and was directed up the stairs to the main auditorium. There he was relieved to see the paintings waiting for him, along with the containers he had ordered. His nephew, Martin, stood off to one side, a gangly youth who waved at Theo as he entered. Theo winked back at him. Also waiting in the room were several women who identified themselves as the members of the commission who would approve or reject Theo's request to export the artwork. These were wealthy wives of businessmen and Communist officials who worked in the arts community. Though they were all older than Theo, some significantly so, he felt instantly at home in their presence.

"Ah, Mr. Král, it's a pleasure to see you back in the city." One tall, rather austere-looking woman whom Theo knew to be the chair of the commission stepped forward to shake his hand.

"Madam," replied Theo, bowing respectfully. "It's indeed a pleasure to be back here. How have you been? The leg is better, I trust?" He pointed to the cane that the commissioner was leaning on. Theo had befriended her a couple of years earlier, and their association had proved beneficial.

"The leg is something I must tolerate," the woman declared. In addition to her height, she was reed thin, and stooped shakily over her cane like a sapling bending in the wind. Her oversized glasses slipped down on her angular nose as she peered over them at Theo. "We have no choice in these matters, do we? But you're young and fit. You aren't yet familiar with the aches and pains of arthritis."

"I must say," protested Theo. "Despite your complaint, you are looking quite well, better than the last time I saw you." Theo smiled broadly at the commissioner, playing her with the skillfulness of a virtuoso.

"I can see that you've been busy," the woman continued, smiling back and indicating the paintings behind Theo. "Let's see what you have brought today. I'm sure this won't take us too long." She turned to address the other members of the commission. "Mr. Král has been doing business with the Gallery for some time. He is well acquainted with our rules, and works well within our regulations. I'm sure you will all agree with me on this."

She motioned for Theo to display the paintings he had brought. Working quickly with the aid of his nephew, Theo lined up the art until there was a long row of paintings in front of the commission. When the paintings had been assembled, the commissioner signaled to her committee and they went to work. One by one, they approached the first painting, examining it carefully, peering at the name of the artist and the date it had been painted, just as Theo had done when he had selected these pieces. A brief conference followed among the commission members, and, when they were satisfied that a painting had passed their test for export, one woman wrote the name of the selection on a form she carried and it was stamped for approval with the official seal of the National Gallery and the Czechoslovak government.

The commission moved quickly, inspecting and stamping the forms like goods on an assembly line. "Show me that! Look at this. Yes, yes. Next!" they proclaimed as they passed each canvas. Theo had done his work well, selecting only those paintings that he knew would pass the practiced eyes of the committee members. There was only one work that appeared to cause the inspectors some concern. Theo watched as they moved closer to study the canvas in question, and then stepped back, huddling in a circle and conferring in half-whispers, like athletes surrounding one another to discuss their next strategic play. One gestured back to the painting while another one shook her head. Theo waited and wondered if perhaps the painting in question was *too good* to be released by the Gallery. Finally, the commissioner raised her hand, glanced over at Theo, and then indicated that the painting was approved. The form was stamped and they moved on.

Theo observed these proceedings from one side of the long room, attentively assessing the progress of the committee members as they walked from painting to painting. His face betrayed nothing of his careful scrutiny. He appeared confident, almost indifferent to the actions of the inspectors. Finally, the members finished walking down the line and the commissioner conferred with them one last time. Then she dismissed them with a bow and turned to limp toward Theo, leaning heavily on her cane. "An interesting collection, Mr. Král," she said.

"I trust everything is in order," replied Theo, accepting the form that the commissioner extended to him. Fifty paintings were listed on several sheets of paper, followed by fifty all-important Gallery stamps.

"Yes, well, there was one painting that caused the members of the commission some unease. But I convinced them that it could be released. I do have your best interests at heart, Mr. Král, as well as ours."

"I'm most grateful for your generous support," Theo replied. "In addition to the fee I will pay for the release of the paintings, I'd like to add a small bonus for yourself."

The commissioner shook her head in a weak gesture of protest.

"Of course, I insist," continued Theo. "And I have a wonderful bottle of cognac at my hotel that I'd like to send to you. I recall it's a favorite of yours."

"You're too kind, Mr. Král," the commissioner beamed. "You're welcome to do business with us anytime."

Theo bowed again. *This is too easy,* he thought. If he could keep this ridiculous woman in bribes and good liquor, he'd indeed be doing business successfully here for some time. He checked the stamped form once more and proceeded to the main office of the Gallery, where he paid the several hundred Czech crowns that he was being charged to export fifty paintings. It was a pittance, he thought as he returned to the main room and, with the help of his nephew, began to roll and package the paintings using the tubes that had been delivered by the blacksmith. When the artwork was secure, he turned to his nephew. "You'll deliver these to the post office for me," he said. "This should cover the shipping fees and a little something for you." He peeled off a few more bills from his wallet and shoved them into the hands of the smiling young man. The entire amount that he had paid – price, export tax, shipping fees – was nothing compared with what they would fetch in Canada.

The sun was shining as he left the building and walked down the front steps to his car, the first time since his arrival, and its warmth penetrated his suit jacket. All had gone according to plan, and this sunshine greeted him almost as a reward for the work he had done. Today had been another good day, but Theo knew that it was time to return to Canada. Perhaps it was the corruption on every corner, or the constant sense of being under observation. Whatever it was, Theo now felt the need to get out of Czechoslovakia like a burning itch under his skin. He turned his face upwards and closed his eyes for a moment. There was still the matter of Karl Reeser's paintings. His meeting with Richard VandenBosch at the Canadian embassy awaited him the following and final day.

CHAPTER TWENTY-NINE

Prague, March 20, 1990

THEO WAS WAITING in front of the dry goods store even before the proprietor had arrived. He nodded at the man who unlocked the door, and bounded up the stairs at the back to knock on the door of the old blacksmith. Their transaction took only minutes. Theo thanked the man for the delivery of the four aluminum tubes to the National Gallery the previous day and accepted the fifth one with gratitude. In return, he placed a wad of American bills in the old man's hands. The man pocketed the cash, first glancing out the front window as if he was afraid that someone might be watching, even here in his own apartment.

"It's always a pleasure to do business with you, Mr. Král," the black-smith said.

"Likewise, my friend," replied Theo, smiling broadly. "I don't know how many more times I'll be making this trip. I guess it will depend on the results of the election."

The man shrugged. "Do you think after forty years, things will change so fast? They never do. I'm here if you need me, and happy to oblige." He patted his pocket, bulging with the money Theo had given him.

The two men shook hands and Theo left his flat carrying the large cylinder, which he deposited in the back seat of his car. It was a tight squeeze, a fact that gave Theo a moment of pause. He wished he could conceal it in the trunk or further down on the floor of his vehicle, but that was impossible. Luckily the drive to the embassy would not take long.

Pulling away from the curb, he merged with the busy morning traffic in the midst of its rush-hour surge to work. The Czech drivers lived up to their reputation for recklessness, ignoring the speed limits and weaving around each other like jockeys at the track, each trying to get to the head of the pack in some imagined race for first place. It was almost as if the drivers, who were so subjugated in every other aspect of their lives, could experience a sense of freedom here on the road. Theo joined in, dodging and zigzagging like the true native he was. Before long, he could see the Canadian flag of the embassy ahead of him and he turned off the main street to approach the gated driveway, stopping at the guard post and rolling down his window.

"I'm here for a meeting with Vice Consul Richard VandenBosch," he announced to the guard. The man stepped outside of the small house and approached Theo's car, glancing suspiciously at the bright aluminum tube stretching across the back seat and over the passenger side of the car. Theo waited, smiling calmly and confidently.

"Your name?" the guard asked.

"Theofil Král. Mr. VandenBosch is expecting me."

Without replying, the guard returned to his post and picked up a telephone. A minute later, he emerged to point Theo through the gates and into a spot in the embassy parking lot. Theo entered the building and was directed down the long, dark corridor to Richard VandenBosch's office.

"Greetings, Mr. Král! I've been waiting a long time for the arrival of the man who will take Karl Reeser's paintings back home to him." Richard VandenBosch welcomed Theo enthusiastically and launched into the conversation as if they were old friends. "Have you been in Prague long?" he asked, inviting Theo to sit. VandenBosch perched himself on the edge of his desk.

"A few days," Theo replied, sinking into a chair and facing the vice consul. "I'm planning to leave tonight, if all goes as planned."

VandenBosch paused. "I can't even ask how you intend to get the paintings out of the country, though I understand that you know something about art."

Theo smiled pleasantly but said nothing.

"I will say, though, that I support whatever it is you are doing," Richard VandenBosch continued. "These paintings have been held hostage in this country for long enough. It's time they were returned to their rightful owner."

"I'm originally from Czechoslovakia," Theo offered. "I know how the Communists work and I am quite familiar with their regulations regarding property they deem to be of value."

"Yes, well, we diplomats have been subjected to the *regulations* of the Communist overseers ever since we arrived here. I know that I am a guest of this country's government, so I have to be careful of what I say. But letting these paintings fall into government hands would be a crime as far as I'm concerned." He thumped his hand on his desk. His mop of sandy brown hair flopped down over his glasses as he shook his head emphatically.

Theo watched him, somewhat amused. He already felt a kind of kinship to this man who shared a last name with his artistic hero, Hieronymus Bosch, and he marveled at the fact that Richard VandenBosch was almost as invested in the paintings as Karl was. He cleared his throat. "Yes, Mr. Reeser is certainly anxious to have his paintings back. So, if you don't mind, I'd like to collect them and get on my way."

VandenBosch paused, seeming to pull himself together. "You probably know that Mr. Reeser and I have been corresponding for some time over this. I think he was becoming quite hopeless about ever seeing his family's possessions again."

Theo wondered for a moment if those were some of the letters that Karl had speculated were being opened by the secret police. He did not voice this aloud. Instead, he focused on the task at hand. "I have a letter here from Mr. Reeser, authorizing you to release the paintings to me." He reached into his jacket pocket and removed the letter that Karl had given to him before leaving Toronto.

VandenBosch took the letter and read it quickly, nodding his head. "Everything seems to be in order here," he said and then looked up. "Mr. Reeser may or may not have told you that we have been displaying several of his paintings here in the embassy. Why not enjoy them while we have them, right? But, about a week ago, we moved all of the paintings into a small building off the courtyard where you will be able to pack them up undetected. The last thing we want is for some nosy non-embassy person in the building to wonder what you're transporting out of here."

Theo nodded. He had seen what appeared to be outside workers in the halls and grounds of the embassy and was grateful for VandenBosch's forethought.

"If you'll follow me, I'll show you where the paintings are." The vice consul stood and walked briskly out of his office with Theo on his heels. The two men left the embassy building and headed across the enclosed parking lot. Their first stop was at Theo's car. Following VandenBosch's directions, Theo pulled the car out of his parking spot and drove up close to a small wooden structure, almost hidden from view by the surrounding garden. He parked again and got out, pulling the large aluminum tube from the back seat and hoisting it up on his shoulder. VandenBosch tugged the heavy door of the building open and motioned Theo inside. He stepped into a dusty, dimly lit room, filled with old desks, a number of empty filing cabinets, and chairs stacked atop one another. This storage shed had no windows and little light except for the glow cast from one naked bulb suspended from the ceiling.

"Little chance of anyone seeing or disturbing you in here," Vanden-Bosch muttered as he proceeded to a canvas sheet in one corner of the room. He flung it aside ceremoniously and stepped back. "Mr. Král, may I present the four paintings," he said, with a slight bow and a wide grin.

Everything seemed to fade into the background as Theo turned his attention to the first canvas that stood leaning against the wall of the shed. It was *Le lavabo à l'école maternelle* by Geoffroy. Face to face with the oil painting, Theo was even more impressed than he had imagined he would be by the detail on each child's face, and the light and dark of the artist's shading. Theo examined the work with the same attention he gave to the paintings he routinely assessed for export, taking a moment to appreciate the simplicity of the faces of the children gathered together. And even in the muted light of this dusty room, Theo could see that the painting was in remarkable condition, given the years that had passed and the state in which the painting had been kept. This was a museum piece, he thought. The National Gallery would never have agreed to part with it – not even with the bribes that Theo might offer. *Pity*, he thought. *This one would bring me a fine price if I could sell it back home.*

"It's a beauty, isn't it?" Theo had almost forgotten about Richard VandenBosch, who was still there behind him. At a loss for words, all Theo could do was nod. "That's the one that was in my office," continued VandenBosch. "The one behind it was in the chargé d'affaires's office. He's going to be sorry to see it go."

Theo pulled the first painting toward him to gaze at the second canvas, in which a young woman was standing, hand on her hip, staring at pages of sheet music. It was *Die Hausfrau*. Theo recognized the work of the gifted German portrait painter, though this one was softer and more appealing than some of Vogel's military representations.

"Well, I'll leave you to your work, then." Richard VandenBosch interrupted Theo's thoughts once more. "I'll have a security officer on the other side of the door – again, just to make sure you're not disturbed. Don't worry," he added. "This fellow is a Canadian with full embassy clearance." With that, he turned around and left the small building, pulling the stiff wooden door closed behind him.

Theo wasted no time. He carefully maneuvered the Geoffroy onto the floor and began the task of removing it from its wooden stretcher. It would be impossible to keep the paintings on their stretchers if they were going to be transported safely and discreetly across the border. This was the same procedure he had used at the National Gallery when he had packed the paintings there for shipment to Toronto. He placed the aluminum tube on the floor, but not before examining it carefully and running his hand along the smooth finish. The blacksmith had done a superb job custom-making the cylinders so that the seam was welded on the inside. A seam on the outside would have created a rough ridge that could easily damage the paintings in transport. Using tools he carried in a briefcase, Theo began to work around the exterior of the painting, meticulously removing the nails and staples that held it in place on the stretcher, being careful not to damage the canvas. He then disassembled the wooden stretcher and laid it to one side. Next, he reached for the aluminum tube and carefully began to roll the canvas around its exterior. The painting was rolled facing out. A sheet of release paper, which Theo had also brought, was layered along the face of the canvas, protecting it, and ensuring that nothing would stick to its surface.

When he had finished rolling the first painting, he turned his attention to the Vogel and began the same procedure of removing it from its stretcher and rolling it around the cylinder over the first painting. *Forest Fire* was next, followed by *Ready for the Ball.* Theo glanced at them briefly before laying them on the floor and beginning the process of packaging them. Both were impressive.

When all four paintings had been rolled around the tube, with protective release paper around and in between each of them, Theo placed the wooden slats of all the stretchers inside the hollow opening of the container. He knew that even though these pieces were cracked and disintegrating in places, they too were valuable, often helping date a work of art. Finally, the entire tube, paintings, stretchers, and all, was rolled in thick bubble wrap and taped securely. By the time he had finished, an enormous wrapped cylindrical bundle lay on the floor in front of him. Theo stood up, breathing heavily, satisfied that the paintings had been safely and securely packed.

He had just completed his work when Richard VandenBosch returned to the shed. "Well, that's done, then," Theo said. "If you and the guard outside will give me a hand, we can carry this package to my car."

The three men lifted the tube of paintings off the floor and carted it out the door and into Theo's waiting car, where they deposited the container into the back seat. What had been a tight squeeze earlier was now a bulging mass, sitting almost upright in the vehicle, pressing against the ceiling of the car and over onto the front passenger seat. Theo cursed under his breath. If only he could have found a way to make it less conspicuous. Here it sat, like a neon sign on a dark night. But there was nothing he could do about that. He closed the door tightly and turned to shake hands with Richard VandenBosch.

"I'm sure you know what you're doing here, but I have to caution you about something," VandenBosch began, grasping Theo's hand and pulling him close. "When you leave the building, go to the left. There's a surveillance car that always sits to the right of the embassy. They're less likely to spot you if you turn in the other direction."

Theo nodded, knowing that the trickiest part of the mission lay ahead of him.

"If they come after you, you're pretty much on your own. Good luck to you," VandenBosch added.

"Thank you for your help," Theo replied. He was turning to get into the car when VandenBosch touched his arm.

"You know," he began, stepping toward Theo, "I must tell you that if you had not arrived to take Mr. Reeser's paintings out of the country, I would have done it myself. My job is winding down here. I'll be leaving at some point in the next year. With the coming restructuring of the country, all of us are going to be going on to new posts elsewhere." He paused and then continued even more earnestly. "If someone hadn't come for the paintings, I was planning to pack them in my own crate and take them out of here when I leave. There was no way I was going to let anyone get their hands on this artwork."

Theo stared at the vice consul. He was an interesting man, not at all like the diplomats Theo often met at government functions and gatherings – those who only thought of themselves and their own interests. Richard VandenBosch's deep and genuine compassion for Karl, his family saga, and the paintings he was so desperate to retrieve was striking. For Theo, so long accustomed to monetary gain in business matters, this altruistic confession took him aback, and he stammered a response. "I know that Mr. Reeser is grateful for all you've done to keep the paintings safe."

VandenBosch dismissed the comment with a wave, suddenly self-conscious. "I'll write to him today and let him know that we had this little meeting," he said. "Please give my best to Mr. Reeser when you see him in Toronto. Tell him that I'm happy for him."

Theo got in behind the wheel of his car, glanced over his shoulder at the package in the back seat, and then moved the car forward.

Heeding Richard VandenBosch's words of warning, Theo drove his car through the embassy gates and abruptly pulled the steering wheel hard to the left, swerving his car away from the building and merging quickly into the throng of heavy traffic. Car horns blared and drivers swore out their windows as they swerved around Theo, but he took no notice. He glanced again at the oversized container in the back seat, and then in his rear view mirror, suddenly seized with a moment of uncharacteristic anxiety, realizing that he was now facing a critical moment in this operation. If they had spotted him, it would only be a matter of seconds before the secret police were barreling after him, ready to seize his cargo and grab Theo himself. Was it possible that he was being followed, he wondered. That black car there to his left, and that gray limousine two cars back – surely they must have seen him. They had to have spotted his cargo bulging like a camel's hump from his back seat. Perhaps he had been too careless on the telephone with Adolfo. Or maybe someone had followed him to meet with the blacksmith. The inside of Theo's mouth felt like chalk. Tiny beads of sweat dotted his forehead.

The black car on the left passed by without slowing. The gray limousine turned off the main road. Theo took a deep breath. There was no one on his tail, he assured himself. But, just to be on the safe side, he swerved his vehicle without warning into a narrow alleyway and deftly maneuvered through an intricate maze of streets and laneways, finally emerging onto another large thoroughfare. He glanced in the rearview mirror one last time. If anyone *had* been following him, they were long gone by now.

Moments later, he arrived at the gates of the Peruvian embassy. After being questioned by the guard on duty, he was admitted and drove into the parking lot. Adolfo was there to greet him.

"No trouble getting here?" Adolfo asked as he eyed the large roll in the back of Theo's car.

Theo shook his head. "You know how careful I am," he replied. No need to confess his own anxiety to this man.

Without another word, the two men removed the cargo from Theo's car and deposited it in the back seat of Adolfo's, which bore the all-important diplomatic license plates. Once the package was secured, Adolfo stood back, lit a cigarette, and glanced at his watch. It was just past noon.

"I'll leave shortly – just a couple of things to wrap up here. And I should be across the border by early afternoon, if all goes as planned."

Everything now depended on Adolfo's ability to drive his car across the border into Germany. While Theo knew that the car would not be searched, there was still the chance that the border guards, if they were the least bit suspicious about the car or Adolfo's activities, might simply send him back. They would not need to offer any explanation for refusing to allow Adolfo to cross the border. If they turned him away, Adolfo would have to return to Prague and Theo would have to find another way to get the paintings out of the country.

"I'll be checking out of my hotel and driving out of Prague in a couple of hours myself," he said, shaking hands with Adolfo. "When are you going to stop that nasty habit, my friend," he added, indicating the cigarette in Adolfo's hand. "Don't you know it could kill you?"

Adolfo smiled and pumped Theo's hand. "We all live a bit dangerously, don't we?"

Theo returned the smile. "I'll meet you on the other side. Good luck and safe travels."

Theo drove back to his hotel, already feeling lighter and more at ease having offloaded his cargo. He packed his suitcase and checked out at the front desk, slipping the clerk a generous tip for his services.

"Always a pleasure to have you with us, Mr. Král," the desk clerk beamed.

Theo tried not to think too much about the paintings as he settled once more into his car. He focused instead on a last look at Prague, wondering again when he would next see this city and under what circumstances. Democracy would be a giant step forward for this country, but it could virtually bring an end to Theo's business here. Free enterprise would mean a more open financial market with respect to art. It might only be a matter of time before the works that Theo was accustomed to buying for next to nothing would begin to command high prices in a competitive marketplace. Still, judging from the state of things, perhaps the dream of autonomy for the country was still far away. A city where uniformity and order had been imposed was also a city in decay. Theo glanced at the boxy concrete apartment buildings that dotted the highway to the airport. These were a remnant of a Communist regime that, in its policy of creating equality for all, had stripped this country of its beauty and individuality. The people, like these buildings, had also become nameless and faceless. It would take years to reverse that, or create something new. Czechoslovakia had its work cut out for it.

The drive out of Prague took Theo on the autobahn west toward the city of Plzeň. He would cross into Germany at Waidhaus and then drive another dozen or so kilometers to the small town of Pleystein to wait for Adolfo. In all, it would take a couple of hours to reach their rendezvous spot and then four or five hours more to drive to Frankfurt. With luck, good timing, and no complications, Theo and Karl's paintings would be on a plane back to Toronto that same evening.

The drive to the border was uneventful and, once there, Theo joined a moderate line of cars waiting to pass through inspection. As he inched forward toward the Czech border guards, he prepared his visa and other documents and rolled down the window.

"How long have you been in the country?" A severe-looking official stepped toward the car and snapped at Theo.

"A week." Had it really been only seven days since he had left Toronto?

"And what was the purpose of your trip?" the guard continued.

"Business," Theo replied, handing over copies he had made of the stamped documents from the National Gallery, which listed the paintings he had purchased. "The Gallery has approved these works of art to be sent to Canada. They were shipped from Prague before I left."

The guard took the papers, inspected them closely, and then lifted his eyes. Theo forced himself to stare back at the guard, his face impassive, and his thoughts unreadable. Inside, however, Theo could feel his blood begin to boil, irritated with this ever-present scrutiny. He clenched his hands around the steering wheel until his knuckles showed white, striving to keep his breathing even. The guard was taking a long time, too much time. He checked and double-checked the passport, matching Theo's photograph to his face. He read through the list of paintings on the National Gallery document as if he actually knew the artists and cared about the paintings that were listed. *He's trying to unnerve me*, thought Theo, *and I won't fall for it.* Cool and calm, that was the image he needed to project.

"Anything else to declare?" the guard asked.

"Nothing," replied Theo, once more in command. It's not a lie if you *believe* you are doing nothing illegal, he reminded himself. Finally, an eternity later, the guard stamped his papers and motioned him through.

Another step completed, he thought with a deep exhale as he checked his watch and headed toward the German border guards and then Pleystein. This small town of only about twenty-five hundred inhabitants had been his meeting place with Adolfo each time the two of them had joined forces on jobs to get special paintings out of Prague. Pleystein was a convenient location, close to the border, and there was a quiet bar where the two men could celebrate the completion of their business deals. The town was dominated by a church whose steeple emerged at the top of a hill overlooking the quaint, cottage-like homes below.

Entering the bar, Theo nodded at the proprietor, whom he had come to know over the years, and settled into a dark booth at the back, knowing he might have some time before Adolfo was due to arrive. An attractive young girl served him, smiling engagingly. Theo returned the smile. He was tempted to ask her name and perhaps even for a telephone number, but then he stopped himself. There was still one piece of important business left to do here and this was not the time to be distracted by anything or anyone.

While he waited, he thought back over the past week and the business he had conducted in Prague. The week had been more successful than he had imagined. He was sending fifty paintings back to Canada, paintings that would bring him a sizeable profit once they were cleaned, restored, and remounted. And if these next few hours went according to plan, he would also be reuniting a family with property they had been pursuing for many years. He had gone to considerable lengths to secure Karl Reeser's paintings. Theo wondered again at the risk he was taking for a man he barely knew. Perhaps it would have been more in line with his personality if he were intending to keep Karl's paintings, fabricating some story about how he had been unable to acquire them, or how the secret police had gotten wind of his plan and intervened, or how the paintings had been confiscated while crossing the border. Was he tempted to steal Karl's property, sell the paintings privately, and profit even more from this mission? The answer, he knew immediately, was a resounding no! He may have been a smuggler, but Theo was certainly not a thief.

There was a sudden commotion at the door of the bar. Two men had entered, talking in animated gestures and half sentences. "Did you see what happened back there at the border?" one of them asked no one in particular. Theo raised his head from his drink. "Someone was stopped for smuggling." The second man took up the story: "That one's gone for good, if you ask me." The men laughed easily and sat down at a table close to Theo.

It's not possible, Theo thought, and yet, more than an hour had passed and Adolfo had still not arrived. "Excuse me," he said, standing and approaching the two men. "Did you say a man was arrested?"

"Yes." The two nodded adamantly. "The Czech police took him away in handcuffs. But he's a fool, if you ask me. Why would anyone take such a risk?"

Theo ignored the comment. "The man who was arrested, what did he look like, if you don't mind my asking?"

"Young, not much more than a teenager," one man replied.

"But he'll be an old man before he sees the light of day," the other concluded.

The men laughed again, raising their glasses and downing their beers. Theo retreated to his table. The encounter had unnerved him. The man who had been arrested was too young to be his friend and colleague. Besides, Adolfo couldn't be detained, he reassured himself. He was a diplomat, protected from being searched. *But why isn't he here?* Theo asked himself, throwing back the last of his drink and glancing at his watch. Perhaps something had gone wrong after all. There was no backup plan here and Theo felt helpless, forced to just wait this out. If Adolfo had been turned back, it would take several more hours before Theo would be able to connect with his contact and figure out where the paintings were. He would soon be forced to make a choice: either he would drive on to Frankfurt, get on a plane to Canada, and leave the paintings behind, or he would have to delay his return and make another attempt to retrieve them. Neither was a desirable option. For Theo, this was the hardest part of this entire scheme: waiting, not knowing, and having no power. He hated the absence of control. It was like skydiving without a parachute.

He was just about to leave his table to look for a telephone – perhaps Adolfo had left a message for him at his hotel – when he looked up and saw a smiling Adolfo Flores enter the bar. Theo stood to greet his contact.

"I was beginning to worry, my friend," he confessed as he grabbed Adolfo's arm and pulled him down into his booth. He signaled the pretty waitress to bring over another round of drinks.

"No need for concern," Adolfo replied. "There was a bit of a line-up at the border. I think somebody up ahead was being stopped. That's what took so long."

Theo filled Adolfo in on the reports from the men who had entered the bar earlier. "I was worried at first that it might be you. Did you have any trouble?"

Adolfo shook his head. "None. The border guard glanced into the back seat of my car where your cargo was sitting. I thought he might ask me something about it. But he didn't – he saw it was a diplomatic car, waved me through, and here I am."

Theo paused and silently blessed the power of the diplomatic license plates once more. Adolfo pounded him on the back, grinned, and lifted his glass to toast the success of the operation. "To you," he said. "And to many more successful transactions."

Theo reached into his jacket pocket and extracted one more bulky envelope, which he pushed across the table into Adolfo's waiting hands. "And to you, my friend," he replied. "Payment for a job well done."

Adolfo glanced inside the envelope and then slipped it into his pocket. "Call on me anytime," he said.

The two men finished their drinks a short time later and left, Adolfo to drive back to Prague, and Theo to continue his drive on to Frankfurt, but not before transferring the container from Adolfo's embassy car back into Theo's rental. He settled behind the wheel and turned the radio on full blast. He still had about four hours of driving ahead on a route that would take him past Nuremburg, Wurzburg, and Aschaffenburg, before he would arrive in Frankfurt.

This time, the hours flew by and before he knew it, the skyline of the big industrial city lay ahead of him. At the airport, Theo returned his car, checked in for his flight, and also checked the large container with Karl Reeser's precious paintings. He knew that, upon arriving in Canada, it would be unlikely that he would be questioned about its contents. And if there were any concerns at Canadian customs, he still had the copies of the National Gallery forms, verifying that he was bringing art into the country legally. On the way to catch his plane, Theo called a woman friend of his in Toronto to let her know that he would be home the next day. They made arrangements to meet. *Something more to look forward to,* he thought.

CHAPTER THIRTY

Toronto, March 21, 1990

ALL TOO AWARE of the date, Karl's brain awoke early that morning even before his body began to stir. In fact, Theo's imminent arrival had haunted Karl for days now, interrupting his conversations, his meals, and his sleep. He had no idea what time he might hear from Theo, so he arose, trying not to wake Phyllis, and went into the bathroom. Quinta was scratching at the door, whining for Karl to let her out. But first Karl splashed cold water on his face and looked up to stare at his reflection. The stark light above the mirror exaggerated the lines deeply etched around his eyes and mouth. He ran his fingers through his hair. What was left of his once bright red hair was now replaced with a more dignified gray. At close to seventy years of age, Karl was still strong and agile. But he felt as if he had aged years in the days since Theo had left for Prague.

Quinta scratched again, Phyllis stirred, and Karl dressed hurriedly and went downstairs and into the family room, sinking into a large armchair to gaze out the back window. This chair was a favorite place to sit. It faced the enclosed backyard with its changing landscape of multicolored gardens in summer, and white, barren snow in winter. Colorful photographs lined the wood-paneled walls of the room, all of them taken and developed by Phyllis and himself on their many tours abroad. Interspersed were pictures of his children and grandchildren at various stages of their lives – this one in infancy, a birthday, a school graduation. Books were stacked in a neat pile next to the chair, reflecting Karl's deep interest in history and politics. He would often sit here with a book in his hands, looking up periodically to gaze out the back, listening to Quinta snoring gently on the couch and feeling the peacefulness of his life. But today there was nothing tranquil in his bearing. He felt jittery and uncertain. All he could think about were the paintings and the possibility, the fervent hope that he might be reunited with them.

What if Theo didn't call today? That thought had competed for space in Karl's mind along with the anticipation of hearing Theo's voice on the telephone. No word from Theo might mean that his trip was delayed and he was still in the process of retrieving the paintings, or that something had gone horribly wrong and he was stuck in Prague. Then there was the possibility that Theo had absconded with the artwork. Karl could not even bear to consider this thought, or the notion that Hana and Paul had been right all along and that Theo was indeed a thief, a con artist who had duped them out of thirty-five hundred dollars and, worse, had run off with the family's treasures. No! That simply could not be. In his heart, Karl believed he had read Theo correctly. He simply had to be patient and the telephone would eventually ring.

What would it feel like to be reunited with the paintings? Karl had barely allowed himself the luxury of imagining that possibility. He had been so consumed with trying to get the paintings back that he had not stopped to fully consider the outcome. But here, in the stillness of this March morning, he pictured the first moment of seeing the paintings in his home in Toronto, and he immediately remembered the day his parents had acquired them from Mr. Schmahl. Fifty years filled with war, family turmoil, uncertainty, loss, and dispossession had passed. There was nothing left from the old days, nothing to remind him of his previous life – no home, no country, few family members. The paintings were the only evidence of what his family had once had.

"Are you going to sit here like this all day?" Phyllis's voice broke the stillness of Karl's morning deliberation. He shook his head, unable to respond. "Come and have some breakfast, and then I want you to go for a walk," she commanded. "I'll stay home in case the telephone rings. But you've got to get out of here and do something."

Karl smiled gratefully. A walk was probably the best thing for him. Besides, there was still one task he needed to complete in anticipation of Theo's call. He ate a quick breakfast, put on his jacket, and headed out the door. The cool and damp March wind swirled around him and he pulled the collar of his jacket up around his ears, thankful that Phyllis had insisted on wrapping a wool scarf around his neck at the last minute despite his protests. It was funny how a day like this immediately reminded him of Prague in early spring, with its comparable bone-chilling dampness. He had been there about a year earlier to meet with Jan Pekárek and Richard VandenBosch, walking the streets of that city a continent away. He reminded himself that, while he and his family had lost so much in their flight from Prague on the eve of the war so many years earlier, he had also acquired so much in Canada: a new life, happiness with a loving partner, children, grandchildren, prosperity, and stability. His life was complete here, with or without the paintings.

There were no customers at the bank when Karl entered. He greeted the manager, who knew him by name, and approached the first teller. "I'd like to withdraw three thousand, five hundred dollars in cash," he said. "Hundred dollar bills would be fine." The teller nodded, unfazed, and began to count out the money for Karl. With thirty-five crisp new bills safely tucked into his jacket pocket, Karl left the bank and returned home to wait once more.

The telephone was ringing as he entered his house and he sprang for the receiver to answer it on the second ring. But it was only Hana, calling to see if there was any word from Theo.

"Nothing yet, Hana," Karl said, trying to catch his breath and slow the pounding of his heart in his chest.

"He didn't say when he would call, did he? Only that he would be back on the twenty-first."

"It may not even happen today," Karl replied, though he didn't want to think of that possibility, either. "I've got the rest of the money here. I went to the bank to withdraw it this morning."

There was a long pause on the other end. "That's being rather optimistic, isn't it?" she finally said.

At that, Karl had to chuckle. His sister had difficulty hiding her ongoing doubt that Theo was going to deliver on his promise. "I'm trying to stay positive, here, Hana. I'll call you when I hear something." He emphasized the word *when*, and listened for her quiet snicker in reply. After he hung up the telephone, and for the rest of the day, Karl tried to go about his business as usual. He answered the mail, paid the bills that were due, lunched with Phyllis, took Quinta for a long walk, napped, and desperately fought to put all thoughts of the paintings out of his mind, futile as that was.

It was evening before the telephone rang again. By then, Karl was a nervous wreck, pacing in the family room, unable to calm himself. Phyllis was out for the evening, attending a lecture at their local library. She had begged him to come. "It will take your mind off of all of this," she had said. But Karl had refused. "No one will be at home to answer the telephone," he had replied. Even Phyllis, always supportive, was beginning to voice her fear that Theo might not call. "Karl, you may have to prepare yourself for the possibility that this isn't going to happen," she had said before leaving for her meeting.

Karl lurched for the telephone and caught it on the first ring. His hand trembled as he brought the receiver to his ear. "Hello," he said.

The voice on the other end was clear and succinct. "Mission accomplished," said Theo. "You can come and get your paintings tomorrow."

By the time Phyllis returned from her library lecture, Karl had opened a bottle of wine and was waiting for her with a huge smile on his face and outstretched arms. "We did it," he exclaimed, as he wrapped his wife in a warm embrace.

"*You* did it," she replied. "This is your accomplishment."

They toasted one another and the arrival of the paintings in Toronto.

As Karl sipped his wine, he experienced a sense of freedom that he had not felt in some time. The burden of having fought to regain the paintings was suddenly gone, lifted from his shoulders like a ten-ton weight. Tonight he could breathe more deeply and perhaps sleep more soundly, knowing that his family treasures had come home to him and were now firmly on Canadian soil. He called Hana to report the news. She was also delighted and relieved that all had gone according to plan.

Early the next morning, Karl and Phyllis walked over to Theo's apartment and knocked on the door. He answered immediately and ushered them into a back room. There on the floor were the paintings, now off their stretchers and stacked one on top of the other. They were dusty, slightly wrinkled from having been rolled around the container for the trip to Canada, but undamaged. Karl stood in muted disbelief. As much as he had prepared, dreamed, obsessed about this moment, he was simply overcome. As he stood in Theo's home staring down at the paintings, he understood it all: his mother's determination to retrieve something of their family's past, her resolve not to separate them or leave one behind. Everything had finally come full circle. Karl had fulfilled his mother's dream and he could be at peace.

He turned to face Theo and grabbed his hand, pumping it furiously. "Words can't express," he began. "I simply don't know how..."

Theo stopped him. "It was my pleasure to help you," he replied, with genuine sincerity. He truly felt the enjoyment of this moment along with Karl.

"You know," Karl continued, "Some members of my family were not as convinced as I was of your honesty."

Theo smiled. "We can all learn something in this, I suppose," he replied.

Karl reached into his pocket and withdrew the envelope containing the remaining payment. "It's the best money I've ever spent," he said, extending it to Theo.

Theo accepted the envelope, reminding himself once again that he had fulfilled the conditions of a contract here. Tomorrow he would go about his business as usual. He had fifty paintings that would soon arrive in a shipment, ready to be restored and sold. There was a lot of money to be made from this trip and he was eager to begin to reap the rewards. No time to be distracted by useless sentiment. He would likely never see Karl Reeser again, and that was as it should be. Theo cleared his throat. "You'll need to get the paintings cleaned, remounted on their stretchers, and framed," he said.

Karl nodded again. "I know someone who can do that. The paintings need to be brought back to their former splendor."

In the following week, Karl met with Joseph Cach, an art restorer who had mounted and framed several other paintings that Karl had collected over the years. When Joseph came to look at the paintings and Karl explained their situation, Joseph was surprised and delighted. The canvases were in remarkable condition, though dusty from years of having sat unprotected in coal-heated homes in Czechoslovakia, where soot layered the furniture, clothing, and paintings. Varnish had been applied decades earlier to try to protect them from dirt, dust, and pollution in the environment. But through the years, it had yellowed the paintings considerably. Several pieces of the stretchers were warped and decayed. They would have to be rebuilt. Both the Swoboda and the Geoffroy were cracked in several places. But other than that, there was minimal damage.

"Can you fix them up?" asked Karl.

Joseph was an exuberant, burly man, with a full head of curly hair. He scratched thoughtfully at his beard and replied excitedly, "They're marvelous, Karl! From what you had told me on the phone, I thought they would be in disastrous condition. All four of them will need to be cleaned and the varnish removed. There is some decay and cracking here, which is normal over time. I'll need to fill in and retouch these two." Joseph scrutinized the paintings like a doctor triaging a group of patients, pronouncing his diagnosis and then stating the necessary remedy. "They'll need new linings on the back. And I'll apply a non-yellowing varnish." His foot kicked the pile of wooden stretchers. "These are pretty bad. This one's practically disintegrated. I'll need to construct new stretchers in some cases." He spoke as much to himself as to Karl. Finally, he turned. "But this will not be a difficult job at all. Once I'm done, they'll be as good as new."

In the third week of May 1990, Joseph completed the restoration and framing of the pieces and called Karl to pick them up. Fifty-one years after his family had acquired the canvases in Rakovník, and one year after Karl had carried them to the Canadian embassy in Prague, the paintings were finally home.

EPILOGUE

SEVERAL YEARS AFTER retrieving the Reeser family's paintings, Theo returned to Prague for another buying spree – and with another commission from Karl. The intervening years had brought democracy to Czechoslovakia, and with it, a loosening of many of the restrictions that had gripped its population. However, it was still proving difficult to export art from the country without going through the complicated red tape that the National Gallery continued to impose. The benefit of this for Theo was that his art-buying business continued to flourish. In addition, he continued to add other paintings to his shipments, smuggling these valuable pieces across the border with the help of several accomplices.

On this trip, Karl had requested that Theo retrieve the portrait that had been done of Karl's father by Rudolf Puchold, Karl's old high school art teacher. Karl had received a letter from Puchold's widow saying she had it and wanted to find a way to get it to him. When Karl heard that this painting of his father still existed, he was desperate to have it, and thought of the one man who could do the job for him. He contacted Theo and asked him to bring this painting out. Theo was happy to oblige, and even offered to retrieve the painting at no cost to Karl. Theo left Toronto with two hundred dollars in his pocket, a gift from Karl to Puchold's widow, and, a couple of weeks later, he returned to Toronto carrying the portrait of Victor, which he presented to a jubilant Karl. That was the last time Karl saw Theofil Král. But the painting of Karl's father hangs in his home to this day.

Several years after the four paintings arrived in Toronto, Hana and Paul traveled to Prague for a vacation. While they were there, they made contact with Jan Pekárek, wanting to thank him for having safeguarded the paintings for their family. He had never asked for any kind of reward, but Hana believed that he was entitled to something. While in Prague, she met with Pekárek and left an envelope with him containing one thousand dollars. Later that same day, when Hana and Paul returned to their hotel, they found waiting for them the envelope with all of the money still inside. Pekárek had returned it and that was last that any of the family heard from him.

There was however, one final and interesting encounter with the Pekárek family. Shortly after Hana and Paul returned from Prague, Paul received a letter from a man who identified himself as Petr Pekárek, Jan's brother. The letter outlined Petr's belief that his family had been entitled to the painting, *Die Hausfrau*, as compensation for having hidden all four paintings during the war. He wrote:

> *I was definitely opposed to my brother surrendering all four*
> *paintings to you. I was of the opinion that we should give you*
> *only three paintings, and that the fourth one, in accordance with*
> *the disposition of the court case, would be kept by our family as*
> *compensation for the problems our family had with these paintings.*

Petr went on to write that since the four paintings were now in Canada and he would have no opportunity to enforce this claim for one of them, he believed that he was entitled to receive compensation and was asking the Reesers to accept what he called the "western custom of paying ten percent of the value of the four paintings." He concluded:

I think that we are entitled to this, even though it is inadequate considering what our family did in hiding the paintings.

No one responded to the letter.

Karl began a search for Richard VandenBosch approximately one year after the four paintings arrived in Toronto. He never felt he had adequately thanked Richard for all he had done to reunite him with his family property. But the diplomat had moved from his posting in Prague, and Karl hadn't been able to track him down. Letters were returned with no forwarding address, and telephone calls and e-mails went unanswered. Karl spent the next few years searching the Internet in an effort to locate VandenBosch, but to no avail – until he suddenly and unexpectedly discovered him working as a member of a Canadian Mission to the United Nations in New York City. Karl and Richard experienced an emotional reunion in Toronto on August 12, 2009.

Even before the paintings were returned to him, Karl had grappled with the dilemma of how to divide them between himself and his sister, Hana. They represented so much to Karl, not the least of which was family unity. After all, Marie had never wavered from her resolve to keep the paintings together. So the idea of separating them now, and worse, doing this in a manner that might be perceived as unfair to himself or Hana, tortured Karl and caused many sleepless nights.

He considered solving this problem with a toss of a coin; he and Hana would each own two paintings and would choose them based on the results of the toss. But that too was unsatisfying. Karl feared that tossing a coin would create a "winner" and a "loser" in terms of the ownership of the paintings and Karl was adamant that this should not happen, not after all that his family and the art had been through. The paintings stood for reunification, family love, and triumph over adversity. Karl was determined to preserve that.

In January 1991, after the paintings had been in his home for eight months, Karl came up with what he thought would be the perfect solution to his dilemma. He resolved that he and Hana would jointly own all four paintings. That was a critical decision, stressing the importance of preserving the paintings as one unit. Karl and Hana would rotate the artwork between their two homes in groups of two over the course of their lifetimes. The rotation would take place in September of every year, the anniversary of the family's arrival in Canada, and the beginning of their new and free life.

It was a perfect solution, and Hana thought so, too. The first time they divided the paintings, Karl asked Phyllis to toss a coin in order to determine the grouping. Karl won the toss and chose *Le lavabo à l'école maternelle*. Hana then chose *Ready for the Ball*, and Karl selected *Die Hausfrau*. The final painting, *Forest Fire*, went to Hana. Karl and Hana discussed that at some point, they would need to determine the absolute ownership of the four paintings, and find a way to divide them fairly and equitably. But they would do that when it felt right to them. They also vowed that, no matter what, the paintings would remain "in the family" forever, if possible, being passed down from generation to generation. In this way, they would establish the family legacy that Marie had always wanted. This property which had been so much about the past of the Reeser family would now also be about its future.

After a couple of years of rotating the paintings in their established groupings, Karl and Hana realized that it was simply too onerous a task to continue to do this. It required art movers, and the constant fear that the paintings might be damaged in the move. Hana, sensing that Karl had a greater affinity for the painting of the children, offered to allow him to keep it. She selected *Forest Fire* as her first choice. Karl kept *Die Hausfrau*, and Hana kept the painting of the Spanish dancer. The four paintings are still owned by Hana and Karl, and they hang in their respective homes to this day.

I hope that my grandsons will understand what the four paintings have come to mean to me. Every time I admire them, they remind me of the dark years of persecution, when our people became nearly extinct.

The torturous road of the four paintings from Rakovník to Toronto symbolizes my innermost and ever-present thought – the good fortune that all four of our family members survived those terrible years. This story is my way of "bearing witness."

May my grandsons understand – and if they do – may they remember.

Karl Reeser, May 1990

Joseph Cach working on the restoration of the paintings

Richard VandenBosch and Karl Reeser, reunited in Toronto, August 2009

References

[1] Adolf Hitler, speech at Koenigsberg, March 25, 1938. "Former frontier" refers to the border into Austria. In Alan Bullock, *Hitler: A Study in Tyranny*, Harmondsworth: Penguin Books, 1962.

[2] Neville Chamberlain, national broadcast, London, September 27, 1938. In Robert C. Self, *Neville Chamberlain: A Biography*, London: Ashgate Publishing, 2006.

[3] Neville Chamberlain, speech, September 30, 1938. Full text available via the Modern History Sourcebook at www.fordham.edu/halsall/mod/1938PEACE.html.

[4] Adolf Hitler, speech, January 30, 1939. Available at www.historyplace.com.

[5] Neville Chamberlain, national broadcast, London, September 3, 1939. Full text available on the BBC website at http://news.bbc.co.uk/2/hi/special_report/1999/08/99/world_war_ii/430071.stm.

[6] "Unconditional surrender," *Toronto Daily Star*, May 7, 1945. Available via the Toronto Star archives at www.pagesofthepast.ca.

[7] Klement Gottwald, speech, Prague, April 1945. In Bradley F. Abrams, *The*

Struggle for the Soul of the Nation: Czech Culture and the Rise of Communism, Lanham (MD): Rowman & Littlefield, 2005.

[8] "We and They," *Toronto Star*, September 27, 1947. Available via the Toronto Star Archives at www.pagesofthepast.ca.

[9] "Lesson for appeasers seen as Bolshevists grab Czechoslovakia," *Toronto Star*, February 26, 1948. Available via the Toronto Star Archives at www.pagesofthepast.ca.

[10] In Ken Lawrence, *John Lennon in His Own Words*, Kansas City: Andrews McMeel Publishing, 2005.

[11] Václav Havel, "The Declaration of the Civic Forum by Representative Václav Havel on Wenceslas Square," *Making the History of 1989*, Item #509. Excerpt available at http://chnm.gmu.edu/1989/items/show/509.

[12] Peter Cipkowski, *Revolution in Eastern Europe*, New York: John Wiley & Sons, 1991.

[13] "Czechoslovaks Celebrate Ouster of Communists," *Toronto Star*, December 11, 1989. Available via the Toronto Star archives at www.pagesofthepast.ca.

[14] "Admirers aplenty for city of romance," *Sunday Star-Times*, May 31, 1998. Accessed through HighBeam Research at www.highbeam.com, July 13, 2009.

[15] "Prague still hasn't gotten the message," *Washington Post*, November 14, 1989. Accessed through HighBeam Research at www.highbeam.com, July 8, 2009.

Acknowledgments

Stories come to writers in wonderful and unexpected ways. This one was no exception. I met Karl Reeser through his daughter-in-law, Elizabeth Forster, who happens to be a law partner of my husband. Elizabeth had given her father-in-law a copy of my book for young readers, *The Secret of Gabi's Dresser*. Karl contacted me to say that he had been touched by my family story that was set in the country of his birth, and that he had a story of his own. I was similarly enthralled with his family saga of four paintings. I knew I had to write this book.

It has been a joyful experience working with Karl on its development, and I can't begin to express the admiration that I have for him. He is passionate, distinguished, articulate, and congenial. His wife, Phyllis, is equally gracious and obliging. They opened their home to me – with a cup of tea and cookies always at hand – endured my thousands of questions, and patiently steered me through the many details of this story. Both Karl and Phyllis embrace life enthusiastically, and retain a great sense of humor and keen interest in world events. My gratitude and affection go out to them. I'd also like to acknowledge Hana and

Paul Traub for taking the time to meet and talk with me. You both have my respect and thanks.

With Karl's blessing, I began to track down the whereabouts of Richard VandenBosch, and was lucky to locate him living and working in New York City. Richard and his wife, Teresa, welcomed me into their home, and helped fill in many of the missing pieces of this story. Richard is a delight – warm, enthusiastic, charming – all of the qualities which I hope I captured in this book. He is also the hero of this story as far as I am concerned, and Karl and others would certainly agree.

It was a wonderful experience to talk with "Theofil Král" and to learn of his unconventional and fascinating life. He was extremely forthcoming about his role in Karl's story. He is also one of the heroes, and I am grateful for his candor and his insights.

I could not have finished this book without the help of Joseph Cach who was particularly open about his own life experiences in the former Czechoslovakia. Joseph is a gifted artist and art restorer who taught me much about the art world here and in Europe.

As always, I am indebted to Margie Wolfe and the fabulous people of Second Story Press – Emma Rodgers, Melissa Kaita, Carolina Smart, and Phuong Truong. Margie's commitment to Holocaust literature is inspiring. Thank you for continuing to support my writing, and for your ongoing mentorship and friendship. Thank you for always pushing me to be a better writer, and for urging me to expand my writing repertoire. And thank you for enduring my anxiety over the many necessary cuts to the manuscript. My esteem for you grows and grows. Special thanks to Carolyn Jackson at SSP for taking me through the final sculpting of the story. Thanks also to Colin Thomas whose encouraging and insightful editing comments were of tremendous help, and to Alison Kooistra for her keen attention to details in the final copyedit.

There are few opportunities to publicly thank ones friends and family members, and many have cheered me on in the writing of this, my first adult book. To Aura and Manny Kagan, Viv and Raefie Epstein, Sandy and Allan Dennill, and all of their wonderful offspring, Lynda Adler, my best buddy Rose Reisman and her husband Sam, my ladies – Sue Weinstein, Marilyn Wise, Shelley Cobrin, and Enid Weiner, Sharna Cohen, Sheila Gordon, Sharon McKay, Loris Lesynski, Frieda Wishinsky, thanks for the faith, the words of encouragement, the laughs, and the love.

I delight in the changing relationship with my now-grown children, Gabi Epstein and Jake Epstein. Their feedback on my writing is shrewd and insightful, and our conversations have evolved into spirited debates on plot, character, and literary style. I love it! And I love them with all my heart. I've always said that my writing is first and foremost for them – to pass the history on. I know that they take this legacy seriously.

And to my husband, Ian Epstein, my friend and love, it's a joy to share the journey.

photo by Negin Sairafi

KATHY KACER is well known as a children's author. She has won multiple awards for her children's books, several of them in the Holocaust Remembrance Series for Young Readers. In 2009 her children's novel *Hiding Edith* won the prestigious Yad Vashem Prize for Children's Holocaust Literature and *The Diary of Laura's Twin* won both the Canadian and American Jewish Book Awards. Her first book was *The Secret of Gabi's Dresser*, which she adapted into a play. Herself a child of Holocaust survivors, Kathy travels around the world speaking to young people about the importance of understanding the Holocaust. A former psychologist, Kathy lives in Toronto with her family.